No Time For Slaves

R.E. McMaster, Jr.

— Books by R.E. McMaster, Jr. —

Cycles of War, The Next Six Years, 1977

The Trader's Notebook, 1978

The Trader's Notebook, 1979

The Trader's Notebook, 1980

Wealth for All, 1982
(Book 1 — Religion, Politics and War)

Wealth for All, 1982
(Book 2 — Economics)

No Time for Slaves, 1986

Reaper Publishing
P.O. Box 39026
Phoenix, Arizona 85069

R.E. McMaster, Jr.

No Time For Slaves

Copyright © 1986
R.E. McMaster, Jr.
ISBN 0-9605316-8-8

All rights reserved. No part of this book may be reproduced or utilized in any form or by any means, electronic or mechanical, including photocopying, recording or by any information storage and retrieval system, without permission in writing from the Publisher, except for reviews of 1,000 words or less, and then only when the complete address of Reaper Publishing is cited.

Published by:
Reaper Publishing
P.O. Box 39026
Phoenix, Arizona 85069

This book is dedicated to
Reverend Carl Nine
for his help in freeing me
from some of the subtle
tentacles of slavery.

— Special Acknowledgement —

I want to express my deep appreciation
to Dave Sczepanski, of Eureka, California,
for his tireless efforts in pulling together,
organizing, editing, and coordinating the
publishing of this series of essays, some
of which originally appeared in my newsletter,
THE REAPER. Without Dave's dedication,
the timeliness of this work
might have been lost.

*"If the Son therefore shall make
you free, ye shall be free indeed."*
St. John 8:36

* * * * *

*"...that they are endowed by their
Creator with certain unalienable rights;
that among these are life, liberty, and
the pursuit of happiness."*
The U.S. Declaration of Independence, 1776

* * * * *

*"Government is always religion
applied to economics."*
R.E. McMaster, Jr.

CONTENTS

Foreword ix
Preface xi

SECTION I: THE CRISIS AT HAND

Chapter		Page
1	EPCOT: Prototype Slavery?	3
2	Security and Dependency	9
3	No Time for Slaves	15
4	Money Chickens — Coming Home to Roost	27
5	The Emperor Has No Clothes	31
6	Foreclosure of U.S.A., Inc.	35
7	The U.S. War Clock	43
8	The U.S. War Clock — More Evidence	49
9	The Climate Crisis	55
10	The Debt Crisis	61

SECTION II: HOW WE BECAME ENSLAVED

11	Human Action Cycles	67
12	"Star Light" — Astrological Slavery	71
13	Vertical Empires and Short-Term Thinking	77
14	Debt Money — Curse and Control of People	85
15	The Real Cause of Inflation — A Simple Story	89
16	Conquest Without Bloodshed	93
17	Taxes: A Barometer of Slavery	103
18	Toward a One-World Order	115

SECTION III: AN OPPORTUNITY FOR FREEDOM

19	Second Chance — Unfreezing the Marketplace	123
20	Second Chance — The Revolution of Littleness	129
21	Second Chance — The Golden Age	137
22	Redeeming The Dismal Science	143

Chapter		Page
23	Overcoming the Slavery of Nature	153
24	Vertical or Horizontal Lifestyle	159
25	The Keys to Human Freedom	167
26	The One Guiding Principle	177
27	Choosing Truth or Tradition	181
28	The Judas "*Sindrome*"	189
29	In a Nutshell	199

Epilogue: An End to Conflict 211

FOREWORD

R.E. McMaster, Jr. has been my friend for several years now. Through my many discussions with him I have learned something important about him. He is a man of careful thought who looks beyond the surface things of life. He is compelled to ask why things work and why they fail. He applies himself to the disciplines of finance and economics, business and politics, and most importantly, he attempts to relate these to the spiritual forces that undergird all human action.

I have listened carefully to the many conclusions R.E. has reached about a diversity of themes vital to the success of our nation and to us as individuals who live and work within this great country. While I do not agree with all his conclusions, one thing is true: I have always been forced to think carefully about the foundations of my own beliefs. No greater service can be rendered to any generation of people than to help them examine the presuppositions and beliefs that guide them through life. In this way, every false conclusion can be challenged and, hopefully, rooted out.

If this country and the world is to remain free in the future, that freedom will depend upon men and women who choose to apply eternal, unchangeable, God-given truth to life. If, however, they choose to ignore God and his laws by trying to find a "better" way, then the slavery R.E. speaks of will certainly come.

I found *No Time for Slaves* to be an uncomfortable book. But then every book that has ever made me think has been an uncomfortable book. The books I have the easiest time agreeing with are pleasant novels that merely reaffirm all of my positions and make me feel well. But they do not help me. This book, though, made me uncomfortable because it made me look more closely and critically at the conclusions I have drawn about my own life. I believe you will find the book has a similar effect on you. For this reason, it is an important book. It makes us think.

Throughout *No Time for Slaves*, R.E. repeatedly refers to principles that are drawn from the Bible. These eternal truths help us understand the true nature of the world. By espousing various theories and philosophies, men have attempted to disprove or change these God-given principles or laws. But they cannot be changed or improved upon. Therefore, when R.E. says that if these laws are violated there is serious trouble ahead, he speaks with authority.

Today, because God's laws are being violated in our nation, there is trouble, serious trouble. In this book, R.E. looks not only at the obvious problems, but he probes to the roots. He helps us see why debt, irresponsibility, greed, envy — and a host of other human ills that surface when men turn from God — always lead to slavery. In *No Time for Slaves* R.E. has given us both positive direction and workable answers to our present problems.

The troubles we face can be avoided. But if they are avoided, it will depend on men and women who have the courage to hear an uncomfortable message, turn to God, and change. Then we will see the title of this book fulfilled. We will see that instead of this being a time for slavery, it is a time for freedom.

James Durkin
Director, Gospel Outreach
Eureka, California

PREFACE

The grand unveiling of the Statue of Liberty at the celebrations on July 4, 1986 again turned America's attention to the freedom this Lady of Liberty symbolizes. But what does the liberty she represents mean to Americans today, and to the people of the world who look to her for freedom?

Does the substance of liberty still match the symbol? Are we indeed free in the sense that our Founding Fathers intended? Have we kept the faith? How do Americans now bear the risks, responsibilities and burdens of freedom? How are we handling the encroaching slavery that inevitably comes through personal irresponsibility, debt, and a longing for security at any price? And finally, what is the likelihood that we will continue to enjoy our tradition of freedom, peace and prosperity? These are just some of the critical questions I confront in this book.

Freedom can be compared to a garden. In any garden weeds spring up. In the garden of freedom, there are persistent weeds of slavery which must be uprooted. These weeds choke the garden unless we are eternally vigilant. Slavery exists to remind us that freedom is never free, never without cost. In a real sense, *No Time for Slaves* is meant to dig hard and deep at the roots of human slavery that persist in our garden of freedom.

In this book, I take a holographic look at the issue of freedom versus slavery. In viewing a hologram, we benefit by looking at the subject from a variety of angles. By observing freedom versus slavery from many viewpoints — in terms of the governmental and political bureaucracy, taxes, agriculture and the farm crisis, mounting global military tensions, economics, personal finance, and religion — we are able to see the depth of the crisis we now face.

Truly, today we are at a crossroads in history. On one hand, the benefits of freedom are enormous. But the price of freedom is also high. On the other hand, slavery does provide immediate, short-term security and benefits. But ultimately slavery is unbearable, in the end crushing the human spirit, leaving in its wake insecurity and poverty. Will we choose freedom or slavery? As I attempt to convey, we really have no choice. Freedom is our only answer. This is no time for slaves.

R.E. McMaster, Jr.
April 9, 1986

SECTION I

The Crisis At Hand

Chapter One
EPCOT: PROTOTYPE SLAVERY?

Over a decade ago, Yul Brynner and Peter Fonda teamed up for the popular film *Future World*. The theme of this movie was that human beings were too unstable and unpredictable to be free, and thus had to be controlled by totally rational and consistent robots. In the world's greatest amusement park, *Future World*, robots produced other robots to take the place of world leaders. The robot duplicates were identical to the world leaders, who were replaced and eliminated at *Future World*.

Science fiction is often a prelude to reality. Today, the real thing, an alive and kicking *Future World* exists. It is part of the billion dollar Walt Disney entertainment center located near Orlando, Florida. This Future World is called *Epcot*. Does *Epcot* significantly reflect a frightening reality that is nearly upon us?

This real *Future World* is brought to us by the multinationals. (Do they want us to feel secure with them shaping our future?) Exxon, General Motors, Bell, Kodak, and Kraft are represented. Also in attendance are Sperry and American Express, among others.

One-half of *Epcot* is literally named *Future World*; the other half is the *World Showcase*. Putting their best foot forward in the *World Showcase* are China, Mexico, France, the United Kingdom, Canada, Japan, Italy, Germany and, of course, the United States. It is literally a United Nations, a One-World Order of sorts. (It is more than just a little discomforting to see Red China, France, and Mexico represented on equal terms with the United States in this *World Showcase*. All three of these countries are socialistic/communistic. Should not such a presentation be expected as part of today's movement toward a socialistic One-World government?)

Epcot is a sensory and illusionary, technological extravaganza. To the average American, a trip to *Epcot* is nothing short of a technological and educational revelation. To some trained eyes, however, particularly to those knowledgeable in occult literature and music, there is abundant evidence of a possible "religious" connotation.

C.S. Lewis, in his book, *That Hideous Strength*, observed that the occult and technology combined would be the threatening death knell for human freedom in the future. Do the vast majority of Americans who visit *Epcot* ever see the possible connection? Visitors are easily captured by the powerful statement made by this impressive and expensive work of art.

Epcot awes or intimidates most individuals. There has never been a better designed and orchestrated system for mass processing, controlling and dictating collective human behavior. Perhaps not surprisingly, and appropriately, the focused attention in many of the exhibits is on robots that look and act human. Robots are the mechanized version of programmed human behavior. The human response to the artificial and overwhelming sensory input at *Epcot* is one of submission. Scores of films subtly emphasize the greatness of collective man.

Is *Epcot*, perhaps, an intense educational propaganda statement, as well as an amusement center? Clearly, it is intended to indoctrinate the American people in the brave new world we are entering — a world of centralized technological control of people, managed by benevolent multi-national interests. One lady commented, "Isn't it absolutely amazing what the mind of man has created?" Another said, "How can anything go wrong in this world when we are able to do all the things that we see here at *Epcot*?"

Epcot indeed leaves one with the distinct impression that all is well with the world. Of course, we are also left with a sense of individual helplessness, in the face of all this technological power. Does the sun of individual freedom set at *Epcot*?

We have to search carefully to find out what *Epcot* really means. The answer is not surprising: *Epcot* means *Experimental Prototype Community of Tomorrow*. Future World! Sounds like the name of your typical amusement park. Right? No way.

Epcot is not at all what Walt Disney himself personally intended it to be. Walt Disney, a man of great vision, as well as a business entrepreneur, wanted *Epcot* to feature an actual living-and-working American community of the future. But since Walt Disney's death, the $1 billion 260-acre *Epcot* project has been transformed into a One-World-type spectacle, which is nowhere close to Disney's original vision.

Does the American public love *Epcot* because it makes them feel secure, taken care of, like slaves? Disney World, patterned after Disneyland, was almost abandoned by the public when *Epcot* first opened. Walt Disney Productions' stock shot up $4.00 a share on the news that *Epcot* was a "winner." Attendance at *Epcot's* opening ran 30% above projections. Ten percent of all Americans will pay good money to go through the *Epcot* center each year.

Until this century, whenever and wherever people were oppressed, such was accomplished in an obviously brutal and tyrannical fashion. Today, however, the American people are far more easily manipulated than are the people of Poland, for example. The Polish people know they're not free. In Poland, the harsh hand of government control, originating in the Soviet Union, is easily recognized. Conflict and poverty are apparent. In this country, however, as possibly exemplified by *Epcot*, control is far more subtle and effective. *Epcot's* control is by design and suggestion, coming under the guise of group "cooperation."

For example, at *Epcot*, gone are the signs that say *Keep Off The Grass*. Nowhere to be found are chain fences blocking *Epcot* visitors from walking on the grass. Far more effective, instead, are the red, textured concrete sidewalks, which mark all paths where tourists are supposed to tread. Thus, one becomes quickly and easily conditioned to staying on the red concrete. To ensure this crowd control — control by design — high curbs separate the grass from the sidewalk. And, for added measure, none of the beautifully landscaped grassy areas at *Epcot* are level. Resistance is built in. Landscaped areas either slope up or down, so much so that one cannot see what is on the other side. Therefore, one won't risk taking a short cut across the grass. By design, people do not walk on the grass at *Epcot*.

In the two days I visited *Epcot*, of the thousands of people who toured all the attractions, I saw only one person on the grass — a girl who decided to take a nap. She was the only "free spirit" who overcame the "control by design" environment.

Epcot is truly a master model of how easily people can be conditioned and manipulated by the subtleties of design and technology. Americans are incredibly pliable. Americans obey what they perceive to be properly-constituted authority almost without question. They emotionally respond and react on cue to man-made, unnatural and artificially created input. The idea that they possibly have been processed or propagandized never crosses their minds, either. Americans are simply awestruck by the power of it all. Are they willing to be subservient, to be slaves?

(If a UFO landed, one wonders if we would turn over the reins of our government to an *"E.T."* if it could convince us it was benign and technologically superior.)

The Experimental Prototype Community of Tomorrow probably would not make Davy Crockett very happy, or Andrew Jackson, James Madison, Thomas Jefferson, or George Washington. These men were independent, freethinking individualists.

There is much to be gleaned from *Epcot*. Man-created odors, fogs and lakes, along with all the robots, mark the surrealism of this "entertainment park." Such a contrived escape from reality is a vital part of the logical working out of the humanistic evolutionary spiral, rendering the ordinary man impotent as master of his own destiny. Such inevitably leads to technological control by a few at the tip of the spiral. Is evolutionary humanism, the mind of man playing God, the clear statement of *Epcot*? *Epcot* is overwhelmingly big — big business, big technology, big bucks — with a big message. And, true to form, the humanistic media reviews have been glowing.

While Disney World is fun, harmless and entertaining, by contrast, is *Epcot* awesome and sinister? *Future World* in *Epcot* has completed the metamorphosis from science fiction to reality.

The natural and best use of technology, according to basic Christian scholars, should be to decentralize society, to help move man from vertical, pyramid-type, bureaucratic, slavelike institutions into horizontal, contractual, freedom-loving, marketplace-type relationships. But with man's irresponsibility, technology — particularly the technology of the computer — can be used for identification and control of man. As psychiatrist Matthew P. Dumont wrote in 1973, "The history of technology is the history of the invention of hammers and the subsequent search for heads to bang with them."

Does *Epcot* hammer the individual into submission so he can be easily controlled? Sadly, have most Americans already lost their individuality and true self-identity? Eighty-five years of conditioning have taken their toll. Most Americans find *Epcot* welcome relief. Their senses are saturated there. They are totally entertained by their welcomed hosts. For too many, the pain and responsibility of freedom long ago became too high. Does *Epcot* reinforce this benign status as comfortable slaves? The God of the Bible has no time for slaves.

March 25, 1983

"It is often said that 'all people wish to be free.' I have doubts about that. In a long lifetime of experience, I have found no compelling evidence that it is in fact true. Freedom of choice places a responsibility on the individual for his own life that millions of people experience simply as a burden that they can't or won't shoulder. Many people prefer to escape from the pain of this burden by handing over this freedom of choice to some authority."

Leo Cherne, Executive Director
Research Institute of America

"Television can control public opinion more effectively than armies or secret police because television is entirely voluntary. The American government forces our children to attend its schools, but nobody forces them to watch TV. Americans of all ages submit to television. Television is the American ideal, persuasion without coercion. Nobody makes us watch. Who could have predicted that a free people would voluntarily spend one-fifth of their lives sitting in front of a box with pictures? Fifteen years sitting in prison is punishment. But fifteen years sitting in front of a television set is entertainment. And the average American now spends more than one-and-a-half years of his life watching television commercials, fifty minutes every day of his life watching commercials. Now that's power."

From the movie, The Looker.

"What computer scientists are proposing today is computer evolution that within the next decade will bring into being a living element — a computer with eternal life, a god-like super human entity that will be infinitely more intelligent than man."

Coming Changes, November 1982

Chapter Two
SECURITY AND DEPENDENCY

We may be on the verge of the biggest outbreak of mental illness in the history of this country. We are set up for this sorrow because dependency, security and slavery have become the new American way of life. As dependency increases, a person's sense of security is more easily shattered. As economic and spiritual slavery becomes a clearer and more frightening reality in this country, and as economic troubles increase, Americans will "flip out" in droves. Children often panic in a crisis. Slaves are children who are dependent and never grow up.

Since the FDR years, in our quest for security, we have slipped rapidly into the bondage of dependency, which leads to slavery. Today over half of all U.S. residents are dependent upon the federal government for their income. Big Brother. Dependency. Too many Americans look to big corporations, big government, big labor unions, big bureaucracies, to take care of them. Folks look to TV and big religion for escapism. These people are dependent and insecure. They rely upon a military/industrial complex and a bureaucratic Pentagon for defense — a military monstrosity that cares first and foremost about its own interests.

Americans have also become dependent upon a life support distribution system which is breaking down at an accelerated pace. Our transportation and distribution system now requires $2.5 trillion to rebuild.

Americans are also dependent on utilities for life support. These complex systems are increasingly targeted for terrorist attacks.

Americans are dependent upon interest income, Social Security and pension funds, which have little long-term hope of surviving. In the slave-like drive for irresponsible security, the fearful collective mindset fomented by this *Epcot*-type environment will break down at an accelerated pace as real world insecurity becomes increasingly evident on all fronts beginning in the late 1980s.

Escapism from reality is a form of mental illness. Recognizing this public mood, *U.S. News*, reported, "'Escapism' is the word for the new TV season."

Real economic security is only achieved by the assumption of risks.

Thus, economic security follows successful risk assumption in the marketplace. This is why the development of individual talents, in an environment which promotes individual freedom, productivity and creativity, is so vital to collective human security. Only such an environment allows for collective long-term security. Historically, a stable local family, local church, and local community have provided the secure environment necessary for individual risk assumption in the economic arena.

In recent years, security has been primarily couched in economic and financial terms, generated by the political establishment. In the latter days of a civilization, where business and materialism predominate, money is king. Thus, money is security. Part of the trauma, leading to mental illness, is due now to the illusionary money/security complex breaking down.

People no longer deny that there is insecurity in the financial and banking system. They also affirm that there is insecurity regarding political leadership and the runaway federal debt. These two "gods" of our society — the financial and political systems — are breaking down so rapidly that fear has seized the hearts of the dependent slaves, the security-oriented Americans.

In past years, most of us have been concerned with increasing our financial assets (i.e., obtaining financial security). We have also been somewhat concerned with preserving those financial and economic assets which we acquired in the past. And yet, in the reality of today's financial world, there is no pat road to security. Diversity of assets has been the best approach, but even this tactic is increasingly insecure.

The most important of all securities is spiritual/psychological security. It is also the most difficult to obtain. Spiritual security begins when people, in faith, look up, place their trust in a sovereign God, and then move out, exercising dominion over their environment. This results in economic security. Such efforts have been rewarded consistently and faithfully throughout history. The "evidence of things not seen" kicks in, and the "Unseen Hand" joins this combination of faith followed by works.

When men assume basic humility before a sovereign God, they are then receptive to the input from their environment. They can listen. They can hear and then respond quickly and efficiently. This is a far cry from the proud and arrogant humanism which grips us today. Today men (with pride as the status quo), become the measure of all things as gods, while shivering in the insecurity of their own limitations. In far worse shape are those who have bought the self-serving programs of this organized, centralized, bureaucratic, humanistic religion, which has promised a drug-like escapism from the present world of expanding socialistic slavery.

Slaves are dependent and irresponsible. Slaves own no property. Free men are reponsible. Free men own property. Thus, there is no escaping the interrelationships between freedom, personal responsibility, morality, and the ownership of property. (Men cannot be held morally responsible unless they are free to choose.)

The moral, free marketplace is the only proven system in history that not only solves problems regarding consumer demand for goods and services, but also best anticipates future needs. When men are seen as uniquely-created individuals, having specialized talents to be developed, they not only serve their self-interest, but also first serve the interests of their fellow man. Through the production of goods and services then, godly free enterprise economics is in force. "Self interest is best served by service." Also Say's Law, a basic axiom of free market economics, is fulfilled: "Supply creates its own demand." In other words, free, morally responsible men, producing goods and services, create a demand which previously did not exist.

By contrast, the philosophy of evolutionary humanism is a philosophy of slavery. When man is seen as primarily a product of his environment, the logical result is a depressing hopelessness. Man is not only a slave to nature, he also does not accept accountability for his actions since they are environmentally determined. Evolutionary humanism therefore fits very nicely with Marxism, and its doctrine of "dialectic materialism." Under "dialectic materialism," man is a product of his environment. According to Marx, man's condition is determined by his economic environment. Stated differently, man is a slave to his environment. This is in stark contrast to the aggressive, confident, hopeful, traditional American creative free enterprise perspective that "man is a spiritual being with a physical nature." He rises up, drawing strength from above and from within, to subdue his environment and to exercise dominion.

Because thoughts precede action, and ideas have consequences, it therefore follows that the approaching bankruptcy of our institutions is a direct product of the preceding bankrupt, evolutionary, humanistic philosophy.

In this modern era, we have not given much thought to our personal physical security. And yet, over 30% of all American homes are victims of crime of one sort or another each year. Movies like *Nighthawks* have brought to the public's attention the ever-increasing threat of terrorism in this country. Over twenty thousand Mexicans crossing the southern U.S. border every day, is one of the kinds of trends which have led to increasing personal violence and crimes against property. Personal security protection is now a major growth industry.

Even the Wild West days of territory controlled by outlaws has returned. North and west of Sacramento, California, and up into southern Oregon, lie vast sections of the U.S. National Forest, literally off limits to both National Forest government personnel and tourists. These lands have been staked out by roving bands of "human animals," armed with violent twentieth century technology (automatic weapons), who threaten the lives of all who trespass on their domain. The federal government and the state of California have done virtually nothing to eliminate these twentieth century outlaws. The worst of the Old West has returned with a new twist. These hippie-type barbarians are using National Forest lands to raise the extremely profitable crop of marijuana to feed the American escapist drug culture.

The insecurity brought about by our failing institutions will move toward a state of anarchy as our collective humanism breaks down. But anarchy never lasts long. Historically, it is quickly followed by dictatorship. And, we are now being conditioned by the media for this bureaucratic type of slavery.

The middle class has been virtually destroyed. We are returning to the divide-and-conquer extremes of the few very rich and the many very poor. This paves the way for bureaucratic dictatorship which fills the vacuum left by the middle class. The age of kings, Caesars, philosopher kings and dictators is about to dawn again. Consider how we are being prepared for it.

President Reagan's first inauguration, the "Gala," was effectively a tribute to a king. Reagan's entire inauguration was Camelot, twentieth century Washington, D.C. style. The media coverage of the death of Princess Grace, the media saturation with the comings and goings of Prince Charles and Princess Diana, all speak to the growing collective human (or humanistic) urge for a king and queen, for a human elite.

U.S. News, in discussing the 1982 fall TV season commented, "Fantasies about royalty and chivalry propel at least two new shows...as well as TV movies about Britain's Prince Charles and Princess Diana." The October 1982 *National Geographic* featured, "Thailand's Working Royalty." All around us the stage is being set for the tyranny of "royalty."

If these trends continue, mass poverty and slavery will become the inescapable, distasteful lot for our children. Rather than reaching out for freedom as our oppressive institutions break down, too many American slaves are clamoring for even greater tyranny. They are throwing away the little freedom that remains in exchange for slavelike security. These wretched individuals, in avoiding the morality of personal responsibility, have not only given up their freedom, they have also given up their property, thus condemning themselves and their children to poverty. Slaves own little or nothing!

Bureaucracies are basic to slavery. All bureaucracies are vertical in nature — whether they are religious, political, economic, educational, military, corporate or labor-related. They stifle freedom, independence, individual creativity, morality and accountability, while promoting dullness, irresponsibility, a lack of morality and accountability, dependency and slavery. Bureaucracies also promote pride and arrogance because bureaucrats exercise their egos and build empires, based upon their position of unaccountable authority. Bureaucrats do not have to face the real test of having the worth of their efforts directly evaluated by the marketplace.

Stated differently, bureaucrats are not held accountable.

Because bureaucracies are potentially so dangerous, particularly in the hands of a tyrant, any vertical bureaucratic hierarchy, where men rule over other men, must be kept local, so bureaucrats can be held accountable.

Bureaucracies are tremendously wasteful and expensive. It costs little for an extended family, a neighbor, a local church or charity to feed a family which has fallen on hard times. By contrast, when this local responsibility is forsaken, the army of faceless, unproductively-employed government bureaucrats take over. Tax collectors, Postal Service employees, IRS bureaucrats, U.S. Treasury employees, USDA employees, food stamp printers, and local bureaucrats who then distribute the food stamps make up the army. The bureaucracy fills the vacuum of personal irresponsibility at least four times the cost of personal, local effort.

The evidence is in, for those with eyes to see; the age of slavery is upon us.

October 8, 1982

Chapter Three
NO TIME FOR SLAVES

The economic equation is composed of only two parts: land and labor. Properly organized, they produce capital surplus — savings — which is the basis for prosperity in all societies. This capital/savings/surplus comes from one of four sources, and preferably all four, if society is to have an adequately balanced economic system, which produces wealth for all. These four sources of wealth are:

1. Real, free, renewable wealth, created through photosynthesis, whereby solar energy is transformed into matter (plus earth's resources).
2. The specialization and division of labor, leading to trade.
3. Technology.
4. Inheritance.

When all four of these wealth-producing factors are operative in an honest, financial system, if there are no natural or man-made disasters, the inevitable result is increasing wealth for generation after generation, coupled with falling prices, if men also take the long-term view and work hard.

Since the sun shines freely every day, we have the potential for producing huge agricultural surpluses (as well as animal surpluses) year after year since the specialization and division of labor allows us to cooperatively produce more and better goods and services within the same limited amount of time; since technology is ever increasing, which makes higher and better use of the factors of land and labor in the economic marketplace in less time than before; and since inheritance taxes do not exist, each generation should have a higher economic starting point than the preceding generation. It stands to reason that we have had to muddle up things pretty badly to avoid increasing wealth for all in our society.

Notice, too, that all four of these wealth-producing factors, all involving land and labor, also require individual responsibility, cooperation in the marketplace (not conflict), free contractual exchange, and a long-term view. The very nature of capital/surplus/savings requires a long-term view. We are talking about the economic essence of life itself.

The opposite of capital/surplus/savings is debt. In fact, debt consumes capital/surplus/savings. Thus, it should come as no surprise that one of the root meanings of the word debt (which consumes life) is death! Therefore, given the pervasive debt in the public and private sectors of Western civilization today, it should also come as no surprise that we are dying — economically, politically, ecologically, militarily, socially and religiously. Debt/death permeates our lifestyle. And we are presently in the eye of the economic hurricane.

With the advent of evolutionary, debt-based capitalism, brought on by the economic adoption of the evolutionary philosophy in the late 1890s by the robber barons, we have moved ruthlessly toward the comprehensive crisis we face today. It is a crisis which threatens the very life of our civilization. What once existed economically in this country, and produced great prosperity, was a Christian antagonism to debt in the free enterprise system. But for at least the last seventy years, with the establishment of the Federal Reserve, and its systems' monopoly on the making of fractional reserve money, we have inevitably moved at an accelerating speed toward the extremes of the only three events which a central bank monopoly and fiat money, fractional reserve system can give us: hyperinflation, deflationary depression, and/or world war.

We are living at the end of an economic age. If we continue on the present road, our only options are either cataclysmic destruction or the tyranny of slavery in a One-World order. One other radical option does exist: the option of a glorious "golden age." But a "golden age" demands that we essentially turn our backs on debt capitalism and not only re-establish what made us great, Christian free enterprise, but at the same time, produce the logical synthesis of what is best in both the debt capitalistic and communistic economic systems.

Let's now look more closely at debt, which is economic death long-term. Since ancient times, debt has always been viewed by the knowledgeable as a form of slavery. Before the Assyrians conquered a people militarily, they first enslaved them through debt. The ancient Hebrew, Greek, Roman and Middle Age Christian cultures warned us against the use of debt. These ancients were particularly antagonistic to a debt-based economy. The horrors of the debtors' prisons (slavery) come down to us in bleak detail in our history books.

Today, we see that Third World developing countries have become slaves to the Developed World due to reliance on debt in an ill-placed hope to secure their economic futures. Many of the Third World developing countries, particularly those with excessive debt, such as Brazil, Argentina and Mexico, have annual debt service which exceeds 100% of their yearly exports. This is economic slavery.

In a root sense, all tangible slavery is economic. Economics deals with the basis of life. So the political slavery in communist countries makes heavy use of slave labor for economic production. Economic freedom allows an individual to spend his time where he pleases, with whom he pleases, when he pleases, doing what he pleases, as he pleases. Debt strictly limits this freedom. Today the banks, which have loaned billions of dollars to these Third World developing countries, dictate their economic and thus, political policies. Alien austerity programs are in place. Effectively, policies of state are now established in bank boardrooms of other countries. Slavery has been established.

The use of debt assumes that the future can be accurately predicted. Men borrow from the future based upon expectations for the future. But experience shows that such predicting is quite difficult. How many major banks made large loans to Third World countries, agricultural loans and oil industry loans just before the economy peaked in 1980?

Men are capable of only one thing perfectly — mistakes and errors, especially when it comes to predicting the future. Men have imperfect information. Isn't it evident now in our economy how dangerous debt can be if the future is not accurately predicted? Presently, we have over $7.3 trillion of debt, including over $2 trillion of federal debt, and $1 trillion in loans to Third World countries and communist powers. Isn't the economic essence of our present global crisis in reality a debt crisis? Isn't most of the pain and suffering being endured now by the Third World countries, by those who formerly relied upon government wealth transfer programs, by farmers, real estate speculators, consumers, and businesses, the result of the use of debt where the future was not accurately predicted? Doesn't it follow that nations totally engulfed by debt are also nations enslaved, and the forerunner of a global slave state? Do we really want such a lifestyle for ourselves or our children?

Rather than have steady consistent, reliable, linear, predictable growth, which provides security for all in a properly constituted non-debt honest-money economic system, we have opted for the insecurity which comes with the cyclical booms and busts of a fractional reserve debt economy. Debt is the source, the cause of all economic booms and busts!

Debt brings misery in an approximate fifty-year cycle because human nature has not changed. This fifty-year economic progression of human action looks like this: We begin with a depression. As a result of the depression, people become thrifty. This thrift, or savings, creates confidence. Confidence then leads to investment. Investment creates economic activity. Economic activity results in prosperity. But by this time, the lessons of the depression have been forgotten. Prosperity is followed by easy credit. Easy credit results in overproduction. Overproduction leads to the inflationary use of credit and inflationary sales, collateral and values. This inflation leads to insecurity, not to mention financial, psychological and physical exhaustion. Finally, a type of social self-destruct mechanism sets in, often in the form of a panic, which brings us back around again to the contraction and depression.

We see that debt is inherently unstable and the source of economic cycles. Debt is based upon confidence. And we all know what confidence is. Confidence is suspicion asleep.

Debt makes everyone a speculator, rewarding the shrewd, the clever, and the quick, while punishing the hardworking and simple. Debt eventually destroys the middle class and produces a wider span between the very rich in a society and the many poor. Thus debt (death), when it is mature, provides the breeding ground for communism/socialism among those who have been the victims of the inflationary debt-cycle. Perhaps through no fault of their own, these victims are left with bewilderment and bitterness from having been run over by the debt-caused realities. The end of debt therefore is class conflict, revolution and warfare. Eventually in this terminal stage of the debt-cycle, government bureaucracies naturally arise to both keep the peace and as agents of totalitarian wealth redistribution. Bureaucracies flourish, transferring economic basics from the few, debt-created rich to the many debt-fleeced poor. The bureaucrats, as well as those who rule over them, are the only real long-term beneficiaries of a debt economic system. Bureaucracies put into effect socialism, the brother of communism.

We can further say that debt violates human rights. Human rights are property rights, because it takes property, such as food, clothing and shelter, to sustain human life. Furthermore, both mental and physical work require property in order to be fulfilled. The poor end up with less and less property to do their physical and mental work because they cannot predict the future accurately, nor act on it. The rich get richer and the poor get poorer in a debt capitalistic and cyclical economic system. This produces an evolutionary survival of the fittest in a most ruthless way, carried out by man as the ultimate predator, in the city primarily, which is today's modern jungle. Widows and orphans are easy prey.

There is no rest, no sabbath, in a debt-based economic system. Due to compound interest, debt is an ever steeper treadmill that exhausts the society which bases its economic system upon its use. Do we dare exhaust our physical, economic, psychological, political and social reserves on a debt treadmill, when we have sworn political and military enemies who seek to devour us? (Perhaps we have done so because our greatest enemy is within.)

To add insult to injury, the evidence is now overwhelming that Western civilization's multinational debt capitalists and banks have not only financed but have continued to ensure the survival of the external enemies who are sworn to destroy us. I am speaking of the reality that we, by our monetary and economic irresponsibility, have allowed power-lusting, ruthless and greedy debt capitalists to finance the Russian Revolution, which produced the U.S.S.R. Furthermore, we continue to keep the Soviet Union and its satellites on their feet as a global power. Through our bank loans, grants and transfers of food and technology, we allow one of the bloodiest powers in all of history to further promote revolution and bloodshed, and to create poverty while establishing tyranny and slavery worldwide. The arms race is truly insane, particularly since we could easily bring the communist powers to their knees by ceasing to support them economically and financially.

A perhaps even darker blot on Western civilization's debt capitalism is the now indisputable confirmation that our debt capitalistic banks and industry actually financed and supported Adolph Hitler's Nazi Germany. The works of Dr. Antony Sutton have documented this in detail.

Capital/surplus/savings is the basic wealth producer in all societies, the evidence of a long-term view. Debt, by its very nature, is a short-term perspective. We borrow from the future by mortgaging the past to consume in the present. We can see then that consumer debt is particularly suicidal. It produces nothing of future value. And even productive debt leads to excess capacity in capital-intensive industries long-term as error-prone men continually overestimate the consumer's ability to buy in the accelerating debt-based inflationary auction. It is no small wonder that today, too much of our industrial capacity is idle.

Because all loans require collateral, debt is usually assumed by the rich and powerful in an attempt to get even richer. Thus, debt has benefitted politically-powerful special interests, such as multinationals like Chrysler and the Westlands Water Project in California. The February 14, 1983 issue of *U.S. News* discussed how the Farmers Home Administration loans aided primarily the rich and powerful instead of the poor and needy. Nepotism was also involved. And yet, 80% of the jobs created in this country are created by small businesses (like farmers), which are the first to be squeezed out of the capital markets in a credit/debt crisis. Small businesses go bankrupt and lay off their employees because they can't get loans. And the waste and poor use of money in such government agencies as the Small Business Administration is so well documented that such agencies have now become a sad political joke. (Government bureaucrats regularly make a bad problem worse long-term.)

Indeed, one primary evidence that we have reached the end of our rope in this debt capitalistic crisis is the fact that we are experiencing the highest real rates of interest in this century, last seen during the Great Depression. Some major banks report that the federal government is consuming more and more of our national savings. If the Fed monetizes the federal debt in an effort to lower real interest rates, the fear of inflation can quickly return and turn interest rates higher, weakening the economy. This is followed by the destabilizing withdrawal of foreign deposits from U.S. debt instruments and banks. If real interest rates remain high, as debt service continues to consume the available funds which otherwise would be put to productive purposes, we inevitably slip into a greater economic slump. It takes ever expanding credit use and inflation to keep a credit-based economic system alive. It's no different than with a drug addict who requires ever increasing amounts of drugs to get high.

Soaring inflation has been checked by soaring real interest rates, with a very short response time. When an economic system has reached the point where it can only give its people painful hyperinflation, severe unemployment, high real interest rates, a depression, or a war — which is all we have available to us now long-term — the system is bankrupt.

The appeal goes out today for honest money, for some type of a commodity standard, perhaps a gold standard, or free market money. Honest money is money that is owned, not owed. It either represents a commodity or is a commodity. And yet, the effect of an honest money system is both thwarted and defeated if a fractional reserve banking debt system is not also eliminated. In such a system, debt, based upon honest money, can multiply and pervert each honest dollar numerous times, depending upon reserve requirements. This is monetary inflation. Fractional reserve debt banking prevents an honest money (gold standard-type) system from functioning as intended.

Inflation is caused primarily by the creation of credit/debt in a fractional reserve banking system. Inflation is a tax upon savers. Debt-created inflation is also theft. It steals from the trusting savers, and the simple, naive poor.

Banks, when they create credit through a fractional banking system, or the federal government, when its debt is monetized by the Fed, are both acting as gods, creating something out of nothing. The inflation which results is the corruption of money. Can institutions that have created corrupt money remain untainted?

The U.S. dollar is the world's reserve currency. But the U.S. dollar is, in and of itself, a debt. A Federal Reserve Note is a debt, by definition. It is counterfeit (fiat) money, because real money, honest money, is a commodity or has a commodity backing it fully. Debt money is borrowed into existence at interest, not earned into existence as is honest money. Thus, the Federal Reserve central bank monopoly today, by controlling the supply of the medium of exchange (fiat debt money), controls the global marketplace. Whoever controls money, controls society. The borrower is the slave of the lender.

Economics is basic to a social order, and money is the lifeblood of an economic system. Furthermore, an exclusive monetary cartel that issues debt money, by the very nature of cartels, depresses the price of other competing monies such as commodity prices. This is why OPEC, to compete, had to establish an oil cartel. We see this warped distortion today in the commodity futures market, for example, where leveraged (debt) commodity futures contracts set the price for physical copper, which copper producers follow. Put another way, instead of copper producers setting the price of copper, leveraged debt speculators in the commodity futures markets set the copper price and then the copper producers follow this speculative lead. The tail is wagging the dog, so to speak. It is no different in the global economic system when it comes to debt money and the price of commodities or raw materials. This is why when the U.S. dollar soared, commodities fell through the floor globally. Do we desire to trust our economic destiny long-term to international debt capitalists and trading/distribution cartels?

What government, once in debt, ever gets out? The U.S. federal debt doubled in the last five years and is projected to again double in the next three years, based upon present interest rates and compounding. As a distraction from debt-created economic crisis, governments often move their people to war. The debt-induced economic crisis which engulfed Argentina, for example, was a primary motivation for its invasion of the Falkland Islands. Wars are expensive. When people have to compute the cost of the wars and pay up front, they seldom fight. But debt, and the inflation created by debt, makes wars easier to fight; it disguises their cost. This is why nearly all wars are financed. And, wars are extremely profitable for the multinational banking interests who finance both the war and the reconstruction efforts which follow, not to mention the profits for the munitions suppliers and multinational postwar reconstructionists.

The use of debt is a pagan practice. In primitive (pagan) cultures, the aborigines take their wealth to the priests — at celebrations known as "potlatches" — who then smash it. We have done the same thing. We have taken our hard-earned productivity to the bankers, who have loaned over $1 trillion to developing Third World and communist countries; and we have loaned over $2 trillion to the federal government. Both, in their spendthrift ways, have smashed our hard-earned productivity. We'll never see the return of our wealth. It's gone. It has been smashed, squandered, and transferred just like in the pagan potlatches.

Bankers today are the equivalent of the pagan priests. Both smash wealth. We have financed our own unemployment through U.S. debt-financed industrial production abroad. And, of course, there is the irresponsibility that runs hand-in-hand when we give up control of our productivity, our money. Embezzlement by bank employees, and the siphoning off of funds by corrupt politicians and bureaucrats, is frequently in the news.

Most bankers know as much about money as most car salesmen do about automobiles. Bankers tend to lend for the wrong project at precisely the wrong time. Why? Bankers are security oriented. Thus, bankers only feel secure in making a loan when all the apparent risk is removed, and all the information concerning the investment is known. But markets are discounting mechanisms. Markets anticipate the future. Profits only accrue when risk is evident and total information is not available. Therefore, bankers tend to lend at precisely the wrong time, when risk is maximized, when all information is absorbed by the marketplace concerning an investment, and the investment potential in the particular project is already maximized.

Were all the real estate/oil loans that banks and savings and loans made in 1979 wise? Who in their right mind considers the multinational banks' loans to Poland, Yugoslavia, Romania, East Germany, Mexico, Brazil, Argentina, Peru and Chile prudent? This same thing happened in 1929, too. And now these bankers have the audacity to tell us that these countries have a "liquidity" problem, when the real problem is *insolvency*! How are we going to solve the problem of Third World countries' poverty (a relative concept in and of itself), when we can't solve the problem of our own U.S. city slums? How are these Third World and communist countries going to import American-produced goods when their very debt crisis has already dictated that they follow austerity programs, particularly when it comes to U.S. imports? (This in turn aggravates our trade deficit.) Where is the foreign aid which built this country when it was undeveloped? The United States was developed by hard work and equity!

Why did we allow ourselves to be financially raped by having the big banks use their bought-and-paid-for politicians to expropriate $8.4 billion of our taxpayers' funds and transfer it to the International Monetary Fund (IMF), so the IMF could then give these funds to the Third World deadbeats so they can pay back their loans to the big banks? It's the Panama Canal giveaway, all over again.

We put our money in these banks supposedly for safekeeping. And then we had to pay to get it back — our own money! The Caribbean pirates never had it so good. Not only was the $8.4 billion gift to the IMF from U.S. taxpayers multiplied four times by way of so-called loans, the IMF further refused to sell its 103 million ounces of gold, the marketing of which could have raised some of the money it needed. What hypocrisy!

We are seeing the working out of the Hegelian synthesis of banking and government, both powerful, at the epitome of the evolutionary spiral. All of us serfs/slaves look up and pay homage with our taxes and bank deposits. It is economic warfare, nothing more, nothing less. And we have not even taken into consideration our taxpayer subsidies to the Federal Financing Bank, the Export-Import Bank, the World Bank, the International Development Association, the African Development Bank, the Asian Development Bank, the Inter-American Bank... ad nauseam.

Debt capitalism truly makes greed — the love of money — the root of all evil. The British economist who got us into this mess, John Maynard Keynes, in his 1930 work, *Economic Possibilities For Our Grandchildren* wrote: "Beware! For at least another 100 years we must pretend... that fair is foul and foul is fair; for foul is useful and fair is not. Avarice and usury and precaution must be our gods for a little longer still."

By startling contrast, the father of our country, George Washington, who established the basis for economic prosperity in our early history, warned: "Avoid likewise the accumulation of debt, not only by shunning occasions of expense, but by vigorous exertions in time of peace to discharge the debts which unavoidable wars have occasioned, not ungenerously throwing upon posterity the burden which we ourselves ought to bear."

We are at the end of a 510-year civilization cycle. Our banking institutions began approximately 500 years ago. Again, under our present economic system, our long-term options are only hyperinflation, deflationary depression, high interest rates and soaring unemployment, and/or war.

The logic behind atheistic evolutionary humanism is clearly anti-American. The relative Hegelian dialectic of thesis and antithesis leads to synthesis. Debt capitalism, the thesis, created communism, the antithesis. We are moving toward the synthesis, a One-World slave empire, made possible by debt. And yet this approaching synthesis, which is taking us to economic purgatory, offers another alternative, the potential of economic salvation.

At its point of apparent greatest economic strength, debt capitalism is exposing to us its point of greatest vulnerability. Now is the time for an honest monetary system. We must overcome evil with good. We have our contract with our government, based in the U.S. Constitution and the Declaration of Independence; we have our contract with our God, found in the Bible. These are the contracts upon which this country was built, and are the legal tools necessary to ensure our victory.

The greatest drawing card of communism is that the workers own the means of production. This is in theory a legitimate and moral goal. But what we have seen historically, is that where this goal is attempted by coercion, by government force, it fails miserably. Communism is everywhere an economic failure, in Eastern Europe, in the Soviet Union, in China, in Vietnam, in Angola, in Mozambique, in France, in Cuba, in Nicaragua — everywhere.

In the system of debt capitalism, it is the appeal of independent, personal economic freedom, which is attractive and moral. We have seen clearly, historically, where men are free, they are economically productive. The United States, West Germany, South Korea, Taiwan, Singapore and Hong Kong are shining examples. And yet, debt capitalism does not work. Now its ultimate crisis is clearly evident. Debt capitalism increasingly results in vertical, slavelike employer-employee bureaucratic relationships, rather than a horizontal, contractual, prosperous, free enterprise approach.

The economic answer to our dilemma comes from the correct synthesis, pulling from the best of both systems — the workers as the owners of the means of production drawn from communism, and mixing them with the individual freedom drawn from debt capitalism. This will result in the synthesis and a potential economic explosion heretofore unknown by mankind. This synthesis is, providentially so, also one and the same thing as Christian free enterprise. It is the Biblical condemnation against debt and usury, which gives rise to equity financing and free enterprise, with the workers as the owners of the means of production in an environment of personal freedom. Then and only then does the God-intended financial harmony and cooperation between workers, management and ownership exist, whereby each individual is an investor in a sole proprietorship, a partnership, a joint venture, or nondebt-burdened stocks or commodities. This helps trigger the long-term view which creates capital/surplus/savings, the basis of wealth for all.

The elimination of debt in an economic system produces the "land" surplus and also stimulates the "labor" long-term view, which is the human surplus. Surplus is the source of wealth, the product of land and labor. The problems with labor unions, government wealth transfers and bureaucracies, environmental distress, technology, Third World development, military conflict, defense and human rights all begin to melt away. A nondebt economic system solves or moves toward solving all materialistically-related problems.

In the economic arena, debt is a primary contributor to all of our economic problems. Debt encourages man to act short-term and be the ultimate predator or parasite, rather than act long-term and be the ultimate resource.

As I painfully documented in the "Pedigree" chapter of my book *Wealth For All: Economics*, the creative, productive, job-producing, driven entrepreneur, who is an economic blessing for society in a nondebt, equity-based economy, often becomes the ultimate predator and curse of mankind as a debt capitalist. When an empire oriented entrepreneur uses debt, rather than equity financing, he not only becomes enriched far beyond his personal productivity by OPM (other people's money), he also cuts the links of human checks and balances which keep his tremendous drive under control, and keep him from becoming ruthless. The over achieving entrepreneur fears and distrusts people, particularly those in authority. He wants to play God. He, therefore, seeks personal power and control. Debt allows these shortcomings to become magnified.

The only way that the insecurity of an entrepreneur can be channeled constructively, as a blessing for both himself and mankind generally, is through the use of equity financing, not debt. For, when such entrepreneurs become debt capitalists, they give unbridled vent to their insecurities and pride (the worst of sins). Their unchecked lust for power and accumulation of material goods, status, and control takes over, leading to oppression of their fellow man. The insecurity of the debt capitalist entrepreneur are so great that he never has enough power, wealth, prestige, or status, and so he works relentlessly to enslave everyone and everything. Other men work under him, in a vertical slavelike, bureaucratic relationship, rather than equal to him in a horizontal, contractual relationship, which is the case with equity, nondebt financing.

Under equity capitalism, wealth will overflow to every segment of our society, and then cooperatively into all areas of the world, as all men have an effective stake in the economic production of the goods and services of every other man. Computers and robots should eliminate the need for work, which is mindless physical drudgery, and make possible the development of individual talents as never before. Individual freedom and inequality will be a blessing, as men produce and then exchange the goods and services which their natural talents enable them to best produce, bringing about true contractual equality. Global computerization will make possible a worldwide marketplace of heretofore unequaled efficiency because knowledge will be so pervasive and instantaneously available. Families, the basic religious, social, political, educational, economic and welfare units in all societies, which create surplus-oriented men (men with a long-term view), will be strengthened as the economic pressures dissipate.

Debt and capitalism are antagonists. Debt involves borrowing from the future. Capitalism demands saving for the future. So debt capitalism in its final analysis is an impossibility. The only way out is socialism/communism.

A sovereign God obviously knew what He was talking about when He pinpointed the love of money (greed) as the root of all evil and linked it with His prohibition against debt and compound interest (usury). Religion comes down to economics.

Our battle for justice, freedom and economic prosperity will require moral courage. But the alternative is unacceptable and repugnant — death or slavery. Slaves are always poor.

Truth is on our side. Nothing long-term ever stands in the face of a better idea. Nothing. Ever. The world has reached the point in its history when it has no time for slaves. It's time to slay, once and for all time, the debt dragon.

June 10, 1983

"The control of the production of wealth is the control of human life itself."
Hilaire Belloc

"In a country where the sole employer is the State, opposition means death by slow starvation. The old principle: Who does not work shall not eat, has been replaced by a new one: Who does not obey shall not eat."
Leon Trotsky, 1937

"The failure rate of employee-owned companies is phenomenally small compared with traditionally owned firms. When you consider that so many of these

firms are growing out of the discards of industry and being turned around, it holds real promise for the future."

Dr. Warner Woodworth
Professor of Organizational Behavior
U.S. News — April 18, 1983

"In the last decade the big failures in financial institutions — banks and gold bullion companies — have a message, there is a common thread: where one man runs the show, without delegation of authority, without strong outside directors, there is danger."

Dr. Antony C. Sutton
The Phoenix Letter
April, 1983

"The ideas of economists and political philosophers, both when they are right and when they are wrong, are more powerful than is generally understood. Indeed, the world is ruled by little else."

John Maynard Keynes

"There is one bit of advice given to us by the ancient heathen Greeks, and by the Jews in the Old Testament, and by the great Christian teachers of the Middle Ages, which the modern economic system has completely disobeyed. All these people told us not to lend money at interest: and lending money at interest — what we call investment — is the basis of our whole system...I am not an economist and I simply do not know whether the investment system is responsible for the state we are in or not. This is where we want the Christian economist. But I should not have been honest if I had not told you that three great civilizations had agreed (or so it seems at first sight) in condemning the very thing on which we have based our whole life."

C.S. Lewis in Mere Christianity

"Owe no man any thing..."

Romans 13:8

Chapter Four
MONEY CHICKENS — COMING HOME TO ROOST

There are only three ways money can be created: 1) A fiat act of government; 2) The creation of credit; 3) The monetization of commodities. The first two creations by men are dishonest, and result in inflationary money, poverty, revolution and tyranny over the long-term. Such money is not tied to reality. The third is honest money, rooted in reality.

Regarding government creation of money by a fiat act, monetarist economist Milton Friedman stated, "I have demonstrated on the basis of a twelve-year analysis spanning five centuries that inflation has always only one single cause: the creation of money by the State. Governments today are thus solely responsible for inflation."

In our fractional reserve banking system today, credit money is created out of thin air and is the main source of inflation. Each dollar can be multiplied (loaned) up to seven times through the issue of credit, its redeposit and reissue. Thus, the creation of something, credit, out of nothing simply adds to the total amount of money chasing limited goods and services. When the money supply is increased via credit and the amount of goods and services remains relatively constant, prices rise because the money is watered down and worth less. This is inflation. The creation of credit money is clearly inflationary, and particularly so as the velocity or turnover of money increases with the excessive monetary growth.

Honest money, on the other hand, takes the form of commodities that are monetized. Man must always be rooted in physical reality if he is to be successfully anchored long-term when it comes to financial matters. What we literally need in this world today is a supermarket of money, where people can either choose to hold commodities, paper receipts for commodities, or even computer entries for commodities as money. Sure, the commodities and the representatives thereof will fluctuate. There is no *absolute* security or stability in this physical world. There is, however, *relative* security amid diversity. And a supermarket of money would allow such diversity; it spreads the risk around.

No doubt that eventually a type of money would spring up, which would hold a number of commodities in storage, sort of a money mutual fund, which would be attractive to many people. Money would be traded as it is today, just like stocks and commodities, only with no leverage. We presently have a fiat, floating, trading monetary system which is increasingly unstable. This is what the daily fluctuations of the U.S. dollar, British Pound, Swiss Franc, German D-Mark, and so on, are all about. What we really must do is separate the economic parasites — governments and banks — from their ability to create and control money and credit. We should require a separation of church and state and money.

Today many of the natural economic processes are out of kilter. Real money is created in the country. That is where commodities, the basis of real money, originate. Fiat money is created in the city. So the natural balance between country money (land) and city population (labor) is distorted because the city today has both the economic and political clout. This has led to a widening spread between debt-based city prosperity and rural poverty. People in the city are becoming more politically liberal and are assuming increasing loads of debt, while the country folk are becoming increasingly conservative and seeking to get of debt, just as depression has seized agriculture.

In terms of basic economics, there should be a natural harmony between the city and the country. Country resources (land) are the economic lifeline to city manufacturing (technology and labor). Land and labor are the two harmonious parts of the economic equation. Our politicians do recognize this in a warped sense. Urban representatives team up with rural congressmen in order to back farm welfare programs. In exchange, rural representatives join with urban congressmen to back the food stamp giveaways. Both programs are legalized theft and are based on conflict.

The widening spread between fiat and credit-money-fiction and commodity-money-reality can only last for so long. At some point the stretched rubber band breaks and society comes tumbling down to the hard concrete of reality. First the farmers are hurt. (How desperate the situation is for farmers today is evident in the foreclosures and liquidations so common now in the key farm states.) But in the end, the city suffers the most. The city, unlike the country, cannot with self-sufficiency provide its residents with the basics of life.

The move back toward real money has been accelerating over the last decade. First gold was again legalized. Gold and silver became not only hedges against inflation, but a source of real commodity money. Numismatic coins caught on. Now, a decade later, we're getting even further back to basics. The March 28, 1984 issue of the *Record Herald* of Cando, North Dakota reported:

> Over 400 coordinated gulf grain block meetings will be held throughout the

nation's grain belt on March 29 to continue building the massive grain block farmers started on February 23 when an unprecedented nationwide grain meeting was held, consisting of ninety meetings in fourteen states, all tied together by telecommunications.

Rodger Schlottach, Director of National Farmers Grain Department, announced the 400 meetings for March 29 and said that since the first meeting that was held in Illinois, farmers have put together millions of bushels of wheat, corn and soybeans...

"These meetings are not just meetings to talk about the problems," said Gary Larson. "These meetings are being held to offer a solution by building onto the existing mammoth grain block. This is not a farm organization program. It is a farmer program of all grain producers."

Not only does this type of thing mean that real money is again becoming rooted in the country, it also means that the country will be the place to be, almost overnight, when our fiat and credit monetary system breaks down. It is also extremely bullish for the "protein gold" complex (cattle, grains, etc.) and metals.

Human beings are energy machines. We need food to operate. Food is produced in the country. It will take the military machinery of the city to come out and conquer the country in order to take food from these farmers in a time of monetary breakdown, particularly after the federal storage programs are exhausted. But such domineering action by the city will only be killing the goose that lays the golden egg, precipitating widespread starvation due to famine.

We are getting very close to crossing the line where our thin veneer of civilization breaks down into barbarian anarchy. There is no real sense of personal, cooperative human community in this nation any longer, only the illusion of such, held together by an unraveling fiat and debt-based monetary system. The money chickens are coming home to roost.

May 3, 1984

Chapter Five
THE EMPEROR HAS NO CLOTHES

Despite the all out thrust by the socialistic, bureaucratic establishment to move this country toward a One-World slave state, Americans generally will not yet openly admit that they are economic slaves and that the government is a parasite. Americans are, however, in terms of their own "human actions," already acknowledging these facts. Actions speak louder than words. The slaves are crying for more tyrannical government security. The free men, by their "human actions," are acknowledging that government, the parasite, is an "emperor who has no clothes." The division in the country grows.

At this time in history, as in all periods when the economic times have turned tough, and the climate has turned harsh, free men are throwing off the bonds of their oppressive governments. Let's just look at some of the evidences of breaks with the establishment:

1. *Business Week* (10/11/82) reported, "As many as 30% of all American households have some member working in the underground economy...The underground economy may approach $400 billion a year."

2. Multinational corporations are now subject to attack in this country, as witnessed by the planting of bombs by an extortionist at the Gulf Oil Chemical Company's petrochemical plant in Baytown, Texas.

3. The fallout from the cyanide-laced Tylenol tragedy is that people will increasingly distrust goods which are not locally produced and grown. This is a move toward decentralization.

4. A Gallup Poll found that 60% of voters in political elections now split their tickets. So, Americans are no longer adhering to the "party line." They are becoming more "independent."

5. Major publications such as *U.S. News* are reporting that the U.N. isn't working, that foreign aid isn't effective, and that women in the Army are a failure (10/4/82). Such evidence increasingly makes people independent as they recognize that the solutions sold to them by the establishment all these years were in error.

6. This move toward economic self-reliance is most graphically illustrated by the fact that in this economy, which has damaged the financial statements of multinational banks and corporations, business start-ups for small businesses are at near-record highs. Entrepreneurship is again becoming more sociably acceptable than it has been for years.

This trend of free men moving away from the parasitic, federal government is coinciding with severe economic problems. Presently, there are two pythons that have a long-term death squeeze on both the U.S. and world economy: debt and bureaucracy. History teaches us, however, that it takes cataclysmic events to break the grip of either of these life-squeezing snakes.

There is no easy way out from under the debt load which has choked governments at all levels, and businesses and consumers worldwide. Compounding interest is now off and running exponentially in a world all its own, with productivity having no chance of ever catching up, and in too many cases, of even matching interest payments. Thus, this debt can only be liquidated by being inflated away, or through defaults and bankruptcies.

During this disinflationary interlude, we have seen some normal marketplace responses to excessive debt. Defaults and bankruptcies have been common in the free marketplace. Where loan "rescheduling" has taken place, special considerations in the political/financial establishment have come into play. This has simply put off the day of economic judgment.

The Federal Reserve decided to substantially ease up on the growth in the money supply and to throw in the towel on monetary restraint. However, the still burning embers of inflation run the risk of igniting the entire economic forest again if extreme care is not taken. For this to occur now, however, would threaten the entire bureaucratic multinational debt capitalistic order, a power bloc that does not give up control easily. It is the power of this entrenched debt capitalistic bureaucracy that prevents the marketplace's supply and demand response to the distortion of excessive debt.

One root meaning of the word debt is "death." As I wrote in *Wealth For All*, "When economists tell us that the only effective way to fight inflation is to throw millions of people out of work, as economists admitted in the *Business Week* of February 22, 1982, we know the economic system is bankrupt." Bankruptcy is the "death" of debt. True to this observation, we have gotten lower rates of interest and declining inflation, but the high cost paid has been either soaring unemployment or high real rates of interest, which have eroded our economic institutional base. The sacrifice has been made by the free market sector.

Economic reality ultimately will be manifest. Supply and demand, while blocked and frustrated short-term, will win out long-term (except in a totalitarian state where the black/free market emerges). The result of honoring the special interests of frozen, entrenched bureaucracies has been the devastation of the market-sensitive sectors of our economy. To achieve lower interest rates and lower inflation, we have sacrificed the jobs of nonunionized labor, small businesses, manufacturing, and the real new wealth-producing sectors of the economy — agriculture, timber, oil, mining and fishing.

The very fact that unionized labor has also been so negatively impacted, along with the likes of big steel, speaks of how marketplace economic reality is rising up to strike down rigid, frozen, entrenched, power-vested bureaucratic special interests, which have refused to respond to the needs of the marketplace. The grinding demise of steel is more than a signal that we have lost to foreign competitors. It is a sign that the python of special interest bureaucracy is slowly dying. The tax revolt is a sign that the federal government is dying. The rescheduling of loans and the patchwork efforts of the IMF to hold communist bloc and Third World country loans together in the international banking bureaucracy is a sign that it, too, is dying. Only a One-World socialistic order can save the system now.

Debt, with its compound interest, and bureaucracy, with its inability to respond to the needs of the free marketplace, are being confronted and slowly defeated by the realities of the way the world really works long-term. Because this happens so slowly, it is difficult for us to recognize that we are in the midst of a massive global readjustment.

For interest rates to stay down long means that the private sector has to be flat on its back and/or the federal budget borrowing requirements cut dramatically (or rise slowly). The latter, as we have seen all too clearly, is unlikely. If the Fed continues to ease, it cannot be too long before the euphoric drop in interest rates is replaced by a fear of rekindled inflation, leading to higher interest rates, as bond holders again scramble to escape the brutality of monetary inflation. And, of course, an exploding federal deficit, triggered by a depressed economy, is a tremendous burden on the capital markets, capturing huge pools of savings. Thus, interest rates have fallen in an "air pocket," so to speak. The influx of foreign money and the cancellation of corporate capital expenditures also help hold rates down. But historical precedence suggests that interest rates will not stay low indefinitely.

October 15, 1982

Chapter Six
FORECLOSURE OF U.S.A., INC.

This piece is a "war game," so to speak. It is a thought-provoking and possible perspective on the future. After all, every ally the United States has had against the communists in recent years, our own government has eventually betrayed economically and/or politically. The long list includes China, Cuba, Taiwan, Vietnam, Rhodesia, Nicaragua and now South Africa. Why then, when the time comes, will not this government betray its own people? History is replete with such cases, where power turns on and enslaves those it is sworn to protect, particularly when men are ill-informed and irresponsible, as they are today. How can a government which consistently supports centralization of socialistic power abroad do anything else at home?

Most critics of the Federal Reserve point out that the Fed is a privately-owned corporation, owned by its member banks. They seem unaware that *Sec. 283, Title 12, USC* permits individuals, co-partners and corporations to own up to $25,000 in any one bank or $300,000 total. As a co-partner and corporation, it is possible for an individual to own or control $900,000 in the System. According to *Moodys*, the subscribed capital of the Fed is double that of paid-in capital. There is little or no mention of the fact the FDIC, FSLIC, and the other classes of "federal" insurance are privately-owned stockholder corporations.

Perhaps the reason these institutions escape criticism or review is because they do not directly affect the supply of currency. But, as banking and insurance are entangled in the financial world, with banks owning insurance companies and insurance companies owning banks, then they are all linked to the "federal" world. (An insurance company today is as much of a financial institution as is a bank or credit union.)

In the America of the 1980s, all financial institutions are being enticed or coerced into joining the interlocking network of privately-owned "federal insurance." *The Wall Street Journal*, December 9, 1983, reported how all of Nebraska's joint stock industrial banks were stampeded into joining the FDIC after one such bank, Commonwealth Savings Co., was selected for persecution as a scapegoat by the FBI. What jurisdiction the FBI had in the case of a state-chartered bank is a serious question. What seems important here is that all financial institutions, which in any way contribute to the money creation process (or impede that process), must be brought under control of this insurance company, which is intertwined with the Fed.

In 1933, in a sense, the U.S. went bankrupt and was placed in receivership, said receivership administered through Federal Reserve, Inc. (Of course, it was FR, Inc. that bankrupted us in the first place, and thus it bears the responsibility and liability.) This event led to the privatization of the U.S., making us U.S.A., Inc., the liabilities of which are covered by a massive insurance company operating under the auspices of the U.S. Treasury, IRS, Social Security, Department of Health & Human Services, as well as so-called "independents" such as the FDIC and FSLIC. These agencies protect the monetary debt/credit system. An event which took place at that same time, probably prior to bankruptcy, was the passage of the public liability statute.

The public liability statute limited the liability of ship owners and passed the liability to shippers. It also moved maritime law inland, thus replacing allodial common law with feudal common law. It further introduced the concept of limited liability upon the citizenry.

The concept of limited liability means mutual responsibility and lack of personal responsibility for one's actions, a clearly un-American communistic/socialistic value. This concept feeds into criminal law and could explain the relatively light sentences given for heinous crimes. The only exceptions are crimes against the state, which evoke the most severe sentences. It also might explain plea-bargaining, in which an arrest and appearance before the court (captain's mast) presupposes guilt and allows negotiation of the sentence. (Jury trials, where allowed, are the only safeguard.)

In other words, all of us are contributing to a central fund on a maritime voyage. If anyone suffers a loss, the neighbors pick up the tab. *This is financial communism.* (Recall that it was Karl Marx who recommended the graduated income tax and public school system.) Our passage into maritime law explains why those who attack the income tax as unconstitutional usually lose, unless there is an informed jury trial. We are not paying taxes as such. The system is "voluntary." But we are paying insurance premiums, and the IRS is the premium collecting agency.

Here's the kicker. One would think that participation in an insurance plan is voluntary, but not under maritime law. We, the passengers on this ship, cannot remove ourselves from the manifest once our names are placed on it. Our names were placed on the manifest by ourselves if we were old enough, or by our parents or guardians in the act of declaring dependency, when the income tax was filed. When the head of household claims that he (or she) is a dependent, he is not claiming dependency on himself but is claiming dependency on the ship owners. This means, of course, that the only truly free and immune persons from the upcoming, possible repossession are illegal immigrants. This could explain the citizenship-granting provisions of the *Simpson-Mazzoli Act*.

There was an interesting *pro se* lawsuit that was put together, but never filed. The complaint cites in clause after clause TransAmerica Insurance Co. and its controlling shareholder, TransAmerica Corp., and their affiliated corporations and their directors, and Karl V. Hermann, Wesley Kinder, Richard D. Barger, Gleeson L. Payne, Ludlow Kramer, Bruce K. Chapman, Richard G. Marquardt, H.W. Edmiston, Richard Milhous Nixon, Gerald Rudolph Ford, Jr., C. Douglas Dillon, Henry H. Fowler, Joseph W. Barr, David M. Kennedy, John B. Connally, Jr., George P. Shultz, William E. Simon, Giovanni Batista Montini (Pope Paul VI), Elizabeth Alexander Mary and their beneficiaries and fiduciaries. It alleges that each of them has willingly and knowingly conspired to deprive the people of the State of Washington of their constitutional right to receive gold or silver coin as a tender in payment of debt. It is obvious, if we are under maritime law, that the case would have been lost.

Elizabeth Alexander Mary was Chancellor of the Exchequer of England and Paul VI was head of the now notorious Banco Ambrosiano. The Bank of England was ostensibly nationalized in 1946, as was recently the French Central Bank. Yet both banks continue to pay dividends to their shareholders. According to the *Great Soviet Encyclopaedia* (Vol. 1, page 490c), the Bank of England continues to pay 12% per annum dividends to its shareholders. The Bank of France probably does also. (At least Baron Rothschild shed few tears when that event happened.) A nationalized bank would not pay dividends. What happened in 1946, because of war debts, was that England was privatized; the Soviet Union was privatized in 1917 (See *The Federal Reserve Conspiracy* by Eustace Mullins). Apparently the U.S. was privatized in 1933. WW II was fought because a certain German tried to repossess his country, which itself was privatized after WW I. Hitler, for all his racial madness, had to have some sound appeal to capture the hearts and minds of so many skeptical Germans. Finance, along with elitism, was at the root of Hitler's appeal, even though U.S. debt capitalists helped finance Hitler's rise to power. (See Dr. Antony Sutton's book, *Wall Street and the Rise of Hitler*.)

The question of insurance company identity is also a problem. All states of the union, it seems, have laws that require all other insurance companies to cover the liabilities of any one of them. In essence, this eliminates the distinction of corporate identity. Instead, it makes all shareholders liable for all insurance companies and in fact creates one large insurance company. Combine this with interlocking directorships, subsidiaries, controlling interests, and holding companies and one gets the picture of one large insurance company insuring the business, commerce, possessions, income and lives of all Americans. Nobody should starve in America since we are all insured. (Doesn't this sound like communism/socialism?)

Is the insurance cover for America, TransAmerica Insurance Co.? Its symbol is the pyramid, just like the Federal Reserve's. Is the insurance cover for England, Lloyds of London? (Lloyds is reputedly controlled by DeBeers and Oppenheimer, who control a large amount of South Africa possibly own the gold and diamond mines of Russia. They allegedly at least manage and control them under contract.)

An interesting point is taken from Eustace Mullins, *The Federal Reserve Conspiracy*, which quotes a 1922 edition of *Fortnightly*. Apparently the Soviet Union was privatized by a combination of trusts. The shareholders of these trusts may have even been the very same Wall Street financiers who originally funded Trotsky to the tune of $25 million. They include the J. P. Morgan and Kuhn-Loeb banking houses. Loans were arranged by Paul Warburg, Jacob Schiff, George Guggenheim, all of whom had close ties.

The December 20, 1983 *Wall Street Journal* noted a virtually unheralded event. The Office of Comptroller of the Currency was being given (under a committee headed by The Order member George Bush) the responsibility of supervising national banks as well as bank holding companies, thus removing this responsibility from the Fed, which supervises bank holding companies. Also, the Office of the Comptroller of the Currency was being given semi-independent status, separate from the Treasury. This distinction is important because the Treasurer is, according to *Title 12, USC*, responsible for supervising the Fed. He has never exercised this authority, probably because it is the Fed that effectively selects him for the job. Is it for them (shareholders of the Fed) that he works? These men also select the chairman of the Fed, and have a reserve of reliable and dependable men in the Senate who would not be so foolish as to not confirm their nominations.

There are two other important points: First, according to *Black's Law Dictionary*, maritime loans are not payable if the loss incurred happens at sea or under a *vis major*. *Vis major* includes acts for which the principals are not responsible. Again, according to *The Wall Street Journal*, November 1, 1983, "The greenback may get its first face lift in over fifty years." It is projected that the currency exchange will take place in 1986. This could constitute a *vis major*.

It appears that we are being primed for a debt repudiation. This debt repudiation could take place in the late 1980's, when the independent Office of the Comptroller causes to be put into circulation a new money system. It may or may not have the same value, but that is not germane to the action which will follow. The new currency will constitute a *vis major*. The financial institutions that issued the current Federal Reserve Notes based on debt will find themselves unable to collect payment in the same form in which they issued the debt.

(Don't be surprised to see the Comptroller issue the money directly, ostensibly under a gold cover. This would constitute a sour grapes victory for the "Fight the Fed" and "Return to Gold" people.)

This debt repudiation would not benefit the citizen debt holder, for a currency exchange does not affect him negatively regarding his ability to pay his bills. It affects the banks in their ability to receive payment and could force them to call all loans and foreclose on liens and mortgages. (See my book, *Wealth For All: Economics,* Chapters 2-5.)

Since insurance companies own the banks and the banks own the insurance companies and the whole system is tied up in a web of reinsurance, then liabilities between parent and subsidiary are self-cancelling, and in fact are eliminated when preparing consolidated balance sheets. The act of *vis major* will wipe out the liabilities and obligations since they will no longer be able to honor their obligations and they are not responsible for the act. Entitlements, retirement incomes, and pension funds could disappear, as would Social Security and the much troubled welfare system. The property of the U.S. would be privatized with the same effect as if it were communized.

It is frightening to realize that *debt capitalism is economic socialism just as communism is military/bureaucratic socialism.* We truly are moving toward a One-World socialistic order. (Recall *The Wall Street Journal* article, September 30, 1983, by Nancy J. Needham, "Banks Must Acquire Equity in Debtor Countries.")

It is an undeniable trend that all financial institutions that loan money are being brought under the monetary authority of the Federal Reserve and the supervisory authority of the FDIC, FSLIC, and so on. Under the auspices of deregulation, financial institutions in the U.S. are actually being consolidated.

In complete defiance of the *McFadden Act* (Congressman Louis T. McFadden both knew and feared the power of financial institutions), large banks are spreading across state boundaries and consuming non-bank financial institutions (*WSJ,* 12/9/83 — "Interstate Banking Spreads Rapidly Despite Laws Restricting Practice"). This process was facilitated by the *DIDMC of 1980* and the *Garn-St. Germain Act of 1982.* We will soon resemble Canada, which has eleven banks and thousands of branches. Those banks which are solvent and well enough managed to escape the umbrella, could be forced by the FBI under threat of investigation to join one of the "federal" insurance companies. No institution that loans money or can affect the monetary base will likely be allowed to escape this net.

People who own or believe they own unencumbered property on which the mortgages are paid off would find that they, too, could lose their titles, via the taxing authority of the city, county, and state. Because of uneven revenue flows, communities (or counties) borrow funds in the form of tax anticipation notes. By the authority to tax (place a lien on private property), they issue tax anticipation notes backed up by the full taxing power of the county. In other words, private property is pledged as collateral on their purchase of short-term loans.

All of this will probably evoke a civil disturbance. But, federal plans are already in place to handle it. Contingency plans have long existed, which would move local National Guard units across the U.S. during a time of civil unrest. The Dallas National Guard, for example, could be shipped to Los Angeles, The L.A. Guard to Omaha, the Omaha Guard to Memphis, and so on. In this way, "foreign" U.S. troops control U.S. cities where they have no local ties. The troops will obey orders from the top, from the bureaucratic elite of FEMA (Federal Emergency Management Agency).

A few years ago, *Reader's Digest* ran an article criticizing the Bradley Fighting Vehicle. Among criticisms leveled against the weapon, were its inability to be airlifted, except by time-consuming modifications, and the weapon's vulnerability. The general in charge of development stated that the Bradley Fighting Vehicle fulfilled its mission requirements. Is that mission to squelch civil riots and resistance of dispossessed Americans? It was obviously not designed for foreign deployment, but for domestic use only. Other weapons, like the highly sophisticated Apache helicopter, could, of course, chase dissidents and resisters through forests and into the mountains.

It is unfortunate that laws created by conservative activism in reaction to liberal activism will, like Section 18b of England, be used against their proponents. Of course, liberals and collectivists will enjoy a shallow victory. They will be responsible for the most monumental private property land grab in history, outside of the Soviet Union. (The forces of the atheistic Hegelian dialectic are already moving toward a union of the United States with the U.S.S.R. Timetable: 2010.)

The new world economy could be 100% gold based; countries without gold would have no money. According to *Business Week,* of September 21, 1981, (if I interpret their chart correctly), no government in the free world effectively owns gold. All gold is owned by individuals (in the form of coin and jewelry — 22.7%), while shareholders of the central banks and the Communist bloc account for approximately 77.3%. Federal Reserve Inc. owns 264 million ounces. (Did Nixon's repeal of the prohibition against owning gold enable the Treasury to satisfy an obligation by transferring gold to the Fed?) If 264 million ounces represents 9.4% of the world's gold, it means the world's gold stock is 2.808 billion ounces. If 10.8% of that is lost, then there is only 1.593936 billion ounces for distribution among approximately 4.5 billion people in the world, or .31876 ounces per person. China possesses .5% of the world's gold, Russia 2.1%. (The U.S.S.R., however, is now a primary world gold producer, selling through Switzerland.)

After U.S.A. Inc., is repossessed, we could find ourselves back on a gold standard, with one ounce of gold per capita. The gold, of course, would not be held in general public hands. Only certificates would be issued. If, at time of repossession, our balance of trade is unfavorable, we will have even less gold. This then makes some sense of the recent operation to recover gold from the *HMS Edinburg*, sunk in high seas, outside of international limits. The 480 bars of gold were Russian payment to the Bank of England. Sitting for forty years in storage, they gained value to the point that only 160 bars were necessary to pay off the debt. The joint venture to recover the gold was divided between the owners of England, Inc., and U.S.S.R., Inc. In dollar value, the cost, effort and technology expended in the effort did not appear to justify the hullabaloo and recovery effort. It is the future value and use of the gold, however, that appears to be significant.

Will privately-held gold be confiscated? How about bullion? This will quite likely occur, in exchange for gold receipts. Numismatics? Unlikely. Even tyrants like Stalin and Hitler did not confiscate collector coins.

Only about 3% — 6% of Americans own gold presently. This could preclude a bullion call-in. However, if there is a run on gold, and the price of gold rises dramatically during 1988-92, count on a gold call-in. The long, hard fall in gold from $850 to under $300 washed out most of the general public. One more slight inflationary rise followed by a deflationary collapse would drive gold through the floor, as gold held on margin (commodity futures) is liquidated in a panic. This could occur by 1987.

Interesting. Instead of a biblical jubilee which cancels all debts and leads to decentralization, we have debts cancelled, honest money restored (gold), but centralization of everything unto the one federal government/god. Biblical economic law is sounding better all the time compared to this tyranny.

February 28, 1985

The Banks and Farmers

If anyone has any doubt that there is a concentrated effort underway to bankrupt America's small family farmers, one is simply not looking at the evidence. Federal authorities are encouraging banks to rollover deadbeat, Third World loans, throwing good money after bad, and even loaning more interest money to the Developing World countries who cannot even make their interest payments. On the other hand, federal authorities have been encouraging banks to foreclose right and left on America's small family farms. As a result, eleven of the fifteen states where the banking community is in trouble are agricultural states. The small town agricultural banks are going bankrupt.

This (of course) is providing a field day for the big multinational banks and corporations, who are buying up the small country banks and small family farms by the shovelful. Or, federal lenders are bringing such distress property into the federal domain. Either way, whether the big banks and multinational corporations or federal government own the farmland, it is being centralized. It's the old city versus country problem all over again. Rome, too, destroyed its agricultural community before it collapsed.

Question: How long will rural America be willing to support this government financially, with its taxes, when farmers are seeing their own tax money being used to subsidize and bail out the big banks who made foolish loans to Third World countries?

Question: How long will rural America be willing to place its money in financial institutions, which use that money preferentially for Third World developing countries over its own American depositors?

Dr. Antony C. Sutton, in his February 12, 1985 *Phoenix Letter* reported on the International Institute of Applied Systems Analysis. According to Sutton, IIASA has access to Soviet data banks. Sutton commented, "...this institute, aimed at destroying American farmers, has known Soviet ties."

If anyone had any question that the bureaucracy will resort to flagrant spending, forget the deficit, and run over us in a dictatorial fashion in a time of crisis, just notice what took place at the U.S.D.A.

On Thursday, February 21, 1985, the farm credit aid package fell apart in Congress. It was the typical political war between the Democrats and Republicans, which led to the breakdown. Secretary of Agriculture Block's letter was blamed for the failure. So what did John Block, Secretary of Agriculture, head of that bureaucracy, turn around and do? He made his own law, ignoring the Congress. He dictatorially announced what the U.S.D.A. would do to help farmers and effectively said, "Shove the law. I am the law."

This is a point I have made consistently. *A bureaucracy is its own law.* Those who rule the bureaucracy are tyrants in waiting. The drones underneath simply obey, with no moral accountability. In such a way, great evil is perpetuated. In all bureaucracies — government, religious, economic, educational, business, labor, medical — all of them, bureaucracies allow the men at the top to behave like gods, while those who carry out their dictates, the bureaucrats, have no sense of moral accountability for what they do. So, the top bureaucrats literally get away with murder, which is effectively what Secretary of Agriculture John Block did. Bureaucracy is the greatest manifestation of human evil.

If we had any doubts that the Federal Emergency Management Agency (FEMA) bureaucracy will turn into a nightmarish Attila the Hun, we grimly observe the brutal action of the U.S.D.A., which slams to the canvas any false Pollyannish hope. Crisis brings about bureaucratic dictatorship, slavery and the loss of freedom!

February 28, 1985

Chapter Seven
THE U.S. WAR CLOCK

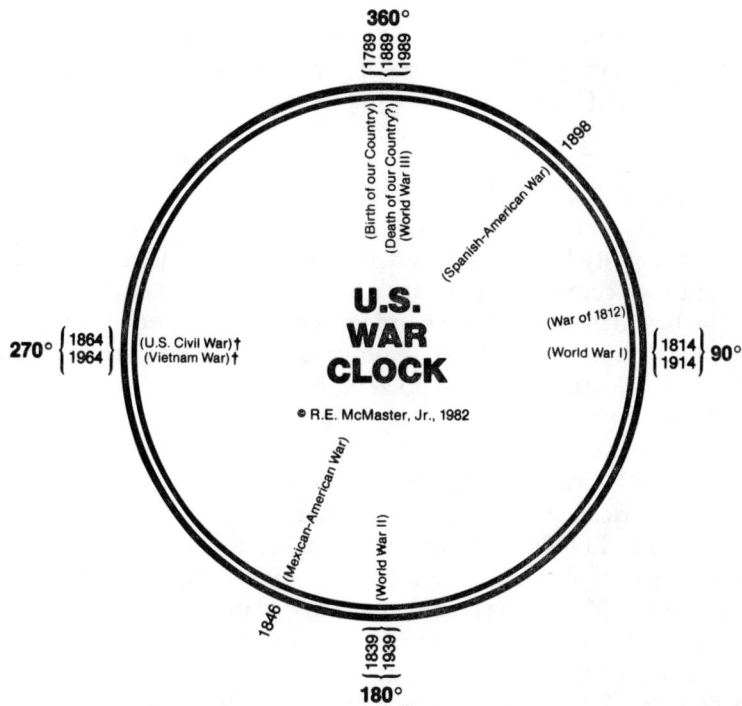

†Although not declared "wars" with foreign enemies in the official sense, and so not included in the Squaring of U.S. Wars, it is nevertheless appropriate to note that Americans were engaged in military combat at the 270° point, both in 1864 and 1964.

In my book, *Wealth For All: Religion, Politics and War,* in Chapter 44, *U.S. Wars Squared,* I wrote, "In terms of U.S. wars, we took the beginning date of each of the five wars and added to those dates significant numerical turning points. What resulted was a 'cluster' of dates between 1988 and 1992. Such a strongly enhanced signal would indicate that the probability of a major declared war by the United States against a national enemy is very likely at that time."

— 43 —

Since writing that chapter, I have continued working on the U.S. War Clock. Here are the recent, grim results of my research.

The birthdate of the United States officially was 1789. This is the starting point for the U.S. War Clock. The U.S. Constitution went into effect when the ninth state, New Hampshire, ratified it on June 21, 1788. George Washington, our first president, took office on April 30, 1789. Rhode Island was the last state to ratify the Constitution in May, 1790. (Rhode Island held back because it wanted "cheap" paper money, something the rest of the states wanted no part of. What a lesson for today!)

In order to harmonize or "square" linear time with cyclical time for the U.S. War Clock, I took a circle, 360 degrees, and divided it into four quarters totaling 100 years. One hundred is the point of completion for a linear time continuum (1-100). Harmonizing the completion of linear time (100 years) with the completion of cyclical time (a circle — 360 degrees) unifies both "kinds" of time. In *Genesis 15:13-16*, the word "generation" means "circle" (cycle) and spans 100 years.

The birthdate of the United States, 1789, is placed at the top of the *U.S. War Clock*. Twenty-five years pass in each 90 degree quarter of the *U.S. War Clock* until we come full circle back to the year 1889, which is 100 years from the birthdate of 1789. This process continues for one more rotation, bringing us to the year 1989. So, in order to read the *U.S. War Clock*, follow the circle clockwise from 1789, to 1814, to 1839, to 1864, to 1889, to 1914, to 1939, to 1964, to 1989.

Next, I marked off the beginning date of the significant wars in American history: the War of 1812, the Mexican/American War (1846), The Spanish/American War (1898), World War I (1914), World War II (1939), and World War III (1989?), projected according to the *U.S. War Clock*.

Notice that the War of 1812 falls only two years short of being perfectly aligned with 90 degrees (off the 1814 date). The next war, the Mexican/American War of 1846 is only seven years removed from being perfectly aligned with the 180 degree position. The Spanish/American War of 1898 is only nine years from being perfectly aligned with the 1889/360 degree first completed cycle. World War I, which began in 1914, falls perfectly on the 90 degree marker. World War II, which began in 1939, falls perfectly on the 180 degree division point. Finally, the projected date for World War III, according to my U.S. wars squared work, falls exactly on 1989, the completion of two rotations (cycles) of the clock, exactly at the 360 degree point, at the end of 200 years.

As you may recall, the average age for a nation is 200 years. Could the point of the birth of this country, the United States of America, in 1789, some 200 years and two cycles later on the U.S. War Clock, mark the effective death of the same country, with the year 1989?

While, in *Wealth For All: Religion, Politics and War,* in the "U.S. Wars Squared" chapter, I addressed myself only in passing to the American War of Independence and the U.S. Civil War, it is interesting to note that at the 270 degree point on the *U.S. War Clock*, we find the dates 1864 and 1964. Of course, the U.S. Civil War was underway in 1864, as was the Vietnam conflict, 100 years later in 1964. The point is this: Wars both declared and undeclared have a strong tendency to cluster at the four division points on the circle (Korean War excepted). The fact that World War I and World War II were right on the button is ominous concerning the projection for World War III. Is the third time a charm? Three is a number of completion, and the projection for World War III falls on 1989, the 360 point of two completed cycles.

If this clock doesn't motivate you into establishing some meaningful priorities in your life, I don't know what will. Those of you who have long been students of cycles and patterns, and observers of my deadly accurate squaring of price-and-time work in the markets, will quickly recognize the overwhelming strength of projection that this U.S. War Clock represents.

I suspect the question you have for me is:

"McMaster, do you really believe that the United States will be fighting World War III, a war for its very survival in 1989?"

My answer:

"Given present trends, unless we have a massive change of mind, a widespread reawakening, and a return to the spiritual and moral principles that built this great country, based on humility, responsibility, giving and a long-term view, unless this occurs, I must tell you honestly, from all the accurate work which I have done with 'time' over all these years, that I unequivocally think we'll be fighting for our very national lives in 1989."

There is additional confirming evidence. Climatologist John D. Hamaker is projecting that civilization will be dead by 1990 unless we stop the increase of atmospheric CO_2. Climatologist Joseph Goodavage is forecasting that, due to lack of foodstuffs, there will be political conflicts, a Third World War perhaps, in 1989. According to the Mayan study of the sun, the hell period for our civilization begins in 1987. Stan Deyo's work projects the 98% probability of a major war accompanying the earthquake and volcanic activity forecast by the Mayans. The French forecaster, Nostradamus (born 1503), projected world-wide drought, earthquakes and volcanic eruptions following Halley's comet in 1986.

Let's get a grip on this grim reaper. We must face the truth. Truth kills those who hide from it or ignore it. We don't have to be a slave to such human action cycles — ever! We can overcome them. Neither do we have to be helpless slaves to natural cycles that exist outside of our physical bodies. We can plan, work, and adjust to the natural cycles in a way to effectively overcome them.

To overcome, however, we must not see ourselves as evolved animals, subject to the natural order. We must see ourselves as spiritual beings who can rise above and rule over the natural order, thanks to our relationship with the Creator of this natural order. In a logical and legal sense, didn't Jesus Christ provide us with that transitional bridge to the Creator with the completion of His work on the cross? Because of that we can now overcome and subdue this world. Do we even have a choice? The *U.S. War Clock* declares that we will choose death unless we get busy and change things.

War is man's ultimate "animalistic" destructive act, the ultimate in "conflict" among the "survival of the fittest." War demands the maximum forced "cooperation" within each competing army, which is committed to decimating wealth. War is brought about by envy (which is economic), greed and lust (economic) and protectionism (the economic breakdown of the free market).

Economic envy, greed and lust are all "animalistic" characteristics of man and thus character (or spiritual) flaws. Protectionism, the economic breakdown of the free market, is ultimately brought about by the individual irresponsibility of man (a spiritual failing), which has elevated government (an economic parasite) to the level of a god (spiritual blasphemy).

Government fills the vacuum of personal irresponsibility and attempts to "protect" the economy with protectionist measures, which ultimately trigger wars. The free market, by contrast, inhibits wars as men internationally buy and sell (or cooperate) with each other. But this ability to contract (make covenant) demands individual responsibility (which is a spiritual virtue) and a long-term view (a spiritual view) as men, by exchanging goods and services, serve each other. Thus, the answer to the economic problem is spiritual, while the working out of the spiritual problem is economic. On the eternal, abstract plane the issue is spiritual, while in this world, the issue is economics.

Spiritual truth and economic reality are both one and the same in producing the greatest good for the greatest number as well as for the individual in time. Religion flows inevitably to economics. And economic prosperity is a direct throwback to religion. This is true because thoughts precede action; the abstract rules over and determines concrete reality.

December 17, 1982

"The Bible prophesy of Daniel involves a 490-year period predicting the death of Jesus. If His death was 28 to 30 A.D., we have completed four 490-year periods totaling 1,960 years to 1988-1990."

Craig Swain in Ace Reporter

"War is a sign of impotence. A system or philosophy of life which has no power to convert becomes imperialistic...A failing faith resorts to war because it

lacks the contagion of faith and conviction and can only force men into its own system. War is the resort of those who lack true power and are declining."
Dr. R.J. Rushdoony, The Eschatology of Death

"But he that sinneth against me wrongeth his own soul: All they that hate me love death."
Proverbs 8:36

"I am come that they might have life, and that they might have it more abundantly."
John 10:10

"The utter destructiveness of war now blots out this alternative. We have had our last chance. If we will not devise some greater and more equitable system, Armageddon will be at the door.

"The problem is basically theological and involves a spiritual recrudescence and improvement of human character that will synchronize with our almost matchless advances in science, art, literature, and all material and cultural developments of the past 2,000 years. It must be the spirit if we are to save the flesh."
U.S. General Douglas McArthur, 1945

"My greatest fear, quite frankly, is that the tremendous deprivation, the tremendous ramifications attending the lack of material goods, particularly foodstuffs, must inevitably result in political conflicts that may ultimately, considering the characteristic stupidity of Homo sapiens, result in some kind of a war — a Third World War, perhaps. I've looked very closely for the natural cause of this and the most likely time for this would be 1989. If we are going to have a global confict, that will occur in 1989, and this is based solely upon my calculations."
Joseph Goodavage, Climatologist

*"Oh, thus be it **ever** when free men shall stand between their loved homes and the war's desolation; Blest with victory and peace, may the Heaven rescued land praise the Power that hath made and preserved us a nation! Then conquer we must, when our cause it is just; and this be our motto: 'In God is our trust!' And the star-spangled banner in triumph shall wave o'er the land of the free, and the home of the brave."*
The last verse of
The Star-Spangled Banner

Chapter Eight
THE U.S. WAR CLOCK — MORE EVIDENCE

War is the evidence of the failure of men to cooperate with each other. War is the full manifestation of the natural man, man the animal, in the ultimate struggle of the survival of the fittest.

Since government is religion applied to economics, war is the evidence of the failure, the bankruptcy, of man's religious, political and economic institutions.

Religious wars are fought when religious institutions fail to win converts by peaceful means. When a religion can no longer entice converts by philosophy, example, or truth, religious wars are fought.

Political wars are fought when a political philosophy fails. Political wars, wars of pride and power, are manifest when a law system fails to convert new advocates and/or retain old adherents. As von Clausewitz wrote, "War is a political act. It is...a continuation of policy by other means."

Economic wars are evidence of the failure of an economic system to win converts. The eminent economist Ludwig von Mises observed that when goods and services fail to freely cross borders, armies pave the way for them.

In terms of the two parts of the economic equation, land and labor, religious, political, and economic institutions are labor-based. Thus, when the landside of the economic equation, climate, becomes harsh, variable and more niggardly, these land-side pressures aggravate the structural and presuppositional weaknesses of man's religious, political and economic institutions, increasing the tendency to use war as a necessary escape valve. Again, war is the clear evidence of the bankruptcy of man's religious, political and economic institutions in combination.

From a financial market perspective, the *U.S. War Clock* has a high probability of accuracy — 78%. If we were dealing with market turning points instead of wars, the 78% probability would have a higher confidence factor.

Is there any more supporting evidence for the *U.S. War Clock*? Yes. According to climatologist Dr. Iben Browning, in *The Browning Letter* of February 21, 1984, two years before high tidal force quarters, nine of our twelve great wars were being fought. Thus, the probability of linking high tidal forces and wars is 75%, close to my 78% probability. The inflationary behavior of the economy with respect to high tidal quarters is similar to the pattern of wars, according to Browning. Wars are inflationary. They have to be financed, and the use of such credit created out of thin air is inflationary.

The implication is that the economy is sensitively geared to war and that both wars and inflation are tied to times of high tidal force and, therefore, to climate. These wars tend to occur at the time of rising northern hemispheric tidal forces, at the time of increasing volcanic activity. This also corresponds to the time when Russian crop yields are minimized, and the occurrence of depressions and/or recessions in the U.S. are maximized, according to Browning's projections and analyses.

Now, if the U.S. is in a depression in 1988 and the Soviet Union has crop failures, both empires will be subject to credibility questions and civil unrest. Then, war between the U.S. and the U.S.S.R. will be an expedient escape valve to distract the people of both empires.

Browning concludes: "To the extent that the future resembles the past, any war that may involve the U.S. has a maximum probability around the end of 1988. Inflation pressures historically occur in years corresponding to those leading up to 1990 — whether war or peace, but especially war.

"In summary, the list of relations is growing: 1988 is the time of maximum probability of: 1) U.S. war; 2) beginning of a recession; 3) inflation; and 4) severe failure of Soviet grain yields."

Browning's research included the same wars as those utilized in the *U.S. War Clock*.

> The nine major wars were declared in years of tidal scale 3.1...(Revolutionary, 1812, Mexican, Civil, Spanish, World War I, World War II, Korean and Vietnam.)
>
> All revolts, uprisings, labor troubles, etc., that involve troops killing civilians (at least 15 periods out of 28) had years of tidal scale 6.2...The next period of tidal forces similar to the periods of troops versus civilians occurs in 1989-92. (Tidal scale 6.5)
>
> Drought, cold, depression, farmer/labor trouble, riots and possible civil wars should typify the period.

Now, Dr. Iben Browning does not use cycles in his research. So, the conclusions he has reached, although perfectly dovetailing with my own, were based upon different data bases, methodologies and assumptions. Browning comments:

> Cycles, time sequence-analysis, tell little about causes, do not necessarily distinguish fundamental from beat frequencies. Since cycles are regular, they fail to take 'non-linear' phenomena into account such as tidal triggering forces which may list spike responses or other sorts of responses. In contrast with time series, another approach known as "causative periodicities"

compare data series with such causes to determine effects.

And yet tidal forces, Browning's trigger factor, are cyclical. Where is the cyclical tie-in, then, scientifically? With planetary alignments! Tidal forces are triggered by cyclical planetary alignments. Here then is the "natural" human action progression (or tendency), beginning with planetary alignment, ending with war: planetary alignments (cycles) — tidal forces — earthquake and volcanic activity — economic distress (land and labor) — government distress — war — inflation — collapse (?).

This is why the ancient empires put stock (literally believed) in astrology, which is nothing less than planetary alignment influencing human action. It was the highest appeal they could make to nature in an effort to gain an understanding of future human mass behavior. They were slaves to nature. They had no theological basis or methodology to rise above and overcome the conflict, chance, and cyclical basis of nature. So, in time, these ancient empires, too, inevitably collapsed as their fatalistic cycle of conflict-ridden human action reaped what it had sowed. Theological ideas have inevitable consequences. We are now following this same gloomy path.

The Mayan study of the sun resulted in the formulation of a 5,124-year cycle of civilization. According to the Maya, 1987 begins the "hell period" of our civilization, when earthquakes will literally rip the earth apart. The Mayan work was based upon planetary study also. Thus, the risk of conflict is great indeed beginning in 1988. In fact, it may mean a Third World War and a civil war.

The year 1989 will be the trough of the moon's 18.6-year cycle. Doesn't the moon affect tidal activity? Of course.

In July 1980, in Kansas City, Missouri, L. J. Jenson wrote a forecasting piece entitled, "Cyclic Business Trend Prospects: 1981-1990." Therein he commented, regarding the decade of the 1980s, "The initial several years are dominated by constructive, positive or bullish factors. Then the swing rapidly turns to increasing negative implications. These elements become very complicated as the years go by until a climax is probable at the end of the decade."

L. J. Jenson continues,

> The last half of the decade in the 1980s (war) is a very complicated crisis in national affairs. The very foundations of government seem at stake. The so-called Left Wing of intense populism seems the driving force. More than 50 years of the notion that government can manage the nation best, guarantee jobs and security, so-called equality in social and economic matters, comes to war with the American tradition and could smash it.
> The intensity of this crisis could make trade and business simply methods of distributing needs of the people. It is a very complex morass in which business could become a responsibility of government. Therefore, as the area after 1983 is reached, the study of reality should intensify.

Anita Kemp in her article, "Cycles Foresee the Future of International

Violence," published in the March 1981 issue of *Cycles*, used a set of six cycles linked with international violence, arms races, United Nations voting behavior, and business shocks. They were the 2.25, 2.7, 5.4, 6.7, 11.0 and 24.5-year cycles. Peak periods for international violence appear from 1980-1990 and 2003-2008. (Browning confirms the latter date as well.)

An article by Anthony F. Herbst entitled, "A 54-Year Cycle in the Purchasing Power of Gold," appeared in the March 1981 issue of *Cycles* Magazine. Herbst commented: "The next ideal crest for the purchasing power of gold in England is at 1990..." Gold is viewed as an inflation-hedge. Wars are inflationary!

Finally, the May/June 1984 issues of *Cycles* featured, "Cycles of Peace, Sunspots, and Geomagnetic Activity," by Buryl Payne. He noted,

> As sunspots increase and decrease every 11 years, so do geomagnetic occurrences...The evidence at this time points to magnetic storms as likely causes of human upsets, including the triggering of large and small scale wars.
>
> Around 1988, sunspot activity will again be on the increase, and international tensions will begin to mount. June 20, 1988 is one time this writer predicts the occurrence of a large geomagnetic disturbance.

While we have focused on the specific probability of war from 1988-1992, let's stand back now and view the broad perspective. Do historians place us in the general time frame of a potential nation-falling war? Indeed they do. The master mind behind the creation of the Drought Clock, who formulated the 510-year cycle, Dr. Raymond H. Wheeler, chairman of the Psychology Department at the University of Kansas, was a man far ahead of his time. Under his instruction, more than 200 researchers worked for over twenty years studying the influences of weather on mankind. Wheeler was not searching for facts that would prove a previously accepted theory. Rather, he was a researcher yearning for truth. Over 3,000 years of weather were evaluated, along with nearly two million pieces of weather information. Over 20,000 pieces of art were studied, as was literature thoughout history. In excess of 18,000 battles were examined. All parts of the world were investigated. Wheeler's efforts were comprehensive and exhaustive.

Dr. Wheeler saw that the time at the end of the 510-year cycle, our time, would be a time evidenced by massive migrations, devastating revolutions and literally the death of the old world and the birth of a new one. Dr. Wheeler expected the death of our world to begin about 1980 and to last until the end of this century, the year 2000. It was his conclusion that governments break down and nations collapse at the end of the 510-year cycle and that there is a wave of international wars, which are nation-falling wars.

The "natural" historians — Toynbee, Durante, and Spengler — concur.

Toynbee noted we are not responding to the challenges thrown at us. Toynbee wrote, "I am not sure whether it is my daughter or my granddaughter who will witness the death of this civilization. A Western Time of Trouble, which appears to have begun some time in the 16th century, may be expected to find its end in the 20th century, and this prospect may well make us tremble."

We are in the "wintertime" of our civilization according to Spengler, a time when commerce dominates everything. PACs control the Congress. "Money rules this world." Government is an economic parasite. "The business of America is business." In June of 1983 we graduated 61,000 MBAs, a 26% increase in five years.

Alexander Tytler, in his 1770 book, *Cycle of Democracy*, wrote,

> A democracy cannot exist as a permanent form of government. It can only exist until the voters discover that they can vote themselves largesse from the public treasury. From that moment on, the majority always votes for the candidates promising them the most benefits from the public treasury, with the result that a democracy always collapses over a loose fiscal policy, always followed by a dictatorship. The average age of the world's great civilizations before they decline has been 200 years. These nations have progressed in this sequence: from bondage to spiritual faith; from spiritual faith to great courage; from courage to liberty; from liberty to abundance; from abundance to selfishness; from selfishness to complacency; from complacency to apathy; from apathy to dependency; from dependency back again to bondage.

The political cycle is as follows: Rule by one (king) — by few (republic) — by many (democracy) — anarchy — rule by one (king).

As Hegel cynically wrote, "What experience and history teaches is this — that people and governments never have learned anything from history, or acted on principles deduced from it."

The civilization land use cycles are always the same, too. Says Eddie Albert: "Man comes, the trees go...the topsoil goes...the desert comes. We are following that path. We Americans are destroying our earth many times faster than any people who ever lived. Man, deforestation, soil erosion, abandonment — that's the cycle. Another word inevitably follows: famine. Every day we are losing 30 hundred-acre farms down the river, 10,000 farms a year, 15 tons of topsoil a second, a yearly loss of 1 ton per every person on earth. We in America have lost about one-third of our arable land since we arrived."

This is the way out. Natural laws are captured and measured by men of science, and transformed from conflict into harmony for the good of man, because men themselves, captured by God's law, have first been transformed from conflict into harmony. We have to rise above nature and nature's modus operandi of planetary alignments, cycles, conflict and chance.

We have to beat this thing, to stop the U.S. War Clock. It's three minutes to midnight on the nuclear scientist's clock — three minutes to nuclear war.

A recent novel, *Warday*, projected war for this 1988 time frame, too. Literature often predicts future reality.

In my 1977 book, *Cycles of War*, I projected war for the U.S. in 1984 in the Caribbean and the Middle East. We've seen conflict in Grenada, Iran and Lebanon. My *U.S. War Clock* is a much stronger signal.

March 20, 1985

"I happen to be one of those who believes that the future is as rigidly fixed as the past. I believe that it is completely knowable — but not, of course, by human beings. I believe for example that it would be possible for God, the Creator and Preserver of the universe, to give you, if He chose, a copy of next year's newspaper.

"I believe that everything is governed by law. In fact, the phrase 'fulfillment of law' is as close as I can come to expressing my concept of the function of universe. And finally, I might add, holding these views, the universe, as I shall try to show you, is to me ten thousand times as magnificent a creation as it would be if I held more conventional ideas."

Edward R. Dewey, founder of the Foundation for the Study of Cycles.

"He hath shewed thee, O man, what is good; and what doth the Lord require of thee, but to do justly, and to love mercy, and to walk humbly with thy God?"

Micah 6:8

"Let us hear the conclusion of the whole matter: Fear God, and keep His commandments: for this is the whole duty of man."

Ecclesiastes 12:13

"Jesus said unto him, 'Thou shalt love the Lord thy God with all thy heart, and with all thy soul, and with all thy mind.' This is the first and great commandment. And the second is like unto it, 'Thou shalt love thy neighbor as thyself.' On these two commandments hang all the Law and the Prophets."

Matthew 22:37-40

Chapter Nine
THE CLIMATE CRISIS

*T*he following article, "The Essence of the Climatic Crisis," by John D. Hamaker, is reproduced with the permission of the Price-Pottenger Nutrition Foundation, (P.O. Box 2614, La Mesa, California 92041).

John Hamaker holds a degree in Mechanical Engineering from Purdue University. He has worked for many years, experimentally and practically, on the relationships between soil, mineral content, agriculture, the level of CO_2 in the atmosphere, weather and climatic changes, and the destruction of the world's food supply. Hamaker's work has also been published in Acres U.S.A. and Aero Sun-Times. The serious attention given Hamaker's analysis by the scientific community commands our attention. When you read Hamaker's comments, keep in mind the incredible climatic disturbances which we have experienced during the last few years — unexpected and severe volcanic eruptions, blistering drought, numerous destructive tornadoes and earthquakes, floods and unforecasted bone-chilling winters.

"For ten years I have been warning that the world's soils are running out of minerals and that glaciation must inevitably follow. Now there is hard evidence that the temperate zone will become a part of the sub-arctic zone in approximately fifteen years. Somewhere in that time period we will stop eating.

"A report by G. Woillard in the October 18, 1979 issue of the English science magazine *Nature* draws a grim picture from a study of pollen in the mud of a lake bottom in south Vosges, France. At the start of a number of past glacial periods, the vegetation changed from temperate zone trees to sub-Arctic needle-bearing trees in a period of 150 years (plus or minus fifty years). The change was one of gradual deterioration until the last twenty years. During the last twenty years the type of vegetation completely changed.

"The 150 year death of the temperate zone vegetation recorded in the French lake mud corresponds exactly with a curve showing the annual percent of increase of carbon dioxide over the interglacial level. The gradual rate of destruction of the forests corresponds to the rate of increase of carbon dioxide. The curve was drawn simply by extending the actually recorded Mauna Loa Curve backward to the middle of the last century and forward to the year 1995 in a smooth curve with an increasing rate of change with respect to time. By 1995 the rate of increase is so great each year that it is pointless to extend the curve farther.

"Tropical forests change to temperate zone forests during glacial periods according to the evidence in pollen studies by Paul Colvinaux, Ohio State University ecologist (*New York Times,* 1/8/80).

"At what point on the curve does the twenty year collapse of temperate zone vegetation begin? Why does the collapse occur so quickly? We already have the answer to these questions. The mechanism of change in the forests involves several factors.

"Temperature change is one factor. As the carbon dioxide from dying vegetation builds up in the atmosphere, it traps the energy required to lower the temperature over the land masses.

"The process of deterioration starts with malnutrition about 150 years ahead of the collapse. Malnutrition results from the using up of the minerals deposited by the last glacial period. The available minerals decrease in quantity to the point where enzyme systems no longer function vigorously. Disease spreads through the forests and they begin to die out.

"The problem starts with the soil microorganisms. As the quantity of available elements decreases, the soil's organism population must decrease. One hundred-fifty-years ago, a virgin soil may have had twenty-five tons per acre of organisms; today's soils generally have less than five tons per acres. The importance of the soil microorganisms is that their protoplasm compounds are the source of the cell protoplasm of every other living thing on earth.

"The key to awareness of the mineral shortage is the easily measured property of acidity of soil, water, and precipitation. If acidity goes up, it is because the mineral supply has become too weak in acid-soluble basic elements for the microorganisms to maintain a neutral soil in which they can thrive. It is probable that the needle-bearing trees can survive on a reduced availability of protoplasm because the needles have far less cells to fill with protoplasm and because the trees can live with only the top branches green while the resin prevents rot from penetrating the trunk from the dead lower branches. Needlebearing trees have taken over from much of our worn out one-time crop soils. Other such soils are kept in production by periodic applications of agricultural limestone. However, the large quantity of basic elements available are not matched by an availability of other elements from the silicate rocks, because neither the acids of chemical agriculture or those from acidic rain can dissolve the silicate. The result is specific element shortage, malnutrition, and death.

"When the tropical forests are dead and gone, the very badly depleted mineral supply will probably support no life until glacial gravel dust borne on very high winds has remineralized the soil to start the process of plant growth. Temperate zone forests are those which will grow in the cooler equatorial atmosphere of the glacial period. They will begin the process of removing the excess carbon dioxide from the atmosphere and bringing the carbon back to earth to renew life on earth.

"There have been numerous reports of crop damage due to acidic rains. Many lakes in the Northeast have become so acidic that no life can exist in them. Lewis and Grant (*Science,* 1/11/80) report some frightening statistics. On the Colorado section of the Continental Divide where there is very little industrial pollution in the direction of the prevailing wind, the pH of all precipitation dropped from 5.43 to 4.63 in just three years. Neutral is pH 7.0. The precipitation was already acidic three years ago, and it increased in acidity by .8 of a point on the pH scale in just three years. Since the curve is almost vertical at the year 1995, we can go back twenty years to 1975 for the start of the twenty year critical period and not be off by more than a couple of years. The pH must then have been about 6.0

"Temperate zone vegetation (including crops) cannot grow on acid soils. The large numbers of dead and dying trees in our forests is directly attributable to the increasing acidity of the soils and decreasing quantities of available elements. Dead forests burn easily with a hot fire which oxidizes large quantities of atmospheric nitrogen. Lewis and Grant found that the oxides of nitrogen were dominant in the acidic precipitation. The more trees die and burn, the more the soils become acidified and the more trees must die. There are also a number of mildly acidic gases released from burning wood. These, plus the acidic gases from volcanism, are nature's way of bringing on glaciation. Man's fossil fuel fires are a big factor in the destruction. Logically, the twenty years for the change in vegetation should be much less because of industrial pollution.

"The burning of the temperate zone vegetation will carry huge quantities of carbon dioxide into the atmosphere. In the zones of latitude where the sunlight is most intense, the carbon dioxide holds the heat at the surface of the earth providing the energy to increase the evaporation and to move the massive cloud cover to the polar regions. The cloud cover lowers the temperature and increases the quantity of cold air which flows south over the land masses. The temperate zone will become a part of the sub-Arctic zone. We can't grown grain in the sub-Arctic. Growing seasons have already been shortened and interrupted by freeze damage. Furthermore, the acidic rain will destroy growth all over the world. The local areas to survive will be the few near the equator that are blessed with a constantly renewed supply of basic minerals sufficient to maintain a neutral soil in spite of acidic rains.

"Humanity should have seen the impending crisis in the slow rise in atmospheric carbon dioxide and the deterioration in forests and jungles. It would have been easy fifty years ago to remineralize the world's soils and bring the carbon dioxide level back to normal. Now we must stop the rise in carbon dioxide level in six or eight years or we must die shortly thereafter. I all but begged the Carter Administration to institute a massive soil remineralization program and to propagate it worldwide as the condition for survival of all of us. Nobody on this earth has either time to waste or resources to use on anything but soil remineralization and the associated food and energy programs compatible with our survival. There must be a common struggle for survival or we won't stand a chance."

Summarizing Hamaker

Hamaker's basic thesis is that as the soil becomes progressively demineralized, plant growth decreases. The soil has less plant food, and so there are less plants. Plants draw CO_2 from the atmosphere. Plants breathe the CO_2. The increasing build-up of CO_2 around the globe can be traced directly to the destruction of forests through forest fires, clearing (deforestation), replacing plant growth with human development (asphalt for agriculture), poor agricultural techniques which result in the demineralization of the soil, the burning of fossil fuels, and the overall demineralization of the soil which occurs globally from glaciation to glaciation.

The level of CO_2 has increased in our atmosphere by 13% since the time of the Industrial Revolution. Of this 13% increase, 5% of it has occured since 1962! This CO_2 build-up also explains the recent violent weather we have been experiencing worldwide, as well as why the "greenhouse effect" warms the earth while the north pole's ice fields and glaciers have continued to expand since 1940.

Again, simply put, Hamaker's basic thesis is that all this climatic destabilization has been caused primarily by the demineralization of the soil and the resultant inability of the soil to support the plant life necessary to remove excess carbon dioxide from our atmosphere. Nature's way, normally, is for plants to grow faster as CO_2 increases, because plants thrive on CO_2. This is not occurring because the elements in the soil, spread by the previous glacial age, have been used up. As a result, the microorganisms in the soil die. These microorganisms are the source of the plant's cell protoplasm. So plant life diminishes. With the natural cycle of the survival of the fittest, plants (trees) which are weak and undernourished, fall victim to insects, diseases and drought, and are vulnerable to fire. The progression runs like this:

1. Demineralization of the soil.
2. Soil microorganisms die.
3. Plants can't produce adequate cell protoplasm.
4. Plants become sick and die.
5. CO_2 increases in the atmosphere.

The CO_2 build-up, as previously mentioned, accounts for both the "greenhouse effect" and the growth of the polar region (ice). Increased CO_2 in the atmosphere leads to a greater difference in temperature between the equator and the poles. In the tropical, equatorial areas, where the sun's rays strike the earth most intensely, the CO_2 "greenhouse effect" traps heat energy from the earth and increases the atmospheric temperature. As a result of this temperature rise in the equatorial tropical regions, there is increased water evaporation which results in more clouds. The result of this is the increasing meridional flow. This north-south flow has altered the normal west-east flow (jet stream), causing abnormal weather patterns.

From the northern polar region, the high pressure cold air flows south toward the equator, displacing the low pressure, and the hot, moist air in this tropical region, forcing it out over the ocean, where it then flows back up toward the Arctic. This warm, moist air dissipates its heat and moisture over the northern polar region, increasing the polar ice build-up, before it again becomes cold, dry air flowing south toward the equator in the continuation of the cycle. The result in the summer is that day after day of cloudless skies with high CO_2 levels triggers record temperature increases and resultant droughts. In winter, blizzards and the like become more frequent as cloud cover reflects the sun's energy back into space which increases cooling. Thus, we have, in an extension of Hamaker's thesis, the explanation for drought, blistering hot summers, and our bone-chilling winters. Such weather extremes signal that we are in the first stage of glaciation. Volcanic activity is another confirmation.

According to Hamaker's study of the CO_2 increase in the atmosphere, we approach the vertical in 1995 — a blow-off, so to speak. His solution is that we must remineralize the soil and plant trees like crazy prior to then. We also must move quickly from the burning of fossil fuels to solar and other forms of energy.

Hamaker has discovered that farmers can very easily and practically remineralize their soil. The average rocks which cover the earth's surface are composed of the proper balance of elements necessary for healthy plant life. Gravel from glaciers and rivers is excellent, and can be crushed and spread on agricultural and forest lands. Hamaker's estimate is that gravel ground to a fineness of 90% passing through 200 mesh is ideal. Only three tons per acre of this ground gravel dust is required to stabilize forest and crop deterioration. Maximum growth is achieved by the application of twenty tons of ground gravel per acre.

Hamaker's solution basically substitutes man's grinding and spreading of gravel for what glaciers do naturally. As glaciers expand and flow from north to south, they grind up the rocks and gravel beneath them, which is nature's way of remineralizing the earth. Hamaker's warning is that if man does not remineralize the earth now, on his own, the glaciers will do it for us — and soon.

Perhaps we should heed Hamaker's warning. What are the odds that we will be the members of only a handful of people who will survive at the equator during the next glacial age, if Hamaker is correct? The world's excess food supply should by used up by the late 1980s. The age of "protein gold" should be in full stride in the late 1980s, and early 1990s. We should then expect worldwide migrations, wars, and revolutions as a result of these drastically changing climatic conditions. The civilization cycle runs as follows:

    1. Man comes to virgin territory.
    2. Man chops down the trees and clears the land.
    3. Man abuses the land and the topsoil disappears.
    4. Famine arrives and the civilization collapses.
    5. The desert rules (or glaciers?).

April 9, 1982

Chapter Ten
THE DEBT CRISIS

One of the central points I made in *Wealth For All: Economics* was that the love of money is the root of all evil, that greed is at the base of man's economic downfall. I further tied that into debt (which is economic death) and slavery. In this light, I very much appreciate Billy Jones sharing W.D. Gann's words from a pamphlet Gann penned in 1940 entitled, *Face Facts America! Looking Ahead to 1950.* Gann wrote:

> There are many causes for the present troubles existing throughout the world, but the greatest cause of all is greed for power and money. The Bible says that love of money is the root of all evil. Unwise leaders, ruthless and reckless politicians in their greed for power have deceived the people and this is the most important cause of all, in my opinion, of the world's troubles.

How far have we come since W.D. Gann's time? The late David Rhoads, publisher of *The Rhoads Conclusion*, wrote with startling clarity how the International Monetary Fund is pulling together a One-World Order. Greed and the love of money are still at the root of all evil.

> To stem the process, the major nations of the world are transferring power and pledging money to the International Monetary Fund (the IMF, a 146-country fund). It is now functioning fully as an international lender of last resort, a central bank for central bankers. It is now a full-fledged world bank in every respect. (It can even create money, called SDR's!)
>
> The IMF used to be a passive arranger and overseer of a few unimportant government and bank loans to some unimportant international borrowers. Now though, it is dictating loan restrictions and austerity measures for borrowers in trouble; it is collecting funds and arranging direct emergency loans; and it is dictating policy to private banks and nations of all stripes, both debtors and lenders.
>
> The IMF is now dictating internal fiscal and monetary policy to thirty bankrupt nations. Thirty governments are now being run by the world's new central bank.
>
> Then last month, the IMF's managing director demanded that 1400 private banks and creditors *increase* their loans to Mexico before it would proceed to arrange a rescue. Naturally the creditors did as they were told.
>
> And when Yugoslavia began to go under, the IMF called for statements showing what that nation owed to each bank. Reading between the lines, the world's bankers surmised that the IMF was looking for lenders who have

reduced their exposure...it's going to put the arm on them to give the money back, to lend more to Yugoslavia, not less. That frosted the bankers a bit. But they dutifully submitted their reports anyway.

So the gloves are off. In this hour of crisis, all the world's governments and bankers are giving up their sovereignty to save their skins. And the IMF is finally unmasked as the world force that we knew it to be all along.

Unfortunately, your bankers and politicians traded away your sovereignty as well as their own. The IMF director is already sternly directing the U.S. to get its fiscal affairs in order, to close its budget deficit. I agree that it's a good idea. But I resent being told to do it by some non-American, unelected world-class bureaucrat!

The International Monetary Fund has just increased its Special Drawing Rights (SDRs) to $90 billion from $61 billion. This 47.5% increase in IMF quotas effectively doubles the resources of the IMF. (Saudi Arabia has even pledged $2 billion to the IMF.) Only 50% of the present $61 billion of SDRs are in currencies that can be used for loans to Third World countries.

The U.S. total pledge to the IMF is $17.9 billion. Interestingly enough, the IMF holds approximately 100 million ounces of gold to increase its liquidity. When push comes to shove, the bankers hold their gold.

It doesn't really matter from what perspective one views our crisis:

1. *A Biblical perspective* — that the love of money (greed) is the root of all evil; that a debt-ridden world is in fact a world of death and slavery.

2. *A historical perspective* — that debt has been used since ancient times to enslave people, going as far back as Assyria; that, as historian Oswald Spengler wrote in the early part of this century, during the latter days of a civilization commerce dominates everything.

3. *A conspiracy perspective* — that money manipulation and international bankers rule the world, are the basic controlling factor in all aspects of life, including politics and war.

4. *A failure of leadership perspective* — that men (particularly) have become weak and have failed to lead. Strong men draw their strength from above and then from within, develop character, and exercise leadership and dominion over their environment. Weak men are materialistic, with the vacuum in their souls drawing strength from things external to them, seeking dominion over other men.

5. *A financial perspective* — that there is no way the compounding interest on this country's public and private debt (or the world's debt for that matter) will ever be paid, which is bringing us nearer and nearer to a financial holocaust — a devastating disinflationary depression or runaway inflation, possibly a disinflation first, followed by a hyperinflation, triggered by the interrelated Third World/communist country debt, and the oil-producing country and multinational bank interdependency network.

6. *A communist perspective* — that the ultimate crisis of capitalism (debt capitalism) is at hand; that the formerly free and independent people of Western civilization have become dependent upon the government dole and conditioned to be slaves, and are now literally waiting for their collars; that control of man's economic means is control of his will since economics is basic to life. Furthermore, since the people understand nothing about economics, the worldwide socialistic revolution is at hand.

7. *An international perspective* — that free markets always dominate and overwhelm government controls and attempted manipulations, unless the market is totally controlled. In this present case, the government's way out of this mess is to have no free markets worldwide. Instead, internationalists will seek total and absolute control over economics and commerce internationally by a One-World Order economic/financial ruling body such as the International Monetary Fund.

Any way you look at it, we are in one big mess.

Gold, interest rates, and commodities remain the key barometers to watch now. Could we see the simultaneous kingship of gold and cash? Possibly. I have written about this for some time. Cash speaks loudly these days and does buy more. At the same time, fear of runaway government spending, and fear of a collapse of the international banks (a natural market process), has led to higher numismatic gold prices.

Certainly, the battle between real money (gold) and counterfeit money (debt money — U.S. Federal Reserve Notes) cannot last forever. But it could be sustained in this economic and financial crisis which is increasingly imminent.

To be generous, less than 6% of the American public have invested in gold. To the rest of the economic ill-informed, cash is security during a financial crisis. Whichever way we cut it, the debt crisis is here, now.

February 18, 1983

SECTION II

How We Became Enslaved

Chapter Eleven
HUMAN ACTION CYCLES

Predictable sequences of human behavior, also known as human action progressions, are frequently called *cycles*. Cycles in human action are acts which men collectively and naturally tend to take if they lack the knowledge and/or self-discipline necessary to overcome these nonprogressive or destructive spirals.

Running through my years of notes on cycles, I found a number of extremely interesting and important cycles in human action. These cycles provide us with a good feel for the direction life is taking today.

Psychological human action cycle: Humility — peace — wealth — pride — war — poverty — humility.

The failure human action cycle: Success — complacency — mental laziness — moral laxity — failure.

Human power cycle: Humility — truth — self-assurance — confidence — assertiveness — leadership — power — pride — compromise — arrogance — relativity — failure — humility.

Prohibition human action cycle: A product or service is outlawed politically for moral reasons. The black market (free market) then fills the demand. Political authorities respond with severe punishment for the "pushers" and "bootleggers" in the black market. The public reacts with civil disobedience. Eventually law enforcement officials throw in the towel and give up their crusade, or they are replaced. The previously outlawed product or service is legalized and heavily taxed.

The 50-year economic human action cycle: Depression — thrift — confidence — investment — economic activity — boom — use of credit — abuse of credit (inflation) — lack of confidence — panic — depression.

In America we move from shirt-sleeves to shirt-sleeves in three generations: Striving — affluence — decline. The sons remember the lessons of their striving fathers, but the affluent grandsons never hear, receive, or apply the lessons of their striving grandfathers. If we begin with a depression, the father teaches his son about that harsh economic experience. However, the grandson, the third generation, is not taught, does not heed, or does not apply the lessons of the previous generations, which causes the human action cycle to repeat. Men strive to get ahead. Their sons are affluent. Their grandsons squander the hard-earned wealth.

A debt/credit money cycle creates boom (expansion) and bust (contraction). As interest rates rise and fall with expansions and contractions, the fifty-four year cycle in interest rates is formed. Because the use of credit is the primary engine of inflation, economic expansion via debt assumption results in increasing inflation, while a contraction in the use of credit in an economic contraction results in a decline in the rate of inflation. Since 1948, every downturn in the business cycle has been associated with an easing of the rate of inflation. On the other hand, every upturn in the business cycle until 1982 has been accompanied by an upturn in the rate of inflation as measured by the Consumer Price Index. (The economic experience of the United States since 1982 suggests a shift in this cycle. Inflation is not yet in evidence in the 1980s.)

The government monetary cycle: In order to stimulate an economic recovery from recession, the government creates money. This monetary stimulus causes a business boom. Next, inflation becomes evident as the bogus money filters through the society — prices rise. This inflation leads to higher interest rates. Business and consumer borrowing then contracts as interest rates rise. The economy slumps into a recession.

In the early stages of a business cycle, demand equals income plus credit. At the cycle peak, demand equals income. On the downside of the economic cycle, during the economic contraction, demand equals income minus credit. (People pay their debts.)

In the early recovery stages of an economic cycle, wages lag behind inflation. At economic cycle peaks, inflation rises faster than wages. During the early stages of a recession, inflation rises faster than wages. Once the recession is entrenched, wage settlements finally exceed the inflation rate. At the depths of a recession, prior to an economic recovery, wages again fall below the inflation rate. Labor/wage rates always lag behind the economic cycle. Labor is nearly always behind the "Eight" ball when it comes to inflation.

The credit-based boom/bust inflationary cycle is accompanied by optimism on the upside and pessimism on the downside, each growing to a magnitude of error that is so far removed from reality that a change in trend occurs.

Product development cycle: A company produces a new product. The product is a hit; demand is high. Company profits soar. The company expands production and increases employment. Success attracts competitors. Successful competition and overproduction cause prices (and profit margins) to drop. The company cuts back on production and lays off employees. The company produces and markets a new product or waits for a resurgence in appeal for the "old" one, or goes out of business.

Conclusion

When men "naturally" behave like animals and are conflict — and short-term oriented, slaves to nature, their human action cycles typically spiral down. When men rise above their "natural" instincts and operate on the basis of harmony and a long-term view, their human action cycles are a spiral up. (A spiral is an integration of linear with subordinate cyclical time.) The "natural" rise and fall in a human action cycles takes on the form of an "S" curve.

Western civlization has passed the peak of its cycle, and has topped out in its "S" curve.

July 12, 1984

Chapter Twelve
"STAR LIGHT" — ASTROLOGICAL SLAVERY

A *Reaper* subscriber once sent me a copy of an article from the August 1982 issue of *Horoscope* Magazine. He stated, "You talk so much about the 510-year civilization cycle that I thought you might be interested in this." The article is entitled, "Astrology For the '80s."

Now, first off, I want to make it perfectly clear that I neither subscribe to nor do I know the first thing about astrology, except what I learned about the Zoroastrian priests (Magi or Wise Men), whose studies of the stars led them to Jesus. E.W. Bullinger's books, *Numbers in Scripture* and *The Witness of the Stars* discusses the subject in a fascinating way.

The reason this article was brought to my attention was the fact that apparently there is an astrological 496-year economic cycle, which puts it only fourteen years removed from the 510-year civilization cycle, which I have studied, documented, and discussed.

I find it extremely interesting and pondersome that the astrological projections for the 1980s in *Horoscope* Magazine, based upon their 496-year economic cycle, are in such *cyclical* harmony with the 510-year civilization cycle, but in radical contrast to my work on the 510-year civilization cycle when it comes to its human action applications. The *Horoscope* 496-year cycle is as optimistic as I am pessimistic, given present trends. Quoting from *Horoscope* Magazine:

> Pluto and Scorpio after 1984 promises the most powerful economic regeneration since the discovery of the Americas. Pluto's 496-year economic cycle could gradually change the very basis of global economics...
> ...the current cycle of the new decade promises to crystalize in 1988-89 in powerful economic terms.

In Chapter 44 of my book *Wealth For All: Religion, Politics and War*, "U.S. Wars Squared," I projected that the U.S., based upon my squaring of price and time work, in those two years, 1988 and 1989, would see a time of maximum testing, civil unrest, probably a world war, a time when the very survival of this nation could be at stake.

Could my conclusions on the 510-year cycle and on "U.S. Wars

Squared" be so dead wrong? In any case, I am in total conflict with the astrologers. And yet, we are both coming up with almost the same length of cycles and identical years for turning points in Western civilization from now to the year 2000.

Let me give you my basic beef with astrology (Christian religious condemnation against it as idolatry aside). *Astrology is another form of slavery.* I am a free man. I want nothing to do with slavery. Under astrology, men are slaves to and under the subjection and rulership of the planets. Such men are not overcomers. They are still slaves to nature. Furthermore, the slavery of astrology has historically been linked with vertical, political slave empires (Egypt, Babylonia, Rome).

Now, the evidence is increasing that there is a relationship between planetary movement/alignment and the electro-magnetics of the human mind. It seems that the magnetic/gravitational pull of the planets affects the magnetic environment of the sun, influencing and triggering sunspots, solar flares, and solar winds, which in turn affect the earth's magnetic environment, creating such things as the northern lights, which in turn affect the electronics of the human mind.

Men are probably subject to such planetary influences. This is why hospital emergency rooms and police departments, particularly in the big cities (vertical slave centers), staff up during the time of the full moon. Reportedly, more rapes, murders and crimes are committed by human "animals" during the time of the full moon, a time when some say the "crazies" come out in New York City. Knowing or not knowing this, men do not have to be subject to such influences, but can overcome them.

Men do not have to be animals. They can be overcomers, spiritual beings with a subordinated animal nature. Thus, they can be free men, not slaves.

In the Soviet Union, the mentally ill, who are dependent slaves, irresponsible, emotional, undisciplined, and literally crazy, manifesting the animal nature of man, are placed in lead-shielded rooms during times of solar disturbances. This decreases their "natural" tendency toward abnormal animalistic behavior during such times.

Along another line in the same vein, I have been concerned for many years with the growing interest in the occult in this country, a trend we picked up from England. With such undesirable growth has come the increasing effectiveness of astrology in forecasting the trading markets. This is just like during the 1920s! Are men becoming more slavelike? The evidence suggests as much. Occultism and true freedom have never coexisted.

Back to my basic argument with astrology — astrology is slavery! And all slavery is, by definition, denied freedom. But man was created by God to be free.

Now, let's go for the jugular. Just what is the nature of this "economic regeneration" that astrology promises us in the 1980s, and the late 1980s particularly? *It is the "economic regeneration" of slavery!* Continuing to quote from "Astrology For the 80s:"

> ...From 1984 to 1989, traditional concepts of the use of paper money could undergo radical changes. Currency could be replaced entirely by individual computer banking accounts, where funds are transferred directly from one numbered account to another or others. In this 'number on the forehead' financial system, perhaps utilizing social security numbers or similar accounting, payments to individuals from employers, investments, social benefits, etc., would be made directly to personal accounts via computer inputs, while debts, taxes, bills, etc., would be automatically and/or personally withdrawn or transferred. A credit/cardlike financial identification could replace money in all its forms, although such a radical departure in the way we use money would be very gradual indeed, coming into its own perhaps by 1989...
>
> The advantages of this new financial system are many. The elimination of cash could greatly reduce crime and the financing of illegal activities in general. It would almost completely eliminate recession, economic stagnations, and inflation by providing a direct method of selected price and wage controls. But the disadvantages include invasion of privacy, greater governmental control over the lives of individuals, as well as making political abuses similar to the events surrounding the Watergate Scandal much easier. In some nations, this 'numbered' system could make economic dictatorships a possibility. At the same time, the removal of currency in general also eliminates the need for value systems based on gold, silver or otherwise. This could actually greatly reduce or even completely eliminate the value of precious metals or the need for such standards...
>
> For the United States specifically, Pluto's influence in Scorpio after 1984 could be most startling, and given the nature of this country's democratic capitalism and liberal free enterprise system...this suggests some drastic problems with unemployment that could be solved through the institution of such social programs as minimum income payments, mass government-controlled public works, or social welfare work programs, and possible reinstitution of military conscription. Generally, this describes a strongly socialistic trend that could follow many of the present developments of the United Kingdom.
>
> At the same time, government could become a major employer of people as the decade progresses, perhaps through the military/industrial complex or the institution of a particularly large standing army deemed necessary in an increasingly hostile international atmosphere...

Is there any question of the direction these astrological forecasts are leading us? They are urging us into a system no different than that of the militaristic slave empires of old. Astrology is clearly predicting a vertical, bureaucratic, humanistic, evolutionary, slave state empire, where government, the economic parasite, plays the role of God in the maximum distortion of reality. Such distortion can only exist in a slave state empire.

Aside from mental freedom, real freedom on this material earth is ultimately based in economic freedom. If economic freedom is removed, all other types of freedom cease to exist. Control over a man's economic base is control over his will. This desired astrological system is one of economic tyranny and slavery. But beyond doubt, with computers, we are moving into the age of total information, making such total control possible.

An unacceptable alternative to the chaos and misery of the 510-year civilization cycle and U.S. Wars Squared is to yield to the tyranny of an all-powerful state. Recall that if men are not individually responsible, if they do not overcome, they fall victim to the political progression cycle: king — republic — democracy — chaos — king (bureaucratic dictatorship). Today, the chaos phase could be triggered by the collapse of the debt pyramid!

Debt, according to this scenario, is leading to the death of freedom. Small wonder that the Hebrew, Greek, and Middle Age Christian civilizations all warned against establishing an economic system based upon debt. It is the breeding ground of tyranny. During coming chaotic times, free men could be put through "hell on earth," our own "tribulation," as we flee such a repulsive system.

The inevitability of Wheeler's 510-year civilization cycle or Pluto's 496-year economic cycle should and must be rejected by free men. We will die, both spiritually and physically, under the chains of slavery. The solution begins with the application of the principles I outlined in Chapter 3 of *Wealth For All: Religion, Politics and War,* under "Life, Liberty And The Pursuit Of Happiness." We must reconstruct our republic with a humble, responsible, giving, long-term view, looking to our own long-term self-interest by so doing. The alternatives are totally unacceptable.

Star Light: On The Horizon

If we were to adopt a plan to repay the total $5.4 trillion of public and private debt that prevails in the economy today at 13% interest, with annual payments over 100 years, it would cost $702 billion per year for 100 years, principal and interest, a total of $70.2 trillion.

If we postpone it one year the cost goes up to $783 billion per year, or a total of $78.3 trillion of principal and interest.

The result of the monetary upheaval, in light of the public's willingness to accept responsibility and forego freedom, is for government to assume total control over our economy before this century is out, once a collapse and anarchy occurs — unless we overcome.

Given the presently sophisticated level of computer technology, a totalitarian state will be able to centralize power as never before and institute a national, personal identification system. This is in radical contrast to what the world is screaming for — freedom! This is in radical contrast to what the present technological revolution is all about — massive decentralization and freedom! The artists, the writers, the singers, the poets, the creative geniuses in the Silicon Valley — all these avant garde thinkers clearly see that the next progressive step for mankind is decentralization and freedom! Even the climate is supportive. The Dole, Bush, O'Neill, Rockefeller mentality is warring against the human tide. If we don't overcome, we will be overcome!

November 19, 1982

"What computer scientists are proposing is computer evolution that within the next decade will bring into being a living element — a computer with eternal light, a god-like superhuman entity that will be infinitely more intelligent than man."
Coming Changes — November, 1982

"If the government ever stops mandating inflation and punishing small business, the Revolution of Littleness will sweep all before it. And the Age of Little Business will be an age of greater economic freedom, thus of ever greater creativity, efficiency, and growth for all of us."
Dr. Jack D. Douglas, Professor of Sociology
University of California, San Diego

Chapter Thirteen
VERTICAL EMPIRES AND SHORT-TERM THINKING

There is a growing division in the financial newsletter writing community. There has always been a split between newsletter writers who were technically-biased and those who favored fundamentals. But this is not the nature of the growing division. The rift is between the more conventional newsletter writers and the increasingly unconventional, radical ones.

The conventional newsletter writers tend to "play the game" within the confines of what is socially acceptable and "printable" by the establishment media. These conventional fundamentalists, and "becoming respectable" technicians, are primarily businessmen. They pretty much stick to analyzing investments and the markets as if such investments were immune and unrelated to the growing social/political factors alarming the more unconventional/radical newsletter writers. I find myself increasingly cast in the latter camp, not out of personal preference or bias, but out of dedication to the reality of the way the world really works.

Religion, politics, society and economics are all interrelated. Economics is basic reality. Unless we have food, water, clothing and shelter, we perish. This is an undeniable fact for all of us. But, because we are social animals, who desire companionship and law and order, we establish a government to rule over our social order. People who work for government are dependent upon economics also for their very survival. Therefore, whether through taxes or inflation, government will practice confiscatory economics on behalf of those who work for it or depend upon it. Because government enacts laws which are nothing more than ideas about right or wrong — morality, if you will — government effectively legislates religious beliefs. This is true because religion is concerned with morality, ideas about right or wrong, and thus "laws" for living. Religion is ultimate spiritual reality. Economics is ultimate physical reality. And the two are inescapably related. Government is religion applied to economics.

Down through history, as men have worked out the relationships between economics, government, society and religion, the established social order has determined whether men were either free or slaves. Men have an option: They can structure their relationships with other men either vertically or horizontally. The vertical structuring of relationships, man *over* man, results in dependency and slavery of varying degress, enacted through the vertical bureaucracy. And, it doesn't really matter which human institution one is referring to — economic, social, labor, business, military, medical, educational, political, or religious — a bureaucracy is an institution that limits accountability, responsibility, creativity, authority, and freedom, while promoting dependency and, effectively, slavery.

By contrast, when men have structured their relationships horizontally, man *with* man, freedom has existed. Man with man is a contractual, give and take, cooperative relationship. Its basis is covenants and contracts. It requires responsibility by each party in the relationship. It maximizes freedom and individual (thus collective) human growth. Men who are held accountable for their actions are forced to grow up in horizontal contractual relationships. Bureaucracies shelter men from their folly, and thus fill the world with fools.

The running rule of human history seems to be that men will either rule over themselves through the assumption of responsibility and self-discipline, thus giving them freedom to contract, or men will rule over other men, establishing slaves in bureaucratic empires. The latter, the bureaucratic slave empire, is the organizational rule of today. Whether we look at the federal government, the structure of big business, medicine, military, education, media, labor, or big religion, or even people stacked on top of each other in high rise apartments or office buildings, everywhere we look, we have vertical relationships, not horizontal ones. Our cities, by the very nature of their dominating skyscrapers, are vertical in essence. Small wonder also that men and women who have contracted together in marriage are breaking up. They are unaccustomed to horizontal relationships.

Our social order has what appears, at present, to be an insurmountable problem. The total debt in all sectors of the public and private economy is placed now at $7.3 trillion, with communist bloc and Third World country debt established at $1,000 billion. The few bright minds who can understand these monstrous debts with accompanying compound interest are clearly recognizing that there is no way this huge debt will ever be paid off. Generously assuming that the rate of interest on this mountain of debt is a modest 10%, with only quarterly compounding, this mammoth debt load doubles in slightly over seven years! The guts of this nightmare is that there will be a small number of winners and a large number of losers in our society, whether the debt is eventually defaulted on and/or inflated away.

This debt awareness has led the more radical/unconventional newsletter writers to speculate on how the social/political/economic problem will eventually be worked out. Because money is basic to economic human action today, the disposition of our $7.3 trillion debt and the $1,000 billion in communist bloc and Third World country debt will affect all aspects of our religious/social/political/economic order dramatically. In fact, this compounding interest time bomb could decimate it.

Now, if the American people were responsible, and their day-to-day activities were primarily contractual/horizontal, as opposed to bureaucratic/vertical, we might have a chance of solving our problems. But the sad truth is, American human action is primarily vertical in nature, escapist in tone, and generally unconcerned with religious, political and economic matters. The accepted *social* norm is to "do your own thing...now," a short-term orientation which precludes the sacrifice short-term to solve our long-term problems.

Our *political* structure, despite the efforts of Reaganomics, has degenerated back to the same old "spend and elect" pork barrel methodology. It is frozen into inaction by competing special interest groups. Ronald Reagan's try at cutting the federal bureaucracy, slashing inefficiency in the military/industrial complex, and taking a meaningful knife to social welfare programs, taxes, and Social Security has been, at best, only marginally successful.

So, effectively, the compound interest/debt problem is running wild.

Sensing this financial time bomb is perhaps the reason that, in the last decade, for the first time in forty years, the U.S. population's growth momentum has shifted radically to rural areas (nonmetropolitan areas) from cities (metropolitan areas).

The more unconventional/radical newsletter writers, understanding the catastrophic nature of this compound interest/debt dilemma, have recognized that all investments, business activities and market ventures are akin to setting up a table for a game of checkers on the rim of a rumbling volcano. The explosion of the volcano could render the game effectively meaningless at any time, permanently so.

October 29, 1982

* * * * *

Centralized vertical power always fills the vacuum left by the demise of responsible, horizontal, contractual relationships. Because economics is basic, and because in our technocratic culture today, money is the most important representation of economic reality (prostituted, though it may be), it follows that rich special interests would fill the power vacuum left by irresponsible individuals.

The most financially viable and visible special interest group is, of course, the banking industry, its power base further buttressed by the evolutionary philosophy undergirding our culture. Its influence is enhanced by interlocking directorates with other major multinational corporations.

The question rightfully raised by the unconventional/radical newsletter writers is, "Given the entrenched power — both political and economic — of the banking industry, and the reality of our debt/compound interest problem that penetrates to the heart of this, the most powerful of our ruling elite, what will this banking special interest do to protect and ensure its own survival and its increase of wealth and power?"

Given the nature of vertical empires and greedy special interests throughout history, these more unconventional/radical newsletter writers believe that it's incredibly naive to think that powerful banking special interests will simply let nature take its free market course, even if it means the bankruptcy of these big banks. These writers believe that the banks will fight to save their skins at all costs.

These more unconventional/radical newsletter writers understand that evil seldom comes on the scene wearing a black hat. Rather, evil is simply actions taken by men in their own self-interest *short-term*, resulting in big losses for the masses in the win-lose relationship. (No sane man thinks of himself as evil.) Thus, to better get a handle upon how these power brokers will affect business investments and market reality, these unconventional/radical newsletter writers have begun carefully tracking the political workings of these banking and multinational corporation special interests, as we move toward a One-World order.

Now, it's an old game for the U.S. Export-Import Bank, the World Bank and the IDA to loan U.S. taxpayers' money to Third World countries for the benefit of U.S. multinational corporations. The so-called "sale" of sixty-four diesel-electric locomotives (manufactured by General Electric) at a cost of $64.1 million to Indonesia, which received a $48 million Export-Import Bank loan, is old hat. Where banks make loans directly, there is always the IMF and BIS to bail them out of their lending folly with our money. The common political meeting ground for these economic power brokers is the Council on Foreign Relations (CFR).

Legislation has been passed to protect these elite banking/multinational corporation special interests. Now they won't have to face the natural readjustment that the liquidation of such heavy debt loads ($7.3 trillion plus $1,000 billion) would bring about in the free marketplace. For example, the *Monetary Control Act of 1980* allows the Federal Reserve to reduce bank reserve requirments to zero, declare bank holidays, bring all financial institutions under the Federal Reserve's control, and monetize foreign bonds and foreign debt.

The Federal Reserve, of course, is the bankers' bank. Furthermore, the Federal Reserve, through *H.R. 7080*, can dictate the nature of mergers and acquisitions (takeovers) of troubled financial institutions by more powerful financial giants. The *International Emergency Economics Power Act* allows the President of the United States to effectively control all foreign exchange transactions, while other legislation effectively allows the government, through the FDIC and FSLIC, to totally control or bail out any financial institution they see fit to so bless.

What about the little guy? What about you and me? We're on our own to try to save our ships in this storm. The powerful rich special interests have built their own private financial arks to carry them to safety.

Which multinational banks are likely to be the beneficiaries of this largess? Bank of America, Citibank, Chase Manhattan Bank, Merrill Lynch, Manufacturers Hanover Trust Company, Morgan Guaranty Trust Company, Chemical Bank, Continental Illinois National Bank and Trust Company, First National Bank, Wells Fargo National Bank, Crocker National Bank, Marine Midland Bank N.A., First Interstate Bank of California, and Mellon Bank N.A.

Many unconventional/radical newsletter writers, recognizing the political nature of the present and coming economic bail-out of these banks and associated corporations, have issued the warning that a hyperinflation is both imminent and inevitable. Hyperinflation cannot be ruled out. If commodities, stocks and gold all explode skyward, while interest rates also go through the roof, a hyperinflation, at that point, will most probably be the correct reading of the financial cards. But a hyperinflation destroys a civilization, decimates its cities, and leads to rampant social unrest and revolution, destroying the urban base where these mammoth banks and corporations reside. More likely, if possible, is a *controlled* bail-out of *selected* banks and corporations. This will prevent outright hyperinflation, so that a *normal* debt liquidation/deflation could take place in most of the politically-impotent private sectors of the economy. When the waters calm, these powerful financial interests will be shored up while the rest of us are financially shipwrecked, and effectively slaves waiting for our collars.

An added benefit of this controlled, selective bail-out approach is that these politically powerful financial interests would then be able to legally buy up, at distressed prices, numerous important assets in the bankrupt, deflated free market. Such a scenario is entirely possible, given the ignorant, dependent, security-oriented slavelike nature of the American public, captured by economic and financial naivete and gullibility. Just enough controlled social unrest would allow these banking and corporate special interests to further consolidate their political power and establish rigid controls, ostensibly "demanded by the people." This would further snuff out the flickering flame of freedom as the vertical, bureaucratic, slave hierarchy grows. Watch the banks and corporations with CFR members on their boards. These banks and corporations should survive due to politically-connected financing and information.

It is terribly ironic that a vertical world empire, Babylonia, gave banking to the world. (Remember the Tower of Babel?) Are we seeing such established again, not only in this country, but worldwide as the United States dollar is the world's reserve currency? The pyramid (on our Federal Reserve Notes) has usually represented vertical, bureaucratic, freedomless empires. Furthermore, if it's true that freedom is the most desired state for man, then, at least in this sense, "the love of money is the root of all evil." Furthermore, since our money is based upon debt — and one root meaning of the word debt is "death" — then the resolution of this tremendous *debt* problem is the *death* of freedom.

Our course of action is clear cut. We must avoid debt, maintain liquidity and investment flexibility. The age of easy wealth accumulation via debt is over. Wealth in the future will be measured in part by a degree of personal freedom.

The oft-spoken adage, "Most men live lives of quiet desperation," testifies to the reality that most men are not free. They are slaves, by default, design, or choice. All of us have areas of weaknesses to which we are slaves, that we must overcome if we are to be truly free. Those of us who were born poor have had to overcome poverty and work for financial freedom (to the extent possible in today's world). Those of us born with rigid, overly-strict, and unloving parents, have had to overcome a fear of authority and learn to love defenselessly. All of us have had to overcome our pride in order to be open and learn the real meaning of mental peace, freedom and security. Some have had to fight to overcome a fear of heights, airplanes, contracting cancer, getting fat, dying and on and on. The point is this: *The nature of free men is that they are, regardless of their weakness or area of slavery, continually striving to overcome.* Men who do this individually, as a group will do it collectively; they overcome and subdue their environment. This is why there are 240 million Americans in the United States who live in relative short-term economic prosperity today, while, when this continent was inhabited by less then one million Indians, the Indians regularly starved to death. In many cases, the Indians brutalized their old people as well as each other. The Indians were slaves, subject to nature. The United States, on the other hand, throughout the better part of its history, has brought the natural order into subjection, and exercised dominion over it, although not always with a sense of ecological conservation.

Today, we are still in our economic infancy. We still have not had a practical, workable, successful long-term economic theory. The reason is because all economic theories to date are based upon assumptions that are radically flawed! Man does not necessarily have unlimited wants (which is a basic premise of prevailing theories). He can overcome his desires through self-discipline. And this is not a world of scarcity (which is another false premise of modern economics). Higher and better creative uses of resources are all around us. All we have to do is utilize them. Additionally, the sun gives us free wealth every day. With such cursed assumptions, however, it is no wonder that economics has been called the dismal science, subject to the rule of the dismal, special interest controlled bureaucracy, which redistributes limited resources.

Our general failure to be overcomers now, our inability to see our problems as a challenge leading to greater victory, is at the forefront of our civilization's demise. We have lost our vision. This then is the nature of our frozen, unresponsive institutions. I discussed this in considerable detail in Chapter 43 of *Wealth For All: Religion, Politics and War*, "The 510-Year Cycle." There, I presented the overwhelming cyclical, fundamental, human action cycle, and authoritative opinion data, which strongly suggests that the conclusions reached in that frightening chapter will shortly come to fruition, unless there is a massive change of mind and reorientation.

Evidence coming together to project future events just doesn't come any more powerful than when cycles of human action, fundamental conditions and authoritative opinions are all in harmony as they are regarding our 510-year civilization cycle. This turning point in history, with all its economic, political, social, and religious ramifications, is effectively the dividing line between the conventional and the unconventional/radical newsletter writers today. Remember, while conventional thinkers can be correct during ongoing major trends in markets, they usually get killed at the turning points, which unconventional/radical thinkers tend to both project and catch. We are in the midst of such a historical turning point now.

November 5, 1982

"These loan guarantees are the sleaziest thing going. The taxpayers are getting raped by this system. This administration didn't invent it, but they have no business promoting it. We are paying for the soldiers who are sitting on the heads of the Polish workers."

Dan M. Burt, President
Capital Legal Foundation

"It's high time we stopped subsidizing our enemies: Let's let communism go bankrupt."

Congressman Ron Paul

Chapter Fourteen
DEBT MONEY: CURSE AND CONTROL OF PEOPLE

When Keynes wrote his critique of the quantity theory of money he was writing to, and on behalf of, his benefactors: those who knew and understood the realities and mechanics of the "free" world's debt-based monetary system. Even the Federal Reserve admits that our money is created out of debt. Those who call it fiat money obscure its realities, as do those who claim it is created out of nothing.

The best, albeit deficient, definition of fiat money is found in the *Dictionary of International Finance*, by Julian Wamsley (Greenwood Press, 1979). *"Fiat money: Money not backed by gold or silver and created by the will of government."* Our government does not create money; it has given the privately-owned Federal Reserve the power to do so through a fractional reserve banking system monopolized by international bankers. Every dollar (Federal Reserve Note or bank deposit) owes its existence to, and was created out of debt, not merely by an act of will or fiat. Then again, money, by its very nature, is a deferred satisfaction, or more exactly a debt recognized by the community.

The Federal Reserve was created for one purpose and one purpose only in the words of its author Paul Warburg. Its function is to mobilize and manage the nation's credit. But for whose benefit is the nation's credit managed? For the benefit of the Federal Reserve's shareholders — other banks!

Interest rates are one cause of decreased purchasing power, which the bankers call "inflation." Between 1980 and 1983, this country witnessed the most dramatic increase ever in the change in the money supply ($28 billion between 1980 and 1981; $36 billion between 1981 and 1982; and $42 billion between 1982 and 1983, all periods from December to December). The percentage increase was 7%, 8%, and 9% respectively, yet inflation (according to the Consumer Price Index or CPI), stabilized. With the biggest increase ever in the quantity of money, the CPI almost leveled. What are the explanations? Some of them are bizzare, such as: "The money is being hidden or sent overseas." Not so. Money held overseas (Eurodeposits) is not included in M1 statistics.

There is no secret plot concerning hidden money because Keynes was correct, regarding the debt-based monetary system about which he was writing. Keynes' secret, not a secret to the bankers and administrators who understand our monetary system, is that money created out of debt is limited by the capability of the public and economy to create debt by borrowing.

For every dollar's worth of debt purchased by the Federal Reserve and placed in the monetary base, there are $2.6 dollars worth of private debt. This is the money multiplier of 2.6 that the Fed reports. This multiplier remained relatively constant even though purchasing power decreased.

If ours were truly a fiat money system, with every dollar in circulation created arbitrarily by the will of the government, the quantity theory of money would probably hold. But such is not the case.

There are two ways to exchange goods: 1) barter, and a receipt for a barterable good; 2) by accepting as deferred satisfaction an instrument recognized by the community as a debt, which will be honored by the community. Number two is a description of today's money.

There are three definitions of money: 1) Arbitrarily created by an act or by the will of government, that is, each issue comes from the government's printing press; 2) Money created by the banks as an act of borrowing; 3) A specified quantity or amount of a commodity, which supposedly holds some inherent value (if you want to use that term to describe worth), or a receipt for a commodity.

In definitions one and three above, money can only be made an official medium of exchange by an arbitrary act or will (fiat) of government. That is, it takes legal tender laws to make them money. In definition two, money can be made by legal tender laws, but not necessarily so, for such money historically traces its ancestry to goldsmith receipts for which there were no legal tender laws. In France, for example, John Law set up a bank (Banque Generale), issuing paper money that actually commanded greater purchasing power than circulating gold coins. During WWI, England was prosecuting its citizens under the *Defense of the Realm Act* for melting coins into bullion.

Follow for twenty years the rise and fall in interest rates and compare it against the rise and fall in the purchasing power of the U.S. dollar. In a debt-money system, the quantity theory of money does not hold. The reason: public capacity for debt limits the quantity of money the Federal Reserve or any central bank can put into circulation. In a debt-money system, when debts are paid off, money goes out of existence. It goes to money heaven. There is just one exception to this. It depends on the Federal Reserve monetizing primary issues of government debt directly instead of buying up existing (old) debt in the secondary market.

The purchase of debt by the Fed is accomplished by the Open Market Committee through its trading desk, which in turn deals with thirty-seven dealers who get big commissions. The Fed has never monetized primary issues from the government. If it did it could not manage the nation's interest rates. Some of these thirty-seven dealers own stock in the New York Fed, and some are subsidiaries of those who own stock. (The benefit from owning the Fed and controlling the Open Market Operations is derived from management of the nation's interest rates and credit, and from the subsidiary profits which can be derived from profitting in the world's stock, bond and commodity markets. After all, the U.S. dollar is the world's reserve currency.)

The Fed pays a 6% dividend to all shareholders (*PL 289, 12 USC*); it holds only 11% of the government's securities; it returns (after expenses) 87%-98% of all interest earned to the U.S. Treasury, still leaving itself with a hefty nest egg. By managing the interest rates, the Fed has enabled the mortgages and liens of America to be held (mostly in FNMA, GNMA, and FHMA pools) by foreign and domestic international banks and central banks and governments.

Remember, to pay back $100 at 10% interest an individual must come up with ten extra dollars; a nation must do the same thing. If the supply of money is fixed (and it is to the extent that debt capacity is limited), then the purchasing power of the $100 is going to have to be decreased. (How can you pay back $110 when there is only $100 in existence?) When the extra $10 is brought into circulation, a new debt is created (rolling over the old debt and netting $10 extra). This further dilutes the purchasing power of the U.S. dollar unless the extra money can be put to productive use (other than paying interest).

Money spent by a nation, within that nation, by government or individuals, raises the effective demand for goods and services, thus creating pressure to produce, thus creating and sustaining employment. Here, Keynes was right again. What Keynes ignored, or more properly took judicial notice of, was the devaluation of money via interest rates (in the name of managing the nation's credit). It is the continuous rolling over of debt, and the resulting pressure on interest rates, that creates our so called "inflation" (bankers' euphemism for devaluation).

In economic theory, an increase in supply leads to a decrease in price. The price of debt is interest rates. Thus, an increase in the supply of debt should lead to a decrease in interest rates, and an increase in the demand for debt (i.e., a demand to purchase debt) should also lead to an increase in price (interest rates). Our national debt (public and private) is soaring, yet interest rates have fluctuated. We do not have a free market in money. The increase in debt has not been fully matched by a decrease in interest rates because the Fed keeps the money supply tight enough to keep real interest rates high. The supply of debt exceeds its demand, and has for some time. Otherwise, the money multiplier would be 8.33 instead of 2.6. This would be inflationary.

Are interest rate manipulated by the Fed for the benefit of the stockholders? One mechanism is the Federal Funds rate. Federal Funds are excess reserves held by all depository institutions and borrowed by them so that they can meet reserve requirements. They are the base line of interest rates which consumers pay to banks when a loan is negotiated. Real interest rates need to be kept high in order to keep the U.S. dollar from free falling and the federal debt funded by the private sector, with both domestic and foreign funds. If the Fed is forced to monetize new Treasury debt, inflation and interest rates will explode. This is why Paul Volcker keeps pushing for budget cuts.

Interest rates in the long-term cause pressure on the U.S. dollar's purchasing power and lead to its decline. Future consumption is sacrificed for current satisfaction; the future is mortgaged for the present.

In the world's money markets, the U.S. dollar is fixed by the Bank of International Settlements (BIS) at .29032258 grams fine gold equalling $1.94149; all other currencies (except the BIS Gold Franc) floats against the U.S. dollar. The U.S. stock of monetized gold (280 million ounces) held by the Treasury, but owned by the Fed, equals $58 billion.

The bankers' solution (pages 131 & 183 of the *1983 Annual Report of the BIS*) is to decrease the standards of living for the U.S. and world. The BIS seeks to exert downward pressure on U.S. interest rates (p. 181), but this can only be done by contracting the economy, increasing the money supply, reducing future living standards, causing bankruptcies and foreclosures. By the last two acts, the bankers will take possession of real wealth — property. In short, the plan is deflation. The bankers own the politicians. The government borrows from the bankers. The borrower is the slave of the lender.

June 6, 1984

Chapter Fifteen
THE REAL CAUSE OF INFLATION — A SIMPLE STORY

Part of the following essay is provided by a social credit pamphlet by Louis Eve, The Money Myth Exploded. (*The Institute of Political Action, Saint-Michel de Rougemont, P.Q. Canada). It involves five shipwrecked survivors and an Eastern European (whom I call Izzy) washed up on a deserted island.*

The five survivors include a carpenter, a miner, a farmer, an animal breeder, and an orchard keeper. The Eastern European is a banker who floats onto the island with a printing press and a cask full of rocks, which he tells his hosts are gold.

Izzy, a belated arrival to the island, proclaims, "Well, you can thank providence, because I am a banker and in no time at all I'll set up a system of money guaranteed to satisfy you. Then you'll have everything that people in civilization have." The five stand in awe of Izzy, the all-wise and omnipotent; they swoon (as they have been conditioned to do) over his "gold".

Izzy sets out with his press, printing money (backed of course by gold), which he loans out at $200 per man at 8% interest. After the sun rises and sets 365 times, the "natural," inevitable and "God-ordained" time for collecting interest arrives. The loans, with interest, come due. Izzy demands his total of $1,080. But among the five survivors there is only $1,000 and that amount has been redistributed. They realize they have been duped, so they meet with Izzy.

Izzy guessed what was on their minds, but put up his best front. While he listened, the impetuous farmer stated the case for the group: "How can we pay you $1,080 when there is only $1,000 on the entire island?"

"That's the interest, my friends. Hasn't your rate of production increased?"

"Sure, but the money hasn't. And it's money you're asking for, not our products. You are the only one who can make money. You've made only $1000 and yet you ask for $1080. That's an impossibility."

"Now listen, fellows. Bankers, for the greater good of the community, always adapt themselves to the conditions of the times. I'm going to require only the interest. Only $80. You will go on holding the capital."

"Bless you, Izzy! Are you going to cancel the $200 each of us owes you?"

"Oh no! I'm sorry, but a banker never cancels a debt. You still owe me all the money you borrowed. But you'll pay me, each year, only the interest. If you meet the interest payments faithfully each year, I won't push you for the capital. Set up a system of money contributions, which we'll call taxes. Those who do have more money will be taxed more; the poor will pay less. See to it that you bring me, in one lump sum, the total of the amount of interest and I'll be satisfied. And your little island nation will thrive." So our boys left, somewhat pacified but still dubious.

Production increased, barter decreased, and yearly interest payments were made. Eventually money became scarce (deflation). Again the group went to Izzy.

"Oh! Now boys be reasonable," said Izzy. "Your affairs are booming and it's thanks to me. A good banking system is a country's best asset. But if it's to work beneficially, you must have faith in the banker. Come to me as you would to a father...Is it more money you want? Very well. My barrel of gold is good for many thousands of dollars more. See, I'm going to mortgage your latest acquisitions and lend you another thousand dollars right now."

The national debt goes to $2,000. Only now Izzy holds real wealth in mortgage. Taxes (interest) increase and calamity hits. Foreclosure follows and those dispossessed now have to rent their lands from Izzy. Things are brewing and Izzy follows the lead of the Rothschilds by using his press to print paper. Like Rothschild, Izzy knew that whoever controlled the nation's money controlled the nation. But he also knew that to maintain that control it was necessary to keep the people in a state of ignorance, to distract them by a variety of means.

Izzy had observed that of the five islanders, two were conservatives and three were liberals. And between the factions there was constant friction. So Izzy set up two newspapers, one for the liberals and one for the conservatives, The Sun for the liberals and The Star for the conservatives. The tenor of The Sun was, "If you no longer matter, it is because of those traitorous conservatives who have sold out to big business." The Star: "The ruinous state of business and the national debt can be traced directly to the political irresponsibility of those unmentionable liberals."

Izzy also used his newspapers to stress philosophy, education, and state economics. For the conservatives he stressed liberty and the free market; for the liberals he stressed collectivism and the plight of the downtrodden. He printed exposes and criticized himself at times, although never seriously and always in a manner that would distract and gather sympathy first from conservatives, then from liberals. Money was never discussed, neither was debt and compound interest.

The day of reckoning came when all but Izzy had been dispossessed and impoverished. Then providentially, a pamphlet washed up on shore. The miner, the most neutral politically, read the pamphlet and got the liberals and conservatives together. They eventually unmasked Izzy and his "gold."

* * * * *

Conflict is created between liberals and conservatives for the purpose of obscuring the real issue — money and wealth, of which naturally there is wealth for all.

There is really very little difference between monopoly debt capitalism and communism. Both seek to control markets, eliminate competition, absolutely control money, and exercise power through a bureaucracy.

June 6, 1984

Chapter Sixteen
CONQUEST WITHOUT BLOODSHED

Let's imagine you wanted to take over a country in order to exploit its economic riches — land, minerals and labor. But you didn't want to arouse the people, much less kill them, or harm the capital or infrastructure of the country. How would you do it? How could you have your cake and eat it too?

Today, we don't have to guess at how this magic is accomplished. A classic example of a successful, nonviolent economic invasion, where the local people had the rug pulled out from under them and didn't even know it (until lately), took place in Argentina. Let's explore what happened there, because the story of Argentina reveals a pattern of what is happening here in the U.S.

Argentina, you will recall, was the country that launched the ill-fated invasion of the Falkland Islands. The ruling Argentina military junta got its nose bloodied by a surprisingly tough and determined British fleet and fighting force. So much for Argentina's governmental effort to distract the local population from their economic problems through military action. In Argentina, inflation was running at about 500% a year.

While the government has made a mess of things in Argentina, the people are generally hard working and productive. This is the labor side of the equation. On the land side, some of the richest crop-growing areas on earth can be found in Argentina. Its farms and ranches are legendary in terms of their productivity. In fact, of the CROPEC countries that produce 78%-90% of all the world's grain, Argentina is one of the Big Four. (The other three are Canada, Australia, and the United States.) Argentina is also rich in minerals and petroleum.

Now, the local people in Argentina are flat broke. High taxes, inflation, and low prices for Third World commodities, not to mention social unrest, the high cost of the Falklands' war, and the expensive, corrupt government bureaucracy have all devastated the people. Argentina, in other words, is in an inflationary depression. But they still take American credit and fiat dollars there in exchange for real assets.

The classic hallmark of an economic depression is that things can be purchased cheaply with money, dirt cheap. And this is exactly what is being done in Argentina presently. The problem is that only foreigners have the money. Real estate, prime developed, productive farm and ranch land, can be had at bargain basement prices — for approximately $100 an acre. (One hundred Argentina pesos equals $6.25 U.S. dollars.) U.S., Japanese, and German multinationals and investors are buying up the land by the spadeful — thousands of acres at a whack.

When you own the land and the commercial enterprises of a country, you own the country. The people then become migrants, peasants, tenants, and slaves, whose labor is for rent because they have no roots. The locals can never again get a start through the small family farms which are the starting point for all successful economic development in Third World countries.

Why are small family farms the basis of Third World economic development? Because it is only through real, free new wealth coming via energy from the sun, combining with the resources of the earth, transformed into commodities, mixed with human labor in the basic social unit, the family, that provides man with the incentive and excess necessary to begin making economic progress.

Increasingly, Argentina no longer belongs to the citizens of Argentina. But, it's really no different than in this country, where big city money buys up American farms and ranches. The people in rural areas of the United States are increasingly becoming tenant farmers, at best, as the acreage of the average American farm grows larger and larger, with increasing corporate and absentee ownership becoming the norm as family farms are debt-plagued and foreclosed. In the United States, the federal government owns 42% of all the land. Of the privately-owned land in this country, a startling 95% of it is held by 3% of the people, according to Town and Country magazine.

Let's look at the economics: at $100 an acre, an international investor in Argentina can buy a 10,000 acre farm for $1 million. Let's say he raises soybeans, which yield a crop of twenty-five bushels per acre. At twenty-five bushels per acre, our absentee landowner's revenue on his soybean crop in his first year is $2,250,000, based upon $9 cash beans. In other words, he pays for his entire million dollar farm in one year and also gleans 100% profit, assuming he can operate on $250,000 as expense money. Not a bad return on investment.

(The real value of land is determined by both what it can agriculturally produce, through commercial and mineral development, and by the concentration of people who put demands on it. This is why ground in New York City is more expensive than most land in Nevada.)

The labor segment of running an agricultural operation is greater in Argentina than in the U.S. But labor there is cheap. It's an undeveloped country by comparison to the U.S. It is unlikely, however, that soybean land in Argentina will yield more than twenty-five bushels per acre. It is unlikely, too, that Argentina soybean growers will receive $9.00 per bushel for their soybeans, given the market prices, all the marketing costs and governmental red tape, both in Argentina and in the exporting process. But, in the previously-mentioned return on investment in the first year, a lot of slack can be eaten up by operating expenses, lower bean prices, and governmental export costs and still leave a hefty profit. In fact, Argentina soybeans could be dumped on world markets, competing with U.S. soybeans, and drive U.S. farmers literally out of business or to growing other crops. How can U.S. farmers compete when they have soybean ground that costs $2,000-$3,000 per acre? They can't, if Argentina ground can be bought for $100 an acre, other things being equal.

What's the point? Not only is agricultural land in Argentina now an excellent investment (if you can keep from getting your head blown off as a Yankee imperialist), but it also firms up a point with regard to international free trade: In free markets, investment venture capital and talent, both in industry and agriculture, inevitably and naturally flow to the undeveloped countries of the world, where land and labor are more competitive (cheaper), all else being equal. This is true whether you are considering manufacturing automobiles by computer robotics in Japan or by Chinese coolies for sixty cents an hour. The low cost of foreign labor, coupled with competitive, relatively uniform world steel prices, dictates that the best product (automobiles) at the lowest price will be produced abroad. This is also true in agriculture. A strong dollar helps even more.

Allowing for even a modicum of technological efficiency in the Third World developing countries like Argentina, which makes them competitive with the U.S. agriculturally, these Third World producers can undercut U.S. farmers, producing a crop at much lower costs (at the margin). Why? Because their basic "plant" cost (land at $100 an acre and labor) is so much cheaper than the "plant" cost incurred by American farmers ($2,000-$3,000 per acre).

Again, because the rule of economics is that investment capital flows to where it can receive its highest return, this means that the natural free market movement of investment capital, both industrially and agriculturally, is to the Third World, away from the developed world. So, the natural tendency among free men is to decentralize and spread out all over the globe, to groom the earth, rather than centralize in empires such as we see today in the United States and the Soviet Union.

Thus, empires, contrary to free market economics, are artificial creations, which must be defended by protectionism of all types. Protectionism is a forerunner of war, because where economic goods and services do not cross borders freely, conflict arises. Armies pave the way for them. No wonder wars have been generated repeatedly throughout history by global empires. The operation of global empires is antagonistic to the freedom and cooperation which comes naturally by way of free market economics. Bureaucratic empires, their exploitative colonial activity and their wars destroy wealth!

The United States is a world empire. It is protecting both its agricultural and industrial bases. Such protectionism is a harbinger of war. Furthermore, in the likes of agriculture, by seducing the American farmer and getting him into debt, the American farmer (without the likes of a PIK program), produces record crops due to his incredible technological efficiency. He has to produce in order to cover his never-ending debt service.

These record U.S. crops are then dumped on world markets, at a price below what the technologically inefficient, struggling, emerging Third World producers can compete with (such as the small farmers in Argentina or the highland farmers in Guatemala). This drives Third World farmers bankrupt, as Third World countries looking at the short-term, import (through multinational bank credit) the cheaper U.S.-produced food. The Third World farmers are then forced to give up their family farms and go to the cities where they become wards/slaves of the state, which must feed them. Big outside money then comes in and buys up the land. Conquest without bloodshed! Next, the Third World country government has to borrow more money from the International Monetary Fund and other U.S. multinational banks in order to buy food to feed their own people, who were formerly self-sufficient in agriculture. This debt makes the Third World country government a slave to the U.S. empire. This is exactly what we did to Iran, explaining in part, why Iran hates us and considers the U.S. the "Great Satan."

Third World countries effectively become a colony, selling raw materials to the developed country at low prices, buying back finished goods at high prices, with their political and economic policy set by the likes of the World Bank, International Monetary Fund and U.S. multinational banks. This is dollar imperialism. This increases tension and hostility between Third World countries and the United States. Hostility is a prelude to conflict or a turn toward communism.

No wonder debt capitalism is so hated in the Third World. It was a similar colonial injustice, accompanied by the war between honest commodity money versus Bank of England currency, which led to the American War of Independence. Injustices perpetrated by the British in India resulted in the people revolting against English rule. Absentee ownership of land in Ireland in 1847-49, allowed over a million people to starve while the food they raised was exported.

Harmony between the developed and undeveloped world comes about when absentee ownership of land (and commerce) is severely limited. Then, capital and talent from the developed world, usually following the missionaries, migrates to the undeveloped world, where there can be a cooperative stake in the long-term development of Third World land, resources, and people. Cooperative decentralization and wealth for all result.

One of the messages of my earlier books, *Wealth For All: Economics*, is that cooperation, where each man prospers through the specialization and division of labor (the development and marketing of an individual's God-given talents) leads to trade and the wealth of nations. The limits of free markets, of free enterprise, then become the process of defining the rules that maximize liberty and productivity, specifically with regard to no government involvement in the economy, limitations on absentee ownership of land, equity (non-debt) capitalism, and honest free-market money, which provide a framework for a global order of unified, peaceful prosperity among all men.

With this enhanced understanding of the Third World's perspective on local land ownership and multinational debt capitalism, perhaps we can now better appreciate the violent negative reaction toward this country, which we have witnessed in Argentina.

On October 3, 1983, Argentina suspended payment of letters of credit and interest on U.S. dollar loans to their international lenders, an effective default on U.S. dollar obligations. The suspension was an attempt by Argentina's government to protect their official reserves. Foreign currency restrictions for travel were implemented. Suspension of the issuance of import licenses also occurred. Argentina's central banks had exhausted their reserves. Furthermore, Julio Gonzalez del Solar, president of Argentina's central bank, was arrested when he returned from the late September annual meeting of the International Monetary Fund held in Washington. He was accused by one of Argentina's federal judges of failing to represent Argentina's national interests in its renegotiation of that country's foreign debt.

A twenty-four-hour strike followed in Argentina on October 4th. Some 800,000 public-service employees stopped work at government offices throughout Argentina. These government workers asked for a 30% monthly wage increase.

On October 5, 1983, there was a run on the banks in Argentina. Argentine citizens emptied their safe deposit boxes of U.S. dollars out of fear that the government would nationalize bank deposits to compensate for the drop in foreign reserves. Argentina's central bank's reserves fell from over $400 million to less than $200 million in under a month. Argentina's citizens were forced to take Argentina pesos over any other international currency.

The October 17, 1983, *U.S. News* featured: "As Argentina Edges Closer to Collapse." Some of the highlights of that article are: Workers in Argentina have staged three nationwide strikes in ten months; Argentina is expected to default on its forty billion-dollar foreign debt; inflation is approaching 500%; military police have raided homes without search warrants; telephones have been tapped; private mail has been opened and suspects have been held without judicial writs; disrespect for the law is widespread in Argentina; anarchy and civil war is feared; people are hungry in Argentina; wages are paid hourly; there are few valid contracts and a person's word is valueless; many people are disappearing, believed assassinated; the United States, its multinational banks, and the IMF which is setting Argentina's economic policy are hated; Moscow is viewed more favorably; the Soviets are penetrating Argentina's government.

On Friday, October 21st, the stock share prices of Chase Manhattan, Citibank, and other banking corporations plunged on rumors that Argentina had declared a default on its multibillion dollar debt. An estimated 50% of the new loans from the IMF and World Bank going to Argentina are winding up in personal accounts in Switzerland and the United States.

Observations and Conclusions:

Don't think it can't happen here. What is occurring in Argentina is a preview of what is ahead for this country when the U.S. dollar dies. But the convulsions here probably will be more violent since we are further removed from the land and basic agricultural production, not to mention the spoiled slave nature and economic illiteracy of the American people.

Isn't it interesting that every economic crisis creates a political crisis? An economy can exist without a government. A government cannot, however, exist without an economy.

Argentina's crisis further makes clear that, of the land and labor economic equation, labor is the most important element. Man is either the ultimate resource, the ultimate predator, or the ultimate parasite. When the government establishes rules (laws) of fair play that promote harmony in society, man, a creature of habit, who likes the restrictions and security of laws that promote freedom, becomes the ultimate resource. However, when government establishes laws that promote conflict and special interests, aggravated by bankrupt economic policies, man becomes the ultimate predator/parasite and creates hell on earth.

Man, as we have seen clearly in Argentina, can turn the earth into a garbage heap. Argentina is naturally one of the richest countries on the face of the earth, self-sufficient in energy, and renowned for its grain and beef production. And yet, Argentina is in turmoil. The sad experience of Argentina is that environment does not make man, but rather that man makes the environment.

In contrast with Argentina, Switzerland, long recognized as one of the most desirable countries in the world in which to live, has had land ownership restrictions for some time. The Lex Feugler regulations on land ownership in Switzerland are generally as follows:

1. Foreigners can only buy property in specified areas as approved by the government. Or, if they are going to buy a business, they can buy property only for the use of that business.

2. Only holiday areas are approved as areas where foreigners can invest in property other than for businesses. When foreigners buy this property, they are not allowed to rent it, and furthermore, they cannot resell it for two years. When they do resell, they must resell it to a Swiss citizen.

Where does one draw the line regarding absentee ownership of land? At the geographic distance at which the spirit of community (harmony) ceases to exist, and beyond which a man cannot turn the natural earth into a garden.

Economic prosperity is based upon peaceful human action and exchange. Money (flight capital) always flees areas of human turmoil and confict. These areas become poverty stricken, whether they are war zones, inner city ghettos, places of civil insurrection or locations of economic chaos brought about by bankrupt government fiscal and monetary policies. Ideas always have consequences. The global evolutionary idea of conflict produces the economic consequence of poverty. Flight capital, rather than combining actively with human labor to produce goods and services and jobs, instead becomes passive, seeking safety in the likes of property or gold, which is taken out of the ground in one country and buried back in a safe deposit box in another nation.

The Difference

North America and South America developed simultaneously. Why did North America become prosperous while South America continued to struggle? North Americans instilled the idea of liberty, the worth of the individual, and the concept of decentralization as supreme. South America, by contrast, estabished the old, vertical, class-oriented, status conscious idea of the elite and the peasants. Freedom produces prosperity. Slavery and the peasant class never produce prosperity. Freedom demands individual responsibility. Peasantry does not. Individual responsibility in North America stemmed ultimately from the Protestant Reformation. South America never had a Protestant Reformation.

Ideas have consequences. Religion comes down to economics. The unique cause and effect religious idea that led to economic prosperity in North America stemmed from the religion of the Puritans and the Pilgrims. The Founding Fathers saw a clear distinction and connection between God's responsibility in the eternal realm and man's responsibility in the created realm. North Americans thus felt the tension of time, the call to be responsible and productive, to fulfill their calling, to use and multiply their talents in time. This work led to economic prosperity. Man, made in the image of God, but formed from the dust of the earth, saw his stewardship responsibility as manifest in his work with both the land and his fellow man: "Thy kingdom come, Thy will be done on earth as it is in heaven."

Cooperation, not conflict, was the philosophical and practical basis of human action in North America. Men were morally accountable to fulfill their contracts/covenants. Evil was overcome with good. The workman lived peaceably with all men. Work, the cooperative specialization and division of labor leading to trade, is a root of economic prosperity.

Early Americans, recognizing the reality that God came to man on earth to give, in turn saw their responsibility to also give by serving their fellow man, by which their own best self-interests were also served. This is the exact opposite of escapist institutional North American religious Christianity today, where men seek God and attempt to flee from the temporal world and are thus irresponsible in time.

Man makes the environment based upon his ultimate religious presuppositions, not the other way around. As North and South America developed simultaneously, South America had the apparent, initial advantage. South America had more resources — gold, silver, lead. North America grew poor crops like corn and tobacco. South America was populated by educated aristocrats and soldiers. North America took the poor, religious refugees, criminals and outcasts. South America established its "top-down" religion, noted for its vertical, bureaucratic, centralized, empire nature. North America established its "bottom-up" religion of decentralization and individual accountability, because first God and His law came from above and outside of nature.

South America established the centralization of church, state and economy. Checks and balances were, by contrast, installed in North America because all men were seen as equal under the law of God. Ignorance of the law was no excuse in North America because everyone knew the law found in the first five books of the Bible, the books of Moses. Also, there was free market money.

South America has reaped what it has sown — conflict, dissension, chaos, and economic poverty. South America's religious ideas expressed in economic terms — the idea of a few very rich and many very poor, the idea of centralizing church, state, and economy with great landed estates and nobility and masses of peasants — has proven out its bankruptcy. No wonder three out of four Catholic priests in South America have turned to Marxism and liberation theology. They are looking for a workable economic answer!

North America has fallen away from the religious idea that made it great — the idea of individual accountability and responsibility of man to God and to his fellow man, the concepts of freedom, work, and cooperation. As a result, America has also increasingly slipped into poverty, conflict, and slavery. The vertical, bureaucratic civil government empire is filling the vacuum of unbelief and poor stewardship.

Ideas have consequences. Religious ideas are inescapably and ultimately manifest in economics. However, while religion, politics, and economics are linked in the abstract realm of ideas, they must be separated institutionally in the real world to provide checks and balances, and to prevent conflict and the abuse of human rights.

The structure of an organization, any organization — political, religious, economic, labor, medical, military, or educational — tells us a great deal about its nature. Vertical, bureaucratic organizations are status- rather than performance-oriented. They resist change, and are plagued by rules, regulations and ritual. They strictly limit human creativity, responsibility, freedom and accountability. They waste vast amounts of human and economic resources, while serving the needs of an elite. And the older they become, the more they move toward tyranny and corruption.

Men simply cannot handle the excess wealth and power found in "top-down" bureaucratic organizations. Man cannot play God. A look at our structures today thus condemns our cities, government, military machine, business organizations, medical complex, educational institutions, and religious hierarchies. Proud, rigid and unresponsive, they are ill-prepared to meet this time of trouble requiring maximum humility, flexibility and willingness to change. Our institutions have precisely the wrong structure for these times. This is no time for slaves.

October 27, 1983

"...the 'self-evident' truth that is the heart and soul of the Declaration — 'That all men are created equal; that they are endowed by their Creator with certain unalienable rights; that among these are life, liberty, and the pursuit of happiness!'

"These rights are denied when the equal right to land — on which and by which men alone can live — is denied. Equality of political rights will not compensate for the denial of the equal right to the bounty of nature. Political liberty, when the equal right to land is denied, becomes, as population increases and invention goes on, merely the liberty to compete for employment at starvation wages. This is the truth that we have ignored.

"We honor Liberty in name and in form. We set up her statues and sound her praises. But we have not fully trusted her. And with our growth so grow her demands. She will have no half service!

"We speak of Liberty as one thing, and of virtue, wealth, knowledge, invention, national strength and national independence as other things. But, of all of these, Liberty is the source, the mother, the necessary condition. She is to virtue what light is to color; to wealth what sunshine is to grain; to knowledge what eyes are to sight. She is the genius of invention, the brawn of national strength, the spirit of national independence. Where Liberty rises, there virtue grows, wealth increases, knowledge expands, invention multiplies human powers, and in strength and spirit the freer nation rises among her neighbors as Saul amid his brethren — taller and fairer. Where Liberty sinks, there virture fades, wealth

diminishes, knowledge is forgotten, invention ceases, and empires once mighty in arms and arts become a helpless prey to freer barbarians!"

Henry George, from
PROGRESS AND POVERTY, 1951.

Chapter Seventeen
TAXES: A BAROMETER OF SLAVERY

Somewhere along the line, probably in the government schools, we have been sold the bill of goods that slavery is primarily political rather than economic. Today, we also wrongly hold that slavery was an institution of only the Ancient World or of the Old South. Again, not so. Slavery (economic) is more widespread today than at any time in human history. The slavery of the communist empires of the USSR, Eastern Europe, Cuba, Nicaragua and Red China, the tyranny in Iran, and the black tyrants of Africa dictate and control the actions of far more people than the Ancient World or the Old South ever dreamed of doing.

Political slavery is primarily for the function of extracting economic production. Why else would 400 American businessmen rush to the Soviet Union (late 1985) and their controlled Eastern European bloc countries except to establish trade and build factories? Why else would U.S. multinational corporations, using the borrowed money of hard working American men and women, scurry over to Red China to establish industrial plants? Slave labor is cheap! (Young men drafted for military service are being enslaved against their wills, too. Their production is being captured and put to military purposes. We must never forget than an army travels on its stomach — economics.)

The opposite of slavery is freedom. Freedom is having the ability to determine how you spend your time, where you spend your time, when, with whom, doing what, for how long. (Freedom includes personal responsibility and duty toward others, as well). A person who is not economically free, and particularly someone who is in heavy debt, is subject to the dictates of someone else who determines where that person's time will be spent, when, with whom, doing what, how, for how long. The Assyrian empire of the Ancient World understood this all too well. Before the Assyrians conquered a people militarily, they would first send in their merchants to enslave them with debt, thereby instilling economic slavery. This way the targeted people would be softened up for the military and political slavery that followed.

We all have only two options in how we arrange our affairs with others.

We can either arrange them vertically, which results in slavery (or tyranny), or horizontally, which results in freedom. We come into this world first experiencing vertical relationships. As children, we are dependent upon our parents to take care of us. We are irresponsible. We are accordingly not free. In a sense, we are slaves. People who grow older but are still dependent upon others to take care of them are nothing more than old children. They are still dependent. They are accordingly irresponsible and not free. They are slaves. Older children (who we euphemistically call adults), who depend upon the federal government bureaucracy (Big Mother) to take care of them, are functionally no different than the slaves in the Soviet Union and Red China, who also depend upon those government bureaucracies to provide for them economically.

The government bureaucracy, just like a parent, possesses the ultimate power of force and determines how its subjects spend their time, where, when, with whom, how, for how long, in an ultimate economic sense. Economic? Why? Because economic control is total and final control. If you control a man economically, you ultimately control his mobility and even whether or not he eats, therefore, whether or not he lives. This is why the power to tax is the power to destroy. Taxation is economic control. This is why, according to a January 13, 1986 *U.S. News & World Report* article on millionaires, what American millionaires fear most is the IRS. This is also why big money (multinational banks) inevitably, eventually, controls a debt-ridden government. Government is an economic parasite. It depends upon money, taxes paid and borrowing, in order to survive, in order for its bureaucracy to function. Therefore, the ultimate weapon of a dispossessed, disarmed people against a slave state is economic, the refusal to work, the refusal to produce, even at the risk of starvation and death. Witness Poland and Solidarity's fight against tyranny.

Free men grow from children, born into a vertical relationship, dependent upon their parents, into a horizontal relationship where they learn to covenant and contract in order to meet their personal needs and establish peaceful relationships with their fellow man. Freedom, responsibility and prosperity always run hand in hand. The only way responsibility, freedom and prosperity can be achieved long-term is by the horizontal, contractual method of establishing relationships, thereby balancing power, as well as responsibility, between the contracting parties.

In a horizontal contract, in other words, neither party has the final force of authority over the other. And so, out of this balance of responsible power flows freedom. This is why most government services should be provided by the private sector rather than by the government bureaucracy. In the contracting private sector, not only is there more efficiency, less cost, waste and corruption, as well as more accountability, but there is also the absence of the threat of force, which permits freedom. Of course, it takes personal, moral responsibility to be able to contract. Again, responsibility, freedom and prosperity run hand in hand. Slaves are not prosperous, nor free, nor responsible. Private sector schools, private sector welfare, and even a contract with government for the minimal services of providing for the national defense, maintaining civil order, and the enforcement of contracts should be subject to review.

The direct connection between freedom and taxation should now become more apparent. The higher the level of taxation, the less one's economic wherewithal, which in turn reduces one's freedom of mobility, investment, consumption, and generally limits how one spends one's time, with whom, for how long, where, doing what. Since it follows that the lower the level of taxation, the greater the freedom and prosperity of a people, we can now directly gauge how free we are by comparing our tax bracket against historical standards.

The greatest tyrannical government bureaucracy of the Ancient World was entrenched in Egypt. And yet, the maximum tax imposed by the Egyptian bureaucracy on its subjects was 20%.

In the Middle Ages, your average serf (who, we're told, was owned lock, stock and barrel by the feudal lord) worked an average of only two or three days a week. That left the serf with four to five days a week (on average) to pursue his own interests, plus three weeks vacation a year, and no long-term indebtedness. Figure that the average serf paid a maximum tax of about 25%.

In the Old South, the average black slave forked over only between 10% and 12% of his production to the boss man, the plantation owner. As one conservative black economist recently stated, "In the Old South, the black slaves looked to the white boss man in the white house on the hill to take care of them. Black men today still look to the white man in the White House to take care of them. Isn't slavery as real now as it was then?" Economic dependency is slavery. The Viet Cong took only 30% from its peasant victims in Vietnam.

So, how do we stack up freedom wise? Most of you reading this will have to look at yourself in the mirror and honestly admit that you are paying more in total taxes than did these slaves of history. It follows that the conclusion we must reluctantly reach is that we are not free today. We are economic slaves. Furthermore, we have forgotten that we are entitled to receive benefits for our taxes paid, not just pay taxes for the duty of it.

Karl Marx, in his 1848 work, *The Communist Manifesto*, called for a graduated income tax. It was the second plank in the manifesto. Marx knew that slavery was economic. The most brutal tyrant of the Soviet Union, Lenin, wrote, "The way to destroy the middle class is to crush it between the grindstones of taxation and inflation." This is exactly what has destroyed the middle class in the United States over the past fifteen years. When a civilization destroys its middle class, it leaves only a few very rich and many very poor. This in turn fosters envy and paves the way for a huge parasitic, socialistic, government bureaucracy, intent on redistributing wealth, establishing total control, and stamping out freedom.

The extremely high taxes, bulldog-type tax collectors, and ruthless punishment systems for nonpayment of taxes is common only to the Western World. This brutal tax system exists only in North America, parts of Europe, Australia and New Zealand. In fact, it exists only where the British empire was at one time established. It is part and parcel of the Anglo-Saxon culture, a cultural flaw. (Unfortunately, the Scandinavian countries have adopted it as well.) High taxes, relentless tax collection, and the ruthless punishment for nonpayment of taxes is not found to any great extent in Africa, South America, the islands of the Pacific or the Caribbean, or in Japan, Asia, throughout the Far East or in the Middle East. Only 2% of the world lives in fear of the IRS and their ilk.

Forgetting for a moment that Americans pay $.46 out of every dollar earned for taxes (compared to only $.13 out of every buck earned in 1929), which puts us in a more severe economic slave status than the ancient tyrannies, nevertheless let's look at a little of the history of taxation.

From the time of the Ancient World, up until the 18th century, tax collecting was considered to be a profit-seeking business. Entrepreneurs bought the right to collect taxes from the king's subjects. An entrepreneur would literally make an investment. He would guarantee the king a fixed amount of income, and then he would hire tax collectors to go out and extract as much as possible from the reluctant subjects. One can just imagine the corruption that occurred in such a system. The people considered tax collectors to be robbers who pillaged and extorted farmers, merchants and villagers. In fact, also in the Ancient World, robbers often found it more profitable (and efficient) to simply settle down among their victims, rule and tax them steadily, rather than hit them occasionally with a raid, which impeded productivity and reduced their long-term take. So, in the Ancient World, outside of established profit-motivated taxation, taxes originated as theft.

The Roman empire used the local franchise, local men, to collect taxes for them. How much these tax collectors extracted from the people was often up to them. During Jesus' time, the crowds at tax time milled around the moneychangers' tables in the temple. They were required to change their coins into half shekels. These were the only coins acceptable (by edict) to settle the tax demanded by the Roman government, which had earlier been corrupted by collaboration with the moneychangers. This collusion enabled the moneychangers (bankers of their day) to swindle the multitude by doubling the exchange rate for the sanctuary coins. This provided them with a handsome profit.

Obviously, there is nothing new under the sun. The game has not changed. Today we have the U.S. Treasury, which trots up to the Federal Reserve and asks for a loan. The Federal Reserve creates the money out of thin air by means of a bookkeeping entry, gives it to the Treasury, for which the Treasury owes principal and interest. This is called monetization of the debt. The Caribbean pirates never had it so good. (In all fairness, most of the Federal Reserve's earnings are returned to the Treasury on an annual basis. But it must be remembered that the Federal Reserve is a private corporation, not a government institution, which exists for the purpose of serving its member banks, not for the purpose of serving the people or the government of the United States. The Federal Reserve is a government-sanctioned, private monopoly, whose thirty-seven primary bond dealers make a killing in the trading markets, knowing ahead of time what the Fed's policy is or will be, not to mention the profits generated by huge commissions and fees.)

The United States did not have an income tax for its first 100 years, and the country did just fine without it. In fact, as the highly respected Vermont Royster wrote in *The Wall Street Journal* of July 18, 1982, "The United States got along for a century and a quarter without an income tax. There was an income tax, however, briefly during the U.S. Civil War, and then one was proposed in 1894, but the Supreme Court held it to be unconstitutional."

During the first session of the Continental Congress in 1774, Congress denied that Parliament could tax real property. The property tax came in only very slowly in the United States. It first appeared in New England, coinciding with the spread of deism and Unitarianism. The Christian South was the last area to accept the property tax because biblically, the earth was considered to be the Lord's (Exodus 9:29, Psalm 24:1, 1 Corinthians 10:26). The Old South did not experience a property tax until post-Civil War reconstruction. The tithe to the local church (10%) had supported the institutions there.

The United States has a history of tax revolt. But it is little known that there is a tax revolt globally today. The March 8, 1982, *U.S. News* reported, "Tax Dodging — It's a worldwide phenomenon...Legitimate business is in the doldrums over much of the world, but there is a boom in the underground economy — the shadowy, often illegal activity that flouts tax agents and government rules."

The March 1982 issue of *Psychology Today* featured an article entitled, "The Tax Evasion Virus." Quoting from that article, "In the epidemiology of tax cheating, no vaccine is in sight. The more unfairness the public perceives, the greater the incentive to cheat. In a 1979 survey conducted by CRS, Inc., after interviews with 5,000 people in fifty communities, 'Americans are cheating more and feeling less guilty about it.' One person in five admitted understated income. One in ten overstated deductions. One in six claimed a dependent illegally. More than half said they thought that nearly everyone would cheat if they thought they could get away with it."

Economist John Shannon of the Advisory Commission on Intergovernmental Relations reported in 1981, "Our polls show that the federal income tax is losing the support of the lower middle class." This should come as no surprise. The lower middle class is being destroyed financially. This same commission found that 36% of the people in the United States thought the federal income tax was the least fair of all taxes. Some 30% thought the local property tax was the worst of all. Interestingly enough, the commission also found in its poll that the state sales tax was considered the most fair tax of all. This is consistent with the observations of the 17th century English social philosopher, Thomas Hobbes. Hobbes expounded the idea that it was only just, fair and honest to tax people for what they take out of society, their consumption, rather than taxing them on what they contribute to society, their income from their work, their productivity. Furthermore, such a consumption-based sales tax system encourages savings, which is the foundation of capitalism and free enterprise. Obviously, one of the reasons why the tax revolt is so large today is that people sense, rightfully so, that the present tax system is unjust. It penalizes the thrifty, hard working, honest people.

A 1981 Roper poll found that two out of every three Americans believe the income tax system is unfair, unjust. When people think a system is unjust, they inevitably, eventually rebel against it. Such tax cheating makes normal, ordinarily honest men and women criminals, because in order to do what they consider fair and just, they are forced to break the laws of their government. This then creates an additional adversary relationship between the people and the government, fomenting the breeding grounds of revolution.

The Joint Committee On Taxation found that the two reasons people don't pay income taxes today is because they perceive the system as unfair, and that it is too complex. This committee also found that a 16% flat tax, applied to an individual's gross income base, including capital gains, would generate all the revenue the federal government requires.

The IRS presently says there are 80,000 tax protest organizations. The tax protest is very deeply rooted in American history. The Boston Massacre, the Boston Tea Party, and Shays' Rebellion were all tax rebellions. Contemporary artistic works that have added to the tax revolt include the popular movie, "Harry's War". Johnny Paycheck sings, "To Hell with the IRS". A portion of the lyrics of that song rings out, "The big man pays little, while the little man pays. So I ain't givin' a dime to the IRS." Paycheck's lyrics are confirmed by Thomas Byrne Edsall in his book, *The New Politics of Inequality*. Edsall argues that the power controlling the nation's taxing and spending policies, "...has become increasingly concentrated in the hands of the affluent — and exercised for the benefit of the affluent." (Who else can afford all the lawyers and CPAs?)

Indeed, a 1984 Brookings Institute study indicated that U.S. corporate taxes have been declining rapidly over the past forty years. In 1983, corporate income taxes accounted for 6.6% of federal receipts, 1.3% of GNP, compared with 28.4% in federal receipts, and 5.4% of the GNP in 1953. The Bank of America, Dow Chemical, Union Pacific, and Tenneco paid zero corporate income taxes in 1981. There is, however, a fallacy here. Corporations don't pay taxes. People pay taxes. Nevertheless, such inflammatory statistics increase the tax revolt.

Furthermore, corporations are not generous when it comes to providing for the health, education and welfare needs of the common man. In 1981, less than 30% of the nation's two million corporations reported to the IRS that they made philanthropic donations. How different this is from the 1480-1660 era in Christian-dominated Puritan England, when Protestant businessmen provided nearly all the funds necessary to support the health, education and welfare needs of the people. (See W.K. Jordon's book, *Philanthropy In England, 1480-1660*).

The number of people who refused to pay taxes by filing protest tax returns grew from 6,000 in 1978 to 40,000 in 1982. Presently, more than 250 tax collectors are being assaulted every year. In 1982, the IRS listed three million new delinquent accounts, taxpayers who did not pay after repeated notices. The underground economy is estimated presently to be $400 billion, costing the IRS and the U.S. Treasury at least $100 billion annually in lost tax revenue. There are presently over fifty million Americans who do not file tax returns and/or who underpay their tax bills.

The supreme irony, however, is that wealthy individuals (not corporations) do pay most of the taxes. According to 1981 statistics, the top half of taxpayers paid 92.6% of all the taxes. The top 10% of taxpayers shouldered more than 50% of the tax bill for the federal government. Those individuals who reported more than a million dollars in income paid 60% of income in taxes.

Our taxation has been approximately 46% of national income for several years now, more than twice what the slave state bureaucracy of Egypt exacted from its subjects. To add insult to injury, the carefully documented 1985 book by Bill Benson and M.J. Beckman, *The Law That Never Was*, has conclusively documented that the 16th Amendment to the U.S. Constitution, the personal income tax amendment, was never officially ratified by the states and therefore is illegal.

"Twenty states, almost half of those which were claimed as having ratified the Sixteenth Amendment, had been researched and found wanting...It was a bit like watching forty-eight episodes of the Lone Ranger in which the bad guys win every single time." (Constitutional Research Association, Box 550, South Holland, IL 60743.)

The studies of the eminent British economist, Colin Clark, were discussed by C. Northcote Parkinson in his book, *The Law and the Profits*. He warned us that rates of taxation above 36% of the national income will ultimately prove disastrous for any economy. This is exactly what Art Laffer confirmed with his Laffer Curve, which indicated that at tax rates above 35% national income falls as the tax rate increases. People either move into tax shelters, take their wealth in luxury goods or leisure time, or become criminals by moving into the underground economy.

High taxes create other problems as well. High taxes increase the real rate of interest, distorting market processes. Cornelius Walford in his book, *Hunger and History*, listed high taxes as one of the four primary reasons historically for famine. Progressive income taxation also keeps newcomers, usually the poor, from amassing capital out of their own savings. This, coupled with stiff inheritance taxes, prevents wealth from being passed on from generation to generation, preventing people from being economically self-sufficient and capitalized for expansion.

High taxes discourage excellence, initiative and creativity. With progressive taxation, talent has little incentive to rise to the top. And yet, it is the work of talented individuals, not the collective mob the bureaucracy represents, who have always brought forth the greatest achievements and advancements scientifically, technologically and economically. Bureaucracies, which are necessarily supported by excess taxation, additionally impede progress by attempting to maintain the status quo, effectively attempting to stop time. This is why during times of radical change, civilizations fall. Bureaucracies cannot respond fast enough. They are too rigid.

With high levels of taxation, those who do earn high incomes spend more and more time avoiding taxes than they spend being productive. This results in a squandering of both time and resources. How many otherwise talented accountants and attorneys are employed today in the economically unproductive activities of tax related work? How much money has been lost or squandered in questionable tax shelters?

High taxes slow the economy. A slow economy increases the federal deficit due to reduced tax revenue. This in turn necessitates further tax increases, which further slows the economy. And so, the vicious cycle continues. Rising taxes then result in driving profit-seeking behavior into the underground economy, making ordinary men and women criminals. If more government revenues are in fact raised, government deficits are not decreased, because the government simply spends more.

Additionally, there is no difference between a dollar taken out of the private capital markets by borrowing, and one taken out by taxing, insofar as the competition for money is concerned. Thus, higher taxes slow the economy in this manner, too. Bureaucracies are wasteful.

Additionally, people are so overloaded with taxes that they have to borrow money from banks and other financial institutions to buy the things they need to maintain their lifestyles. Tax slavery moves people into debt slavery in order to maintain a lifestyle. Families have been forced to mortgage their wives to the workplace. This in turn results in less careful, loving, disciplined training of children, which in turn increases the juvenile wards of the state. With both members of a household working for the rest of their lives to pay their debts and their taxes, the average American is next locked into wage slavery. He cannot determine how he spends his time, with whom, where, for how long, doing what. Furthermore, tax money used for welfare transfer payments (legalized theft) further stimulates class conflict which in turn increases poverty.

In the U.S. Senate debate, prior to the adoption of the federal income tax in 1913, several senators expressed concern that the low tax rate then being considered, a measly flat 1% on incomes up to $20,000, was just "a camel's nose under the tent." How right those senators were. Some had the foresight to forecast that the income tax rate would rise to as high as 20%. This speculation was considered by Senator William Borah of Idaho to be outrageous. He declared, "Who could ever impose such a confiscatory rate?" What we wouldn't give for a 20% income tax rate today.

Allan Reynolds reported in the January 23, 1985 *Wall Street Journal*, "...Countries with persistent high tax rates have sustained an actual loss of real tax revenue over the entire seven-year period. Those who attempted to counter this loss with even steeper tax rates, such as Belgium, had even larger revenue losses.

"Countries in which taxes extracted the smallest share of GNP — Japan and Spain — have experienced by far the most rapid increase in real tax revenues. The reason, of course, is that real GDP (or GNP) is the tax base for real revenue, and production invariably grows more rapidly in low-taxed countries, as Keith Marsden of the World Bank recently observed..."

Keith Marsden, the Operations Advisor at the World Bank, found that out of twenty countries examined, in all cases, the countries that imposed a lower effective average tax burden on their populations grew faster over a decade than did those more highly taxed.

The bottom line is simply that high taxes do not work long-term. Slavery does not work. Slaves are irresponsible, dependent and poor. They cannot support a bureaucracy long-term. This is why even the Soviet Union today relies upon loans, grants, foodstuffs, and technology from Western civilization in order to survive. A bureaucracy is nonproductive. It cannot long be afforded by its own people. It has to become imperialistic or die. A bureaucracy takes care of those who are dependent upon it in a vertical manner. These dependents, older children, are effectively nonproductive. A bureaucracy is an economic parasite. It consumes its host in an accelerated fashion when personal income tax rates exceed 35%. Therefore, it follows that any government bureaucracy that exacts more than 35% in income taxes from its productive people is committing suicide.

Government is always religion applied to economics. High taxes are the economic price we pay for irresponsibility and ungodliness. When man has the faith to believe that God, eternal and temporal salvation, and His law come from above and outside of nature, he will tend to take a long-term view. He will sacrifice short-term and assume the painful responsibility of covenants and contracts, which lead to horizontal relationships, freedom and prosperity. Taxes will be accordingly low. High taxes are thus not necessary to finance a bureaucracy to support a "guns and butter" federal economy. On the other hand, when man's gods are simply other men or idols from nature, and when laws come simply from other men, when man sees no future beyond the grave, he eventually becomes disillusioned and becomes his own god, with a focus on the present. This puts him in conflict with every other man, who also claims to be his own god, which increases the government bureaucracy as a referee of conflict.

Conflict is antagonistic to prosperity. (Who wants to invest in Lebanon?) Furthermore, this natural man, seeing the injustice and folly of other men playing god, along with the inadequacy, injustice and corruption of their laws as well as their materialistic gods, has no reason to sacrifice or take the long-term view. Logically, the natural man decides to eat, drink and be merry and take advantage of the pleasures of life in the "now". Ultimately then, the difference between a self-governing man, whose God, salvation and law are outside and above nature (with economic prosperity and low levels of taxation), is contrasted with the man who is a slave to himself and other men. These other men play god with their laws, which come from the natural order, leading to inescapable poverty and high levels of taxation.

Biblical law has only two taxes, the head or poll tax, which was the same for all males twenty years of age or older, and the tithe. Both are logical. The purpose of the civil government is to provide for the national defense, to protect people against civil insurrection, revolt and crime, and to provide for justice through a court system, primarily by enforcing contracts. National defense guidelines, civil and criminal law given directly by God, were implemented by the civil authorities under the biblical system. Since men are the heads of the households (men pay alimony and child support), since men think primarily with the left side of their brains, their legal side (Father Knows Best), and since men bear the burden of national defense, domestic protection and exercising business contracts, it follows that men would be required to pay the head or poll tax. The civil government administered justice for the half a shekel that each man over twenty years of age paid to the civil government. (A militia and civil defense system patterned after Switzerland and Israel are best.) So much for the "gun" tax.

The "butter" tax was the 10% tithe paid effectively to the local church to provide for the health, education and welfare needs of the people. In fiscal year 1984, 42% of the federal budget went for direct transfer (welfare) payments. Thus, one of the reasons the federal budget, debt and deficit are out of control is because the church has failed to do its job of providing for the health, education and welfare needs of its people. This has been increasingly the case since the U.S. Civil War. The year 1907 was the last time in the United States that there was a major organized effort by churches to deal with the problems of social welfare. And yet, if every family took care of its own, as it should, and if every church took care of its own and just one person on welfare outside of its local congregation, the number of people on welfare would be zero. It is no accident following the 1907 dereliction of the church of its biblical responsibilities, that the income tax followed in 1913. Economic judgment was sure and quick. What we have today are too many coffin churches, offering nothing more than comfortable coffee clubs of cultural conformity. Too many of today's churches are slaves to the bureaucratic traditions of men.

The two forms of biblical taxation, the civil head tax (half a shekel) and the religious income tax (10%), established the economic separation of church and state, neither having authority over the other. This delegated responsibility matched by the delegated responsibility of the family, provided for checks and balances and a balance of power. No wonder there were both church and state courts of law in the Roman empire under Constantine. Both were independent godly institutions. The church was not under the state. The state was not under the church. If the church could collect no more than 10% in taxes (tithes), by implication, the state should be unable to do so also. This was the warning of Samuel in *1 Samuel 8*. Taxes above 10% are evil. Furthermore, as taxation increases, the tithe always decreases, because men say to themselves, "If I'm paying money to the state for these health, education and welfare programs, why should I pay it to the church?" Contrary to the philosopher Hegel, the state is not "god walking on earth." The state is an economic parasite playing the role of god today, the maximum distortion of reality.

We reap what we sow. But we don't reap much even when we have sowed a great deal when taxes are as high as they are today. Taxes are high because we have become an ungodly people, who take our pseudo gods and laws from man and nature. We are accordingly not responsible and self-governing. Instead, the government bureaucracy with its alphabet agencies rules over us, consuming our productivity in high taxes, which in turn impoverishes us through debt. Only when we again establish God, salvation and His law as coming from outside and above nature, thereby establishing the head tax by the civil government and the 10% tithe to the socially responsible church (with a possible consumption or national sales tax as an interim measure), will we again help establish the delegated responsibility of church, state and family, leading to the checks and balances of a separation and division of power, resulting in responsible self-government, with institutional government being primarily local in nature, functioning nearly exclusively by means of covenant and contract, resulting in not only low levels of taxation, but in freedom, peace and personal prosperity individually and collectively.

January 30, 1986

Chapter Eighteen
TOWARD A ONE-WORLD ORDER

Recall that *every government's laws are nothing more than the concrete enactment of religious ideas.* To get a feel for what a country's people expect of its government, we should first look at its religion.

Every social order whose god and laws come from the natural order or man, gravitates toward establishing the civil government as god. In turn, every humanistic state, after it reaches the empire level, moves toward establishing a One-World order, as its people become increasingly enslaved.

Along this line, a poll by George Gallup discovered that America's faith is superficial and self-centered. It has little involvement with the real world. It is religious "feel goodism."

American religion does not feel that it has the need or responsibility to go out and change the world. What this effectively means is that the people of this country, rather than being personally responsible, have left the vacuum of their irresponsibility to be filled by the civil government. People in the United States look to the federal government to change the world and solve their problems.

When people are irresponsible with regard to their duties in all areas of life, they are expressing a lack of religious faith. *Government then fills this vacuum of irresponsibility and unbelief.* In the long-term, all short-term government "blessings" turn to a "curse" on the people. The influential songwriter Bob Dylan in the June 1984 issue of *Rolling Stone* confirmed this when he stated, "I think politics is what kills; it doesn't bring anything alive. Politics is corrupt."

What's important to note is that government is the religion "of the devil" in Dylan's words. And big government can be constituted as a curse by either the extreme Right Wing or the extreme Left Wing. Both make use of vertical bureaucracies to implement their evil. Both feed and grow on conflict. In fact, both generate conflict. The Right Wing overemphasizes the individual. The Left Wing overemphasizes the group.

Conflict is the essence of our way of life today, whether we look at politics, business, labor, liberation theology, the military, the professional sports arena, or the number of lawsuits filed. It almost goes without saying that the conflict generated by special privilege has captured members of both political parties today.

The logic underlying conflict today is the Hegelian dialectic. *Thesis* wars against *antithesis* which creates *synthesis*. Debt capitalism has both created and now wars against communism. These two will merge together in the synthesis of a bureaucratic One-World order. Both Stalin of Soviet Communism on the Left and Hitler of National Socialism on the Right used the Hegelian dialectic to build their vertical bureaucracies which oppressed and brutalized mankind. Why shouldn't the Soviet Union and the United States do exactly the same thing? Their philosophical bases today are identical.

Dr. M. Scott Peck in his best-seller, *People of the Lie: The Hope For Healing Human Evil*, noted that conflict was evil, and was generated by people attacking others rather than facing their own failures. He noted that it was bureaucracy that led to "the fragmentation of conscience." In a bureaucracy, people are conscienceless humanoids, morally unaccountable. Too many politicians seek power over others through bureaucracies, due to their own personal inadequacies.

The political action cycle in a "free"(?) society enslaved to nature is from the "rule by one" (a king) to the "rule by a few" (a republic), to the "rule by many" (a democracy), to "anarchy," and back then to the "rule by one."

We are at the end of the age of democracy in this country. A democracy normally lasts only about 200 years. A short period of anarchy is about to befall us. Which "rule by one" will this country experience? A Left Wing bureaucratic dictatorship or a Right Wing bureaucratic dictatorship? History and the odds favor the Right Wing variety, and then the merger with the U.S.S.R. Power unites with power in the synthesis.

As I have pointed out repeatedly, we are following a similar track to that of Nazi Germany. This becomes additionally clear from such works as Leonard Piekoff's book, *The Ominous Parallels: The End of Freedom in America* and Constance Cumbey's work, *The Hidden Dangers of the Rainbow: The New Age Movement and Our Coming Age of Barbarism*. Climatologist Dr. Iben Browning has noted that in our "civilized" world, we are the most akin to being barbarians. We don't do the same thing day in and day out as "civilized" people do. Also, we are heavy red meat eaters, a sure sign of a barbarian, according to Browning.

Hitler and Nazi Germany were considered by the civilized world to be barbaric. The underlying religion of Nazi Germany was occultism. Wilhelm Wulff's book, *Zodiac and Swastika: How Astrology Guided Hitler's Germany*, makes this point abundantly clear. Again, every government is the overt expression of the religion of its people. And every vertical bureaucratic human government empire has had an occult religion at its base, usually including astrology. Our vacuum of spiritual unbelief in this country, our selfish "feel-goodism," is being replaced by rampant occultism. The sensational moneymaking movie hits today often feature occult religion and government empires as their major theme.

The book I've found the most helpful in understanding the occult activity which gave rise to the Third Reich was Jean-Michel Angebert's (McGraw-Hill, 1975) work, *The Occult and the Third Reich*. Angebert gave the specific details on how occult religion gave rise to the Third Reich politically. (This was also confirmed in a general sense by Harvard Professor James H. Billington's book, *Fire in the Minds of Men: Origins of the Revolutionary Faith*. What Billington pointed out was that political revolutions begin with an occult religion and end up with a worse tyranny than what existed prior to the revolution.)

Another book on this government-religion subject has really spun me around. Dusty Skyler's 1977 work, *Gods and Beasts: The Nazis and the Occult*, historically details the direct connection between occultism and the activity of the Nazis. In fact, Skyler stated that Nazi Germany cannot be understood apart from understanding its occult religious roots. Skyler noted that when the Nazis proclaimed themselves to be gods, they became beasts. So it is with men everywhere who proclaim themselves to be God. This is why civil government should never make laws as such, but rather implement the morality of God's laws to specific factual circumstances.

What took place in Nazi Germany prior to the rise of Hitler is very similar to what is taking place in this country now with the rise of our bureaucratic dictatorship. For example, at that time in Germany, taxation and inflation had sapped the strength of the middle class. There was a huge gap between advancing technology and an out-of-date social order. Evolutionary Darwinism was the basis of the Nazi intellectual appeal. Extreme migration of the people from city to city severed traditional family ties. The Germans were rootless. The tremendous scientific advances and discoveries in Germany brought about a sharp decline in religious faith. The people were searching for new religious beliefs and values. They lived in a religious and value vacuum. Eastern religion became influential. Egyptology was extremely popular. A type of romanticism was attached to the East. People longed for the good old days. For Germans, this was a longing for the Middle Ages, a time when men, art and religion were unified. Gnostic thinking was pervasive. Secret societies, composed of men of money, power and influence, competed for government control. The Nazis were looking for a messiah and the dawn of a new age. The swastika became the key symbol of the Golden Dawn.

Astrologers guided high-placed Nazi officials, including Hitler. Men such as Professor Karl Haushofer, a practicing astrologer and fortune-teller, had a tremendous influence on Hitler, as did Karl Ernest Krafft. Hitler spent a great deal of his own time studying Eastern religions, yoga, occultism, hypnotism, astrology, telepathy, graphology, and phrenology, all of which are again growing in popularity today. Hitler had a high level of understanding of medieval occultism and ritual magic. And all of this worked for the Nazis, for awhile. But once the Nazis were drawn into it and believed in it, and saw it work, and put their faith in it, then it turned on them. Demons lie! As Skyler notes, "But in the end, all the prophets failed them, and the Nazis learned that they could not be saved by the stars."

A society reaps what it sows. Ideas have consequences. People pay the price for their actions, which stem originally from their religious assumptions about the nature of reality. I am convinced that we are moving toward a Right Wing bureaucratic dictatorship, which will be historically similar to that of occult Nazi Germany. This will be the sad price we pay for "feel-goodism" religion, leading to lack of involvement in government by moral, responsible men. This dictatorship could begin to exert power in late 1988. Its bureaucracy could attempt to unite religion, government, and economics into one centralized block of power. Persecution will be against Jews, Blacks, Mexicans, Hispanics, rich conservatives, conservative Christians, and free men generally. It will be a good time to live outside of the United States. It will be a prelude to an attempted One-World Order, uniting the "Right" of this country with the "Left" of communism, probably following the Hegelian conflict of a Third World War and/or civil unrest in the 1988 to 1992 time period.

Beginning in 1987, the earth should begin to undergo one of its most catastrophic periods of history. Expect climate variability and earthquake and volcanic activity. Without exception, such periods historically have been times of radical decentralization, as the "labor" side of the "land and labor" economic equation adjusts to harsh "land" changes. So, the movement then toward a One-World Order will be a colossal failure. It is exactly the wrong thing at the wrong time in history. The problem is, those who favor a One-World Order control the economies and governments of the world. This means we will all have to suffer through their insanity and maybe a limited nuclear war.

The laws of any society are nothing more than the religious rules enacted to govern human conduct (economics) in that society. Rules that come from man are inevitably marked by conflict, because man is part of nature and thus cannot on his own completely rise above nature, and nature's *modus operandi* of conflict. Neither does man have perfect knowledge. This also breeds conflict. Conflict is inevitable in nature as it swings from Yin and Yang, oscillating between the rights of the individual versus the rights of the group. There is no stability inherent in nature.

Furthermore, when men make laws and decide morality (good and evil), this inevitably leads to the centralization of power in any culture. It cannot be otherwise. Society (human action) as a whole is ultimately governed by the rules of the highest power (lawmakers) in that society. For this reason, decentralization is only possible if the governing body is benign (very rare), or if the laws that govern man come from outside of and above the culture and nature — from God — such as the Mosaic law. Since God's laws arise from outside and above nature, they also are above conflict and can potentially implement harmony. Thus, for mankind to have both decentralization and harmony in society, his law system must come from God. Decentralization is necessary for freedom. Decentralization, freedom, and harmony are vital for long-term economic prosperity. The prosperity of any culture is thus a reflection of its religion and subsequent law system.

July 6, 1984

"Men must be governed by God or they will be ruled by tyrants."
William Penn

At the federal level today, for every elected official, there are 5,500 unelected bureaucrats.

The World Constitution and Parliament Association's timetable for establishing a One-World Order is 1990: "We're going to have to have a very big fright — perhaps a short atomic war — to obtain world federalism."
J.F. Leddy, Chairman
World Association of World Federalists

SECTION III

An Opportunity for Freedom

Chapter Nineteen
SECOND CHANCE: UNFREEZING THE MARKETPLACE

Second Chance is, appropriately enough, the trade name of a body armor worn by law enforcement officers. *Second Chance* body armor protective vests are designed to absorb the impact of most pistol slugs and thus give police officers a second chance to apprehend some criminal bozo. *Second Chance* is, thus, much preferred to a "last chance."

In pondering again the implications of the fact that we have now past the turning point of Western civilization's 510-year cycle, this writer has begun looking at what it would take for us to have a "second chance."

Through the ages, theologians have expressed a predictable dislike for cyclical historians, because the cyclical view of history presupposes a "fallen" culture. Of course, such cyclical historians are, in fact, more accurate in their projections *if* the civilization being studied has become hedonistic, cyclical and nonprogressive. This is why, effectively, cyclical historians such as Spengler, Toynbee, and Durant have provided us with so much valuable insight during this century. The twentieth century has been a cyclical, nonprogressive, hedonistic civilization, particularly with regard to Western civilization in its bureaucratic, institutional and economic arrangements.

Oswald Spengler was writing his classic, *The Decline of the West*, at about the time the Federal Reserve Act was legislated (1913). Spengler observed then that we were in the "wintertime" of our civilization, a time when our civilization was "frozen." It has often troubled me that Spengler made these remarks some seventy years ago. Have we been "frozen" for seventy years? If so, and if we have been unable to meet the "challenge-response" (Toynbee) for that long, then without a doubt the pervasive economic and financial breakdown we are going through presently is long overdue.

Certainly, with the establishment of the Federal Reserve, the nation turned over its economic lifeblood (money) to a private corporation. In this act, we saw the centralization of power — basic economic power. This central power drew to itself all political, military, religious, education, medical, media and labor power. They all followed the Pied Piper of economic power. Why? Because "bread is basic." Money rules this world. Money is "bread." It takes bread to live.

The establishment of a vertical, bureaucratic, slavelike, centralized, legislated monopoly over money — the building block of an economy — is the pinnacle of the evolutionary spiral of power and control. This maximum institutionalization of money wiped out the vestiges of basic and meaningful financial freedom. As a result, seventy years ago money became "frozen." And everything else has followed. Because economic freedom is basic, this means our children are third generation slaves.

Unfortunately, few Americans are educated in the freedom-oriented basics of economics and finance. These things are simply not taught in the public schools. The General Education Board, established in 1902, in its *Occasional Letter I* declared, "People will yield themselves with perfect docility to our molding hands." How true!

How many Americans know, for example, that the Federal Reserve creates money (credit) out of "thin air," on which it earns interest? Specifically, let's say the U.S. Treasury needs to borrow $100 billion, and the Federal Reserve agrees to monetize that debt. The Bureau of Engraving and Printing prints up $100 billion of U.S. bonds for the U.S. Treasury. The U.S. Treasury receives a credit entry for that amount at a bank; the Federal Reserve receives an interest-bearing U.S. government security. The Federal Reserve (bank) now deposits its $100 billion worth of U.S. bonds with the Comptroller of the Currency in exchange for $100 billion of U.S. currency. (The Federal Reserve, of course, continues to earn interest on the $100 billion on deposit.) Then, the Federal Reserve, with the $100 billion in currency in their vaults as reserves, can make loans or investments as desired through the banking system, and, through the multiplier effect, multiply that $100 billion roughly ten times to its own self interest. What a great way to earn a living, as a legitimate counterfeiter!

It can be astutely argued that the corruption of a nation's currency leads to increased corruption throughout all aspects of society. In our case, the monetization of debt is monetary corruption beginning at the very top. What a tragic example for the rest of us.

This concept, that we have been effectively "frozen" monetarily for seventy years, controlled and manipulated by a central bank (the Federal Reserve), lends credibility to the monetarists' school of thought, which in the last decade has been the rage among contemporary economists. Money is the lifeblood of an economy. Therefore, if there is only one money, and its control, issue, and withdrawal are manipulated by one private corporation, then having a monetarists' perspective makes some sense.

When we look at the real world over the last seventy years, our first-blush impression is to exclaim about how much has transpired, about how much we have progressed. How could we be "frozen?" The real question is, "How much have we progressed in a real, meaningful economic sense?"

One thing we know about debt-money and a fractional reserve banking system (accompanied by compound interest) is that it requires never ending expansion to stay "healthy." The debt treadmill, with its ever growing compound interest, stimulated through the fractional reserve banking system, leads to a red-hot boom, which, once cooled, leads to a contraction and a bust.

Human frailties and our biological limits simply cannot keep pace with the infinite growth of compound interest, created by debt, which is continually expanding through the leveraged fractional reserve banking system. When such a system stops growing, it dies. There is no sabbath, no rest, in a debt economy. It is either on a drugged-up high or in the death of cold turkey. Again, the question is: "How have we expanded during the last seventy years?" Perhaps, in answer to this question, we can discern why we are now eating our tail as the $7.3 trillion of public and private sector debt in this country, and the $11 trillion total of debt in all of Western civilization, now consumes all of our assets. If this "frozen" perspective is correct, it's amazing that we've gone this long and this far without having to pay the piper before now. (Keep the first U.S. depression of the 1930s in the back of your mind for now).

Let's review the high points of what has occurred historically and economically since being blessed (cursed) with a central bank (the Federal Reserve).

First, immediately following the establishment of the Federal Reserve, we had World War I. The one thing we can confidently say about wars is that they destroy wealth, thereby creating artificial demand for both human and natural resources, as well as artificial expansion. Was the monopoly on monetary power in evidence as far back as WWI? Paul Warburg was the architect of the Federal Reserve. He became its first Chairman of the Board of Governors. Warburg was a German immigrant whose family banking institution, M.M. Warburg Company of Hamburg and Amsterdam, financed Germany's war effort. Paul Warburg's own firm, Kuhn, Loeb Company, had five representatives in the U.S. Treasury who issued Liberty Loans to finance the American war effort against the Germans. Pretty slick, financing both sides in a world war.

The actions of the Fed were inflationary during World War I. All wars are inflationary. Wars have to be financed. Otherwise they cannot be fought because they cannot be afforded. However, it's often only after a war that the increase in the quantity of money (inflation) is recognized and felt. As Milton Friedman wrote, in *Free to Choose:*

> ...The additional money was being used not to pay for the government's expenses but to finance private business activities. A third of our total

wartime WWI inflation occurred after the end not only of the war but also of government deficits to pay for the war. Belatedly, the system discovered its mistake. It then reacted sharply, plunging the country into the sharp but short depression of 1920-21.

So, the Federal Reserve created the economic depression of 1920-21, as well as cooperated in the financing of WWI. Alas, we see the effects of the Federal Reserve in its first decade — war, inflation, depression — all "frozen," nonprogressive events.

The artificial stimulation of WWI, followed by the cleansing effects of the depression of 1920-21, carried us through the 1920s, one of the few eras when, for the most part, debt was used for productive purposes (real estate and stocks), and thus was relatively noninflationary. But the 1920 credit-created boom led to the 1930's bust. As things started to break down during the latter part of the 1920s, there was a conspiracy (secret monetary manipulation) between the Bank of England and the Federal Reserve. Economic historian Donald Hoppe commented in *The Donald Hoppe Analysis*:

> In 1927, Montague Norman, the governor of the Bank of England, secretly met with Benjamin Strong of the N.Y. Fed and told Strong that Europe was facing financial collapse because the U.S. dollar was too high in relation to the pound and other world currencies. The only thing that could save the situation, said Norman, was for the Fed to cut its discount rate and thus weaken the U.S. dollar. Strong (whom President Hoover later contemptuously referred to as a 'mental annex to Europe') readily obliged and overstimulated by easy money the New York Stock Market. The New York Stock Market soared to its final, disastrous peak in 1929.

It is well-documented that the Federal Reserve triggered the first U.S. Great Depression. As monetarist Milton Friedman wrote: "...the depression was produced by failure of government in one area — money..."

Friedman blamed the Great Depression on the Federal Reserve system, since the Fed let the supply of money contract throughout 1930. Furthermore, the money supply contracted from late 1930 until early 1933.

It would have seemed, after WWI, with the depression of 1920-21 and the Crash of 1929, that astute Americans would have put a halt to the folly of the central bank. They should have recognized that Federal Reserve funny money, the most critical factor and the most basic ingredient in the economic marketplace, needed to be decentralized and "unfrozen" so its monopoly power could be defused. But, by 1930, Americans were already economic slaves.

The Great Depression convinced the American public that capitalism was radically flawed. Americans were correct with regard to "debt" capitalism, but they stumbled forward to a greater error, the belief that an economic parasite — a centralized, bureaucratic government — would efficiently turn the economy around. Thus, their error compounded. And so did their misery.

The rising socialism of the FDR years, as Americans fled from the responsibility of freedom, was a total failure. The New Deal was no deal at all. It was the artificial demand and expansion created by World War II that ended the Great Depression.

It's a cruel cycle when the economic death of a depression can only be overcome by the artificial stimulation of increasing debt inflation, or the artificial stimulation of demand and expansion created by the physical death of men in war.

Recall that a root meaning of the word "debt" is "death." It is beginning to become more apparent why our civilization became "frozen" economically with the monopolistic centralization of money and power in the Federal Reserve in 1913. Since then we have effectively had no economic advancement. It's all been artificial. Our only options have been inflation, war, or depression. For generations now, Americans have labored productively all of their lives and died in debt and poverty, if they were lucky enough to avoid getting slaughtered in war. (Dollar imperialism, the raping of Third World resources, has added to our debt-induced illusion of prosperity.)

With few exceptions, most who have gotten rich in the last seventy years have done so via speculation, usually with heavy borrowing. Less than two-tenths of one percent of our people are millionaires. The ever increasing debt pyramid has produced only the illusion of prosperity for most folks. Today the middle class is being destroyed. Only 2% of Americans are financially self-sufficient at age 65. Our classic, productive American inventors, real estate developers, natural resource developers, and entrepreneurial businessmen have prospered, aided by inflation, (and usually some debt), but only in the face of high taxation and over-regulation.

January 28, 1983

"In 1982, the twelve Federal Reserve banks earned $16.52 billion, of which $15.21 billion went to the U.S. Treasury. The Fed paid $79 million in dividends to member banks and $78 million to Reserve banks to increase their surpluses. The Fed's expenses were, of course, deducted."

The Wall Street Journal

Chapter Twenty
SECOND CHANCE: THE REVOLUTION OF LITTLENESS

World War II created one whale of a lot of artificial demand and expansion. The military hardware demanded for World War II in both Europe and the Pacific stimulated tremendous industrial activity and employment stateside. Uncle Sam had plenty of jobs available for young, male bodies. The glut of unemployment only came after WWII.

It is now well documented that FDR desperately wanted the U.S. to enter WWII. In fact, he encouraged the Japanese attack on Pearl Harbor. The Hudson Institute study titled *Report from Iron Mountain* stated:

> War has provided both ancient and modern societies with a dependable system for stabilizing and controlling national economies...the permanent possibility of war is a foundation of stable government; it supplies the basis for general acceptance of political authority.

Of course, the reconstruction and rebuilding of Europe and Japan after World War II, through such welfare programs as the Marshall Plan, was again the working out of this artificially created demand and expansion generated by the devastation of those geographic areas during World War II.

War is a type of urban renewal. The war machines are the bulldozers. The banks make a "killing" financing these bulldozers and the subsequent reconstruction. Europe (West Germany) became an industrial power after WWII. Japan became an industrial power after WWII. The same thing happened in Korea, following the Korean War. Today Korea is an industrial power. Will Vietman be next? Evidence suggests as much! The Soviets now occupy former U.S. military bases there.

Given the present economic dilemma for all of Western civilization, will this cruel cycle of human action again repeat? Albert M. Wojnilower, Chief Economist at First Boston Corporation stated, "One way of ensuring a fantastic recovery...would be to raze our industry the way German and Japanese industry were devastated by World War II..."

Wouldn't a theater action now in Central America or in the Middle East, to "save oil for the Western democracies," be an ideal solution to the problems facing Western democracies? We could stimulate artificial demand and expansion by the war, and at the same time, by destroying the likes of Saudi Arabia's oil fields, keep the price of oil high and thus preserve the multinational banks and oil companies. (For further discussion see the chapter, "Oil: The World's Key Commodity" in my book *Wealth For All: Economics*.)

Since World War II, the additional artificial war demand and expansion created by Korea, Vietnam, and by ever increasing consumer, business and government debt brought us to the threshold of runaway inflation in early 1980. In late 1979, the Fed again stepped on the monetary brake, and triggered an inescapable contraction and depression. (Debt money has to keep expanding to prevent a contraction in the debt pyramid.)

Given the immensity of the problem, and our unwillingness to formulate creative new economic and financial solutions, can there be any question that either greater inflation or a bigger war is eventually in store for us? Probably both. A hyperinflation in the late 1980s, leading to civil unrest and World War III in 1989, given the cause and effect human action cycle over the last seventy years, is a terrifying and realistic expectation. Of course, we should expect a depression by then as well.

For the last seventy years, all our expansion and demand has been artificially stimulated by wars or debt inflation. No surprise that we are "frozen," in the "wintertime" of our civilization. Given this grim scenario, one would think that all Soviet Russia would have to do is sit back and wait for Western civilization to collapse, which it is surely doing. But the Soviets also see the realistic probability of World War III. Besides, the Soviet economic problems are worse that those in Western civilization. The Soviet Union is a far more centralized, bureaucratic, economic parasite. And, as Soviet exile Mikhail Makarenko noted, there is only one thing that has sustained the Soviet Union all these years: "Western trade." Also, didn't the Russian Revolution occur in 1917, during the time when Spengler was writing that Western civilization had become "frozen?" And wasn't that Revolution also financed by New York banking interests? It was. The Soviet Union is sustained by Western debt capitalism.

Given the terrifying alternatives of global depression, worldwide hyperinflation, or a third world war — the only three possibilities under our present "frozen" economic system — if past patterns repeat, where is our opportunity for a "second chance?" Two administrations, one Democratic (Carter) and one Republican (Reagan), have both tried their own extreme proposed solutions within the confines of the present "frozen" system and have failed miserably. There is nothing left but failure, collapse and destruction unless a new and creative road is taken immediately. *Such an approach will necessarily come from the grass roots if we are to prevent a One-World Order. Freedom always comes from the bottom up.* It is freedom, the freedom of decentralization, that the world is crying for now. As Willian Pfaff wrote in the *Los Angeles Times* (10/31/82):

> This country has now experienced two populist governments in succession, those of Jimmy Carter and Ronald Reagan. Both men were elected because they seemed to represent decency, common sense, the wit of the ordinary man. Neither has done well. Together, they have proven that good intentions are not enough. The country is in need of brains, new ideas, sophistication, seriousness — and probably of reforms in party and governmental structures. But the elite of this anti-elitist country were plowed under during the political and social upheavals we went through during the 1960s and early 1970s. What takes their place? The country is discontent with what it has, but no convincing alternative is put to it. This is why the mood is bleak.

Well, the alternatives are clearly there. We are in the middle of a second industrial revolution, the revolution of global jet travel, satellite communication, and microchip computers. It is an information revolution. Information processing now involves 62% of our work force as compared to 17% in 1950. This has led to an explosion in the creation of new companies, something to the tune of 600,000 a year compared to only approximately 100,000 in 1950. We haven't seen entrepreneurs shine to this extent since the transition from an agriculture society to the industrial society in the late 1700s and early 1800s. We are moving back toward freedom-oriented horizontal relationships and clearly away from vertical, slavelike, bureaucratic, centralized relationships, such as those now dominating our economy: the federal government, political parties, labor unions, businesses, universities, media, military, medical and religious institutions. It is projected that by 1990, seven out of every ten homes will have a computer. There are now 173,000 computers in the public schools.

Dr. Jack D. Douglas, Professor of Sociology at the University of California, San Diego, commented, "If the government ever stops mandating inflation and punishing small business, the Revolution of Littleness will sweep all before it. And the Age of Little Business will be an age of greater economic freedom, thus of ever-greater creativity, efficiency and growth for all of us."

(Make no mistake about it. Much of our service economy today can go up overnight like a puff of smoke. Too much of it is bureaucratic makework. Goods production is foundational to a service economy. Agriculture is our leading goods industry today. We must use our technology to rebuild agriculture and our basic industry, and work in harmony with the industrially developing Third World.)

The world has always been ruled by ideas, particularly better ideas.

"Frozen" institutions crumble in the earthquakes created by new and better ideas. Our "second chance" opportunity lies with the speed and pervasiveness with which the "Revolution of Littleness" is sweeping the world and challenging our institutional dinosaurs. A depression will accelerate this revolution. A return to the moral virtues of humility, responsibility, self-interested giving, and a long-term view will also accelerate it. The changing, harsh and unpredictable climate will accelerate the "Revolution of Littleness." As Wilhelm Roepke wrote in his 1960 classic, *A Humane Economy*:

> ...our centrist civilization, which has become more and more remote from man and the human scale, has reached the point where its own continued existence is at stake.

If we do not reconstruct our financial and economic system as the present global debt capitalistic structure breaks down, we will have squandered our best opportunity for real economic freedom and "Wealth for All" in this century. The establishment is giving us a broadside shot!

We are in a desperate race. If won by the agents of moral decentralization, we face the prospect of a glorious, free, prosperous, creative, technological new age. If won by the agents of centralization, we face at best a statist, bureaucratic, miserable tyranny, and at worst a humanity-destroying third world war. This is a race that none of us can escape running. It is a race between the "frozen" old economic order and the fast-growing new one. It is a race between a free market and no market at all. It is a race between vision, self-sacrifice, and a long-term view versus blindness and indulgence, culminating in short-term death. In this decade we will begin either creating heaven or hell on earth.

How clearly is the old "frozen" order dying? For seventy years all it has offered us is inflation, depression and unemployment, or war. The May 3, 1982 issue of *Fortune* magazine included an article, declaring that the ten largest mergers among Fortune's 500 largest corporations were overwhelming failures. Present mergers are meeting the same fate. Despite $30 billion worth of direct federal spending for business, we experienced a second great U.S. depression (1982). Agriculture is in the worst shape it has been in since the Great Depression, despite $16.2 billion in spending by the U.S.D.A., primarily via Commodity Credit Corporation loans.

Few seriously believe in Keynesian economics any longer, as Paul Craig Roberts pointed out clearly in the December 21, 1982 *Wall Street Journal*. Globally the countries of the world have given up on the Keynesian approach. And, it is financial rape of the American taxpayer for the Federal Reserve to bail out the bad debts of twenty-six foreign countries with U.S. taxpayers' money, just so that the multinational banks can be saved. Given the historic violence of the WASPs in this country, one wonders how long until federal judges, bureaucrats, politicians, multinational bankers, corporate officers and the like are shot or hung by an alienated, violent citizenry, sick and tired of a "frozen" order. Violence is the way of nature.

Only about 19% of the country is unionized now, compared to 32% in 1950. Three out of the last four presidents of the Teamsters have been convicted for federal crimes. The U.N. can't come close to performing its global peacekeeping function. Speaking of the U.N., U.S. Ambassador Jeane Kirkpatrick said, "Resolution of conflict is the job at which it is the least successful...the U.N. actually exacerbates conflicts..." Put simply, the system is "frozen," awaiting its burial by the "Revolution of Littleness."

In this "Revolution of Littleness," the computer is becoming to man's mind what tools and machines became to man's hands in the first industrial revolution. Mind rules over matter. Thus, human beings have the ability now to learn how to act in their own enlightened self-interest and develop their talents in a way never before possible in human history. As Peter Drucker commented in *The Wall Street Journal*, "We now know that the human being is a learning machine, and the problem is not to motivate people but to keep from turning them off." The present "frozen" system has turned off nearly everyone except the bureaucratic elitists in power. Some 76% of all Americans believe government is run by a few big special interests who look after themselves.

We are in a race against time. Things are happening much faster today than ever before, and we have so little time left. The structural unemployment generated by this transition period could destroy our society unless a "Wealth for All" type of free enterprise system is established. Robotics is on the march. The computer is accelerating our awareness of the time crunch. Will the computer be used by centralized agents for identification and control, or for massive, freedom-loving decentralization and development of human talents? The second option is our "second chance."

Because meaningful change, particularly in the economic arena, begins at the grass roots level by freedom-loving individuals, I have come to define practical good and evil in terms of time! *Good occurs when man acts in his own self-interest long-term. Evil results when man acts in his own self-interest short-term.* The former leads to "win-win" cooperative transactions, the latter to "lose-lose" conflict-ridden transactions. Furthermore, such a definition gives us a fusion of religious morality, economics and time!

The microelectronic computer age should be just the trick necessary to trigger the development of individual talents and instill purpose which leads to widespread cooperative exchange in the free market. Warren Bennis, Professor of Management at the School of Business Administration at the University of Southern California, declared, "People would rather dedicate their lives to a cause they believe in than lead lives of pampered idleness." How many Americans today are living lives of lonely desperation?

Henry Boettinger, in *Harvard Business Review* wrote:

> At every level of management, from shop floor to boardroom, across the spectrum of our institutions, whether government, business, education, armed forces or the church, we need the rediscovery of the value of the individual imagination and a rekindling of that passion for humane purposes which is the authentic light of leadership.

The November, 1982 *Psychology Today* featured an article by psychologist Bernard Rimland of the Institute for Child Behavior Research in San Diego. Rimland had nearly 2,000 people rated by over 200 students in six colleges according to whether they were selfish or unselfish and happy or unhappy. Rimland concluded:

> Selfish people are by definition devoted to bringing themselves happiness. Judged by others, however, they seem to succeed less than other people who work at bringing happiness to others. Conclusion: Do unto others as you would have them do unto you.

That sounds an awful lot like self-interest is best served by service, that good is achieved by man acting in his own self-interest long-term — functions that the computer should facilitate long-term globally, as the influence of our mental/computer/freedom/decentralization revolution expands.

While religious presuppositions, philosophy, ideas and thoughts, and subsequent human actions and habits are inherent in each individual, the basic human activity in our natural order is economic. Without economic basics — food, clothing, shelter — we perish. It is only in a world of plentiful economic basics that all other human activity and endeavors can expand and flourish. If no one worked, if no one took a self-disciplined, long-term view, we would only have available to eat what was provided to us freely by photosynthesis — grain, fruits, nuts, vegetables, and some animals, poultry, and fish. It would most certainly be a world of scarcity and conflict. Only 10 million of us would survive, out of 4.6 billion presently on the earth. What we need to flourish and expand in an "Age of Littleness" is an ethical global free market, pure competition if you will, which leads to cooperation.

There are four requirements for pure competition, that is, in free markets:

1. *Large number of buyers and sellers.* This we have in great abundance worldwide.

2. *Product homogeneity.* Here we have very similar products perceived by the buying public as being equivalent. This exists today.

3. *Free market entry and exit.* Anyone or any organization can either enter or leave any particular industry, profession, or business endeavor. For this to occur, we need separation of government from economics in all areas. This means no government legislated cartels or monopolies, no government licensing of professions. As Milton Friedman wrote in *Free to Choose*, "A monopoly can seldom be established within a country without overt and covert government assistance in the form of a tariff or some other device." This also means upholding right to work laws with labor unions having to compete in the free market against nonunion labor. Labor unions, in every case today, are organizations that discriminate against free, lower priced labor, particularly minorities. It also means no monopolies for the likes of the American Bar Association or the American Medical Association.

(Abraham Lincoln was a pretty fair, self-taught country lawyer. The greatest justice ever to serve on the U.S. Supreme Court, John Marshall, had only one year of formal education. Not until March 25, 1957 were all nine members of the Supreme Court law school graduates...)

("If the medical establishment is truly interested in good health, why does it fight to suppress every new idea that develops outside its sphere of influence, especially when those ideas meet the first commandment of medicine...cause no harm?" Stephen Dorne, President, World Health Alliance)

4. *Perfect dissemination of information.* Here, price, cost, and quality and quantity information is known by all prospective buyers and sellers in the marketplace. The microcomputer age will make this possible to an extent never before known by man.

We face the potential of the most free markets in history! Microcomputers also make honest free market money possible globally.

The age of microcomputers is rushing us into the second half, the completion of the industrial revolution. The mechanical industrial revolution brought us the tools and machinery to aid man's hands to do better, faster, and more efficient physical work. The computer brings to man's mind the greatly enhanced capability of doing superior mental work, while also creating robots to do mindless physical tasks. The usefulness of noncreative human labor is almost past. This is no time for slaves.

Let's return to the observations of Oswald Spengler about the "frozen wintertime" of our civilization, which occurred with the establishment of the Federal Reserve and its monopoly over money. Remember, money is the lifeblood of an economic system. At one time in Europe, the Rothschilds controlled the banking industry in five European countries. (Source: *60 Minutes*). One member of this banking elite family effectively stated, "Give me control of a nation's money and I care not who makes its laws." The borrower, the government, is always the slave of the lender, the central bank. The late Louis T. McFadden, Chairman of the Bank and Currency Committee of the U.S. Congress declared in 1933:

> Every effort has been made by the Fed to conceal its powers, but the truth is — the Fed has usurped the government. It controls everything here (in

Congress) and it controls all our foreign regulations. It makes and breaks governments at will.

For this revelation, Congressman McFadden is reputed to have died from poisoning.

It's time to push for free market money, for basic freedom — economic freedom. It's time to break the seventy-year cycle of debt-death-inflation, war, unemployment and depression. We should exercise our option found in the *Federal Reserve Act of 1913* and buy the Fed back. The cost is about $1 billion.

We have had decentralized free market money in this country before. In fact, it's our tradition. Our Founding Fathers believed so strongly in honest, commodity-based, free market money that it was the major issue that kept Rhode Island from ratifying the U.S. Constitution until May, 1790. A major reason for the American War of Independence was that the American colonists wanted no part of the Bank of England's debt money (after which the Federal Reserve is patterned). Early Americans saw their freedom and prosperity explode with free market commodity-based money.

The relative freedom of the so-called Dark Ages, from 1150 to 1350 A.D., created such prosperity that workers had four-day work weeks, no indebtedness, wore silver buttons on double-lined vests and coats, and had four courses at each meal. What an incredible economic prosperity explosion we should expect with a Christian work ethic, honest free market money, the specialization and division of labor, no inheritance laws, laws that strictly limit the absentee ownership of land, computer assisted mental and physical production, advanced scientific techniques of harvesting, photosynthesis, and other sun-created real new wealth, including cheap energy. It's time to grow up economically.

February 4, 1983

"Most journalists spend their time writing about strikers, or marchers, or protesters whose actions are not worthy of being reported. But, they hardly ever inform the public of something so vital as the subtle acceptance of Electronic Funds Transfer, a system which will result in total slavery for mankind, an absolute '1984'..."

Dr. Mary S. Relfe
The New Money System

Chapter Twenty-One
SECOND CHANCE: THE GOLDEN AGE

One key factor that locked us into a "frozen" economic civilization in 1913, leading to the creation of the Federal Reserve, was the reality that *we ran out of land for expansion*. From 1790 until 1910-1914, we were able to have real demand and expansion from the new land and resources that we subdued. Until then, the curse of fractional reserve debt banking and debt in general was disguised and minimized.

Since 1913, because we have effectively had no new territory upon which to exercise dominion, and because the dollar is the world's reserve currency, we have been "frozen" economically by the Federal Reserve's (central bank) monopolistic control of money and credit. This control, along with the fractional reserve banking system, has only led to artificial demand and expansion through wars and inflation, the checkmates of which have been devastating depressions and unemployment (Third World exploitation excepted). Withdrawal of land from the private sector by the federal government has aggravated the problem. The federal government now owns 42% of the land in the United States.

In the potential golden, electronic, computer robotic age that lies ahead, there will be no need for debt. Instead, human talent will be maximized. Economic prosperity will be able to reach previously unimagined levels, while civil government's income will be restricted to a head tax, sales tax, or a flat tax, and government will have no involvement in economics except the settlement of disputes in contracts. When solar energy becomes cost effective, when the free energy machines hit the market, as they very well should during the latter part of this decade, along with fusion energy, all the pieces will have fallen into place — if the "Revolution of Littleness" wins.

Financial institutions will serve the following functions:

1. *Partnership banks* — computerized institutions where men come together to form general and limited equity partnerships for business purposes.

2. *Joint venture banks* — institutions where men bring their economic equity to discuss and formulate various joint ventures.

3. *Stock banks* — institutions where men bring their economic productivity to exchange it for stock in companies, whose management they carefully monitor.

These first three institutions — partnership banks, joint venture banks and stock banks — are very similar to financial institutions we have today. In fact, present financial institutions could easily operate in this capacity, only without inflation-creating debt. Some Muslim banks are already effectively operating this way. Mohammed took his economics from Moses.

An international computer network among these new types of banks will open up a supermarket of partnership, joint venture, and stock opportunities for the common working man, who will then see his labor efforts in harmony with management, because he too has "ownership." The working man will finally become a capitalist.

4. *Savings banks* — institutions like the present "vault stores" in many shopping centers across the country, or like safe deposit boxes in bank vaults. These institutions simply store wealth much like bank safe deposit boxes do today.

5. *Service banks* — institutions set up by creative service bankers, which involve no exchange of money or goods, only "units" of service. A gardener's work might be evaluated as worth two units per hour, a carpenter's work valued at four units an hour, a physician's at six units an hour, an attorney's work at five units per hour, and so on. People desiring a particular service, or capable of performing a particular service, would come to a service bank and list on computer the service that they require, or were willing to perform, and the amount of units they would be willing to pay (exchange) for it. (Or, the service bank could set the standard and place a value on a particular job done by a particular skilled individual, as agreed upon by the bank and the parties to the transaction.) A truck driver, for example, whose work is valued at four units an hour could work for various clients of the service bank for a total of ten hours. He then would accrue credits to his service bank account in the amount of forty units (10 hours X 4 units per hour equals 40 units), transferred from the accounts of those he serviced. This would enable the truck driver to draw on his service bank account forty units worth of services from other clients of the bank, regardless of their occupation. The computer would easily keep track of all these service transactions, debits, and credits, with no danger of risk or theft.

Such a computerized service banking system would greatly enhance the cooperative division, specialization, and exchange of labor. It would provide a sophisticated barter and service economic function. For example, as an economic consultant wishing to barter an hour of consultation (worth six units) for an hour of electrical engineering work (worth six units), and going to all the hassle to find an electrical engineer who wants my services, all I have to do is provide economic counsel to any client of the service bank for an hour and accrue six units of credit to my bank account (transferred from his account). Then, I simply draw down those six units, by calling out to work for me a client of the same service bank (or a related bank in an interbank system) who is an electrical engineer. When his hour's work for me is completed, as both of us so agree and is certified by the bank, my six units of credit are simply transferred as a credit to his account. And so it goes. (Remember, physical money is only required where goods are involved in market transactions or as bank capital during the start up phase.) Under such a system, service bank handling fees should be modest.

None of these banks would preclude any free market money — gold, silver, or otherwise. Nor would they preclude paper receipts or computer entries serving as money, as long as the paper receipts or computer entries were representatives of real wealth — i.e., stored commodities.

6. *Resource banks* — Here is where real new wealth is monetized and new money can be created, via paper or computer, causing a rippling effect of a higher standard of living throughout the society.

We know from physics that energy can be converted into matter, which is real, new wealth. The sun shines freely, and through the process of photosynthesis, creates real new wealth — grains, fruits, nuts, timber, vegetables, and grass, which feeds livestock, and fish which have offspring. Under the curse of debt capitalism, farmers have usually only been blessed with high prices when they have been simultaneously plagued with poor yields. With the free market resource bank, however, big crops would be a blessing. Everyone throughout the society will rejoice when there are agricultural surpluses. We will have a true "Thanksgiving." Here's why.

Let's say a farmer raises 5,000 bushels of wheat and that the demand for wheat, for purposes of this discussion, is inelastic. If 5,000 bushels is his "normal" wheat crop and $5.00 a bushel is the "normal" price, the farmer receives $25,000 for his crop. Since this is the norm, the society is neither better nor worse off from this production. It is stable. The farmer is issued $25,000 worth of "wheat receipts" from his local resource bank, the grain elevator. He then uses the wheat receipts, as money, to buy what he needs. The value of the wheat receipt fluctuates in the free market, much like the U.S. dollar today. In this system, there would be all kinds of commodity receipts exchanged until the commodity is drawn down and consumed, at which time, the commodity receipts are destroyed.

Next year, the same farmer experiences a drought and only produces 2,500 bushels of wheat. However, in the free market, with inelastic demand, since the number of bushels of wheat has dropped by 50%, let's say the price of wheat doubles to $10.00 per bushel. The farmer still gets his $25,000 (2,500 bushels X $10.00 per bushel equals $25,000), but the rest of the society spends a greater proportion of its disposable income on food (wheat), and so the amount of money available to be spent on other goods and services throughout the society decreases. Thus, the standard of living falls.

Now, let's say in the third year, our farmer produces 10,000 bushels of wheat and the price of wheat drops to $2.50 per bushel. Our farmer still gets his $25,000, but the society rejoices. Why? People have to spend less of their disposable income on food (wheat), and so have more money to spend for other goods and services, business ventures, and investments, and so the standard of living for all rises. "Wealth for All" kicks in. Prices generally should fall as the ripple effect, brought about by declining food prices, leads to profit margin cuts, let's say, in the lumber industry. If the lumberman spends less of his income on wheat (food), he may decide he wants the same income as the previous year and so he is able to drop the price of lumber to his buyers. With greater production, over time, the norm should be falling prices.

Now, no free market works exactly this way. Higher prices usually ration a limited supply. Supply and demand are always changing and include many variables in all markets. But a global computerized economic system will come far closer to giving us perfect information, which is necessary for perfect markets, than ever before seen by mankind. And, it can be seen that with a resource bank, surpluses and abundant harvests are a blessing for all, rather than the warped curse they are today under the debt capitalistic system. Furthermore, it solves the farmers' basic dilemma of parity.

In our example, in a normal 5,000 bushel wheat crop year, the farmer receives his normal $25,000. In the subpar year of a 2,500 bushel crop, where prices will increase (not inflate — remember, inflation is an increase in the supply of *money*), the farmer will still have his $25,000. He will also have first shot at other goods and services before their prices also increase, due to the ripple effect.

Without government involvement in economics, productivity will not be a problem. Those who don't work simply won't eat, thus encouraging productivity (allowing, of course, for merciful local charity). Without debt, the boom/bust cycle won't be a problem. Steady, stable growth, with time to rest, will exist.

While, in our example, the farmer's gross income remains constant, his net income will still be determined by his efficiency, productivity, husbandry of the land and like factors. The farmer could use the commodity futures market for its legitimately created purpose, to forward sell (hedge) his crop when prices are high, probably at a higher price than he could receive at the time of harvest.

A farmer who astutely decides what crop will be in greatest demand by the marketplace the following year should and will reap higher prices. The farmer who moves toward organic agriculture will have fertile soil, requiring less fuel to run irrigation equipment and less fertilizer, which will reduce his costs and increase his bottom-line profit. A farmer who astutely buys his equipment at going-out-of-business auctions, estate sales, repairs his own equipment, and works long hours, rather than hiring extra personnel and purchasing new equipment, will also increase his bottom-line profit, just like with any other business. In short, a farmer becomes like any other businessman, even though he is one of the initiators of the monetization of raw materials for the resource bank. The farmer can even take out insurance for crop failure (inventory insurance), as he can today.

The resource bank can issue the farmer wheat receipts for the wheat which the farmer has stored in the resource bank's elevator, minus storage, insurance, and handling charges. The farmer can then exchange these wheat receipts for other goods and services because it is real money, a commodity substitute — "real" commodity-backed paper money. Or, the resource bank could simply record the number of bushels the farmer has deposited with it on its computer in terms of equivalent wheat receipts. Then the farmer could effectively draw that down in exchange for other goods and services from his resource bank's "bank account."

What a healthy, normal, prosperous, cooperative, economic system this will be. Everywhere, free market banks will spring up, in a decentralized, computerized environment. They will be brought about by the demise of the monopoly on debt (death) money exercised by the Federal Reserve and other central banks, and by the death of debt capitalism and communism.

Finally, with regard to the resource bank, perhaps it can now be more clearly seen how insane 50% and even 100% crop acreage reduction programs are, as suggested by U.S. Agriculture Secretary, John Block, in the payment-in-kind (PIK) program. Farmers not planting crops are killing the golden goose of economic prosperity by destroying real, free new wealth. It is the destructive insanity of a "frozen" economic civilization, captured by maximum economic error.

The "Wealth for All" system of free and efficient markets worldwide is on the threshold of being made available, thanks to the increasingly timely and efficient flow of information, brought about by the microcomputer revolution and, ironically, multinational business interaction. The computer can do for the mind of man in this "Revolution of Littleness" what machinery and tools did for the hands of man in the last industrial revolution. The "Industrial Revolution" was our first chance; this "Revolution of Littleness" is our "Second Chance." If each of us assumes all of his personal responsibilities, the "Golden Age" is upon us. We dare not blow this opportunity. Will we be sane or insane? Will we choose life or death? Our "second chance" could very well be our "last chance."

February 11, 1983

The late R. Buckminster Fuller was one of the geniuses of our time. The most successful architect in history, with 200,000 of his buildings erected, inventor of the geodesic dome, coiner of the word "synergy," poet, mathematician, com-

puter expert, and author of Critical Path, Dr. Fuller made the following comments in the May, 1981 issue of High Times:

"They will either realize it in the next eight years or they will not survive. I am not speaking idealistically, but with total realism. It's all touch and go for the next eight years. Either we all make it, and humanity achieves total success in Universe, or we all go down together."

(Dr. Fuller spoke these words in 1981. Adding eight years to 1981 brings us to 1989. The U.S. War Clock is again confirmed!)

"In the past twenty years, the U.S. Treasury has aided in the financing of both sides in fourteen separate wars.
"We don't have any political ideology and must not, because there is a great variation among our owners."
A.W. Clausen, President
The World Bank

"Since today's paper money achieves its status by government declaration and not by its value in itself, eventually total power over the economy must be granted to the monopolists who manage the monetary system."
The Case For Gold
by Congressman Ron Paul and
Lewis Lehrman

The Congress of 1792 imposed the death penalty on anyone convicted of debasing the coinage.

"I am in favor of abolishing the Central Bank."
Milton Friedman

Thomas Jefferson in 1801, as president: 1) Cut taxes 50%; 2) Reduced the federal debt 50% in eight years; 3) Fired all tax collectors.

Chapter Twenty-Two
REDEEMING THE DISMAL SCIENCE

Economics has always been called "the dismal science." Why? Because economists have never questioned or broken out of their dismal evolutionary presuppositions about the nature of reality.

For as long as they've been around, economists have never seemed to challenge the longstanding fundamental premises upon which economics has been based. The two most basic premises are: 1) We live in a world of scarcity, of limited resources; 2) Human wants are unlimited. Given these two basic premises about the way the world works, no wonder economics has been categorized as "the dismal science."

These two assumptions about the nature of reality assume that man's wants can never be satisfied, and further, because resources are limited, this puts man in never ending conflict with every other man as they vie for control of these scarce resources. Such premises of never ending conflict, of limited goods, of unfulfilled wants, of never having enough, are indeed dismal. They speak clearly of slavery — slavery to one's wants, lusts, and desires, and of slavery to the natural order. And, whether of land or labor, slavery is always dismal.

In any field of human endeavor, the experts in that field tend to "rut think." Experts tend to get into a groove of assumptions and techniques. This is why consultants are brought in from outside by business enterprises. Such outside consultants can and do take a new, fresh and creative look at an organization's operations and find ways to improve its productivity, efficiency and cost effectiveness. These are "improvement areas" that management seldom sees, because management is both too close and/or too ego-involved with the business. This same situation holds true with our investments. We tend to "rut think." Such is clearly the case in economics, also. Few economists challenge these basic assumptions about the nature of economic reality.

These two traditional economic assumptions about the way the world works hold that man is a consuming "animal," who ultimately is undisciplined regarding his wants and desires. Further, the assumption is that nature is a cursed and limited universe that mankind cannot rise above, overcome, and subdue in better and creative ways. Both of these operating economic assumptions lack vision. When men lack vision, they perish. No wonder economics has historically been a "dismal science." Its short-term operating assumptions are those of defeat.

As never before, we need economic assumptions about the nature of reality that allow us to achieve victory. When man sees himself as created by God for a specific stewardship purpose, when he realizes he has developing talents, which benefit him as well as his fellow man, he will move toward the long-term development of those talents. In the process, he will exercise short-term discipline to achieve these long-term objectives. Such discipline, when joined with a strong internal sense of security and self-worth, leads ultimately to a limitation of man's wants, desires and lusts. The greater the character of an individual, the greater his sense of personal identity, security, and strength derived from within as well as from above. Also, this individual will require less from his environment in order to lead a fulfilling life.

So, it is entirely possible, and historically documented, that men can limit their personal wants. In economic terms, this is the essence of savings, of capital formation, of providing stored economic wealth for the future. With savings and inheritance, each subsequent generation is left with a higher economic starting point than the preceding one, providing both the time and capital for human advancement. This is why the classic American economic system has been more rich and prosperous than any system heretofore on the face of the earth.

American men subdued their lusts and exercised dominion over their wants and desires. Their wants were not unlimited. They saved and invested for the long-term. Their deferred gratification led to greater long-term prosperity for both the individual and society-at-large. It was a cooperative "win-win" contract. When men seek dominion over themselves and their environment, they are too preoccupied to seek dominion over other men. Control over others often stems from personal insecurity.

Next, when man assumes that he lives in a universe of scarce resources, such pessimism cannot help but lead to conflict, followed eventually by a sense of hopelessness, despair, and subsequent inaction. Man increasingly consumes and stops building. Scarcity then truly does become a way of life. Poverty-stricken thinking precedes economic poverty.

By stark contrast, creativity always stems from both a latent and active optimism — the belief that there are answers, that there are ways to make higher and better use of both human and natural resources. The results are the human growth and technology which enable us to advance, by using our savings for research and development projects.

Furthermore, we live in an endless supermarket of economic abundance. The amount of solar energy which hits Lake Erie in one day is the equivalent of all the fossil fuels we have burned in the history of this country. Since it's true that energy and matter are interchangeable, then we have an abundant source of solar energy to use to transform into commodities. Commodities are the basics of our economic order. Therefore, unlimited consumption is potentially possible for man, a far cry from a so-called niggardly natural order, a far cry from a universe of scarcity.

Where is our vision, our characteristic "can do" American attitude? Julian L. Simon's 1981 book, *The Ultimate Resource*, shatters the myth that resources are scarce. The earth is an open system, he says, and man is the ultimate resource.

Necessity is the mother of invention. It is during times of upheaval that man's true creativity, new thinking and inventions come to the fore as the comfort of the old ways are shattered. Man meets the challenges that the factual environment puts before him. He must face threatening reality, overcome it, or perish. But to meet such challenges, man must have an underlying confidence that such problems are, in fact, opportunities. He must stop thinking insecurely and selfishly about himself and embrace the opportunities. Thus, man's religious and philosophical view of his world ultimately determines his freedom or his slavery, as well as his economic well being.

Human history points to the conclusion that mankind generally is still in slavery. Men collectively have not disciplined their wants, passions, and desires. Men collectively have not aggressively sought to harvest a universe of potential plenty, but instead have fallen victim to a cursed natural order of scarcity (early America distinctly to the contrary).

We have available to us in the next twenty years the ability to bring about the most glorifying, uplifting, manual-labor-free, prosperous age of human and natural development seen in the history of this world. As our old technology and institutions die, a window of opportunity is opening. Will we have the vision, optimism and courage to capture it?

The turning point, depends upon whether man escapes the pervasive pessimism brought about by the evolutionary humanism that has again gripped him with a vengeance during this century. Horizontal relationships — contractual, decentralized, with checks and balances — lead to "win-win" human relationships, resulting in freedom and prosperity. By contrast, vertical relationships are characteristic of wasteful bureaucracies, slave states, and empires which maximize massive human misery in "win-lose" fashion.

It is no accident that creationist biology holds to only horizontal and limited change, while evolutionary biology's faith is in vertical unlimited change. Ideas have consequences. Vertical empires of all types attempt to stop time and progress, a truly short-term perspective. Vertical empires attempt to sell us the illusion of vertical change, while standing still in decay.

Organic farming, solar energy breakthroughs, robotics, computer technology, free energy generators, satellite utilization — all provide us with the ability to transform our world into one of "wealth for all." In such a world, cooperation through shared knowledge and economic exchange is the *modus operandi* of men, rather than the conflict inherent in the Marxist, socialistic, debt capitalistic, atheistic, bureaucratic, environmental determinism that present slave states embrace worldwide.

The bankruptcy of the perverse, present and historical, economic assumptions has led to our approaching bankruptcy today. A sick trade-off continues between inflation, disinflation, and unemployment, or war, in an ever more terrifying way. We inescapably return to the political and religious issues leading to the economic reality. When men see themselves as created beings with unique purposes and talents to be developed, they move optimistically forward. When men see the natural order as one which is to be harnessed and groomed, where natural laws wait to be discovered and applied, to bring about a greater prosperous economic destiny for man to the glory of God, they smash the enslaving and dismal economic presuppositions. Civil government is then seen as a servant of man, the guardian of families, communities, and the marketplace. Government is limited to regulating disputes, providing for defense and civil order, and ensuring justice. In short, the sole purpose of government is to restrain evil, not save and reform man as it attempts to do in all imperial, bureaucratic government empires, which masquerade as god. God has already saved man.

Horizontal, cooperative relationships mushroom when men are free and optimistic, stemming from their confidence of having been created for a useful purpose. Prosperity follows. By contrast, when men see themselves as the final authority, pessimism creeps in and eventually dominates. This is because men soon see the reality that they have limited minds and limited time, and are also slaves to the conflict, chance and cycles of nature. This makes men insecure and pessimistic. They seek protection under civil government, where more men have seemingly more time and more collective knowledge. Government, however, like all vertical organizations, breeds tyrannical, inefficient, corrupt and wasteful bureaucracies. Few creations are more harmful to prosperous economic reality than wasteful vertical government bureaucracies involved in economics, including the creation of money. Government can't hope to match the power and information exchange that comes when free men cooperate horizontally-contractually and responsibly.

History has often been called "the lie the establishment commonly agrees upon." Truth is nearly always surrounded by a bodyguard of lies. Thus, we find the evolutionary, humanistic historians telling us that "Dark Ages" existed whenever we did not have dominant, vertical, government-run world empires. However, we see instead that it was during the times of vertical bureaucratic empires — with government control of money, government involvement in economics, government attempting to save and reform man through laws, and such things as high levels of government debt and compound interest — that the masses lived miserably in poverty.

I had often suspected that such historical times, which the establishment calls the "Dark Ages," were, in fact, times of real prosperity for the common man because he was free. (The reason these times are called the "Dark Ages" is that there was no wasteful, costly, vertical, bureaucratic record keeping, the rumblings of the Byzantine Empire, the Crusades, the adventures of Genghis Khan and the Ottoman Empire to the contrary.)

Until recently, I could not support this "Dark Ages" freedom and prosperity hunch, other than from the knowledge that the *Magna Carta* was reissued for the third time in 1225 A.D. However, Dr. Hugo H. Fach, an American, along with a Swiss researcher, Fritz Schwarz, have brought to light some important facts about the "Dark Ages":

> After the fall of Rome came the dark ages. This was followed by the dramatic boom from 1150 to 1350...This significant development carried the mind of man to heights which he has not often reached...The historians agree that wages were unbelievably high...that workers decided on a four-day work week...that long indebtedness disappeared...that peasants were wearing gold or silver buttons in a double line mostly on vest and coat, that shoes were worn with large silver buckles...Johanes Butzbach, one of the chroniclers of the time, records that the low people, the workers, had rarely less than four courses at the meals.

Well, well, well! Pretty impressive support for the "Wealth for All" arguments. The so-called "Dark Ages" were, for the common man, a boom time economically, a time of intellectual advancement, a time of no long-term debt (no monetary/debt slavery), short work weeks, prosperity and plenty. There existed freedom and a noted absence of controlling vertical, bureaucratic government empires!

It is not easy for any of us to admit that we've been duped, played for a fool by our government, its public schools and universities. The historic reality, however, is that when optimistic economic assumptions are instilled in man, and where decentralization and freedom exist, he can then exercise self-discipline and limit his wants. In such an environment, he can plan for the long-term, overcome, and subdue his environment — an environment of unlimited abundance — in new and creative ways.

In an environment of freedom, decentralization is prominent. Where vertical empires do not exist and their bureaucracies are abandoned, there will be no government involvement in economics. Instead, self-interest is served by service to one's fellow man, and the free market determines what serves as money. Debt and compound interest are in retreat. Cooperation rather than conflict is the *modus operandi* of mankind generally. The result is a "Wealth for All" available to mankind that staggers the imagination.

This, then, is God's economic gift to mankind. Character plus work plus savings produces abundance.

Scarcity: A Myth

There are only two elements in the economic equation — land and labor. Economics, as an optimistic science, sees "land," or the earth, as an open system. Free energy from the sun is transformed into commodities which are then monetized. Thus, wealth is potentially unlimited. Additionally, man can find new and better uses of the earth's present resources which increases prosperity. Plus, he can harness free energy. This is true technology.

On the "labor" side of the economic equation, man becomes the ultimate resource. By overcoming his natural pride, instinct for conflict and short-sighted selfishness, irresponsiblity, and a short-term view, and instead exercising humility, self-serving giving, and responsibility long-term, he will experience a harmony of interests. He can then turn the earth into a garden rather than a garbage heap. He can be creative, save, and limit his wants. Paradoxically, such savings, creativity, and work end up bringing man short-term prosperity, too.

The known reserves of virtually every major mineral and energy source are larger today than they were in 1950, despite increasing use. "Because we find new lodes, invent better production methods, and discover new substitutes, the ultimate constraint upon our capacities to enjoy unlimited raw materials at one stable price is knowledge...And the source of knowledge is the human mind." Dr. Julian Simon, University of Illinois.

Why have we long operated under the myth of scarcity? Because if scarcity exists, then some agency (government) is necessary to redistribute scarce resources and fight wars to obtain them. Thus today, scarcity is planned by power-lusting individuals and groups who want to use civil government to gain control over land and labor — wealth and people.

Scarcity is abnormal. It is planned, the result of government control. And government control always limits freedom. Destroying freedom, of course, destroys economic progress and brings on poverty. Therefore, government planning and control are a curse on the people long-term.

When the Pilgrims landed, there were fewer than 300,000 native American Indians living on 3.5 million square miles. On average, one Indian per every ten square miles barely kept from starving to death. Life was spartan. Poverty was rampant. The average life expectancy was thirty years. The Indians were slaves both to nature and to the "natural" man. They did not overcome nature, subdue it or return it to harmony. They did not truly overcome themselves. They did not operate under a comprehensive harmony of interests. The noble savage was not all that noble.

By contrast, on average today there are more than 600 Americans on every ten square miles of this country. Only 3% of the American population feeds the entire country and 20% of the rest of the world. Our standard of living and affluence can hardly be imagined by the rest of the world. We have the capability to feed all of the world. Our life expectancy is seventy-three years. All that is necessary for us to move on to a glorious future is to recapture our spiritual birthright and again let it rule over our civil government and economic system. Government is religion applied to economics.

Consider this enlightening look at the Middle Ages from Jean Gimpel's book *The Medieval Machine* (Penguin Books, 1976):

> The Middle Ages was one of the great inventive eras of mankind. It should be known as the first industrial revolution in Europe. The scientists and engineers of that time were searching for alternative sources of energy to hydraulic power, wind power, and tidal energy. Between the tenth and the thirteenth centuries, western Europe experienced a technological boom. Both that boom and the subsequent decline can now be seen to offer striking parallels to Western industrial society since 1750, and to the present situation in the United States in particular. Some of the features that accompanied this first industrial revolution seem strangely familiar.
>
> There was a great increase in population, which led to massive movements of people. They emigrated; they founded and built new towns. Conditions favored free enterprise, and this led to the rise of self-made men. Capitalist companies were formed and their shares were bought and sold. Entrepreneurs were fully prepared to use ruthless business methods to stifle competition. They introduced extensive division of labor to increase efficiency, and their enterprises called into being a proletariat whom they could exploit. The workers retaliated with wage claims, absenteeism, and strikes.
>
> Energy consumption increased considerably. Technological innovations brought about improvements in the efficiency of existing methods and also led to a successful search for new sources of energy. Many of the tasks formerly done by hand were now carried out by machines. Concurrently there was a revolution in agricultural methods, which enabled farmers to produce enough food for an expanding population and provide a more varied diet. There was a marked increase in the general standard of living. The growth of industry and the search for new sources of raw materials led to extensive industrial pollution of waterways and, on a wider scale, posed a severe threat to the environment, with grave long-term consequences.
>
> The entrepreneurs, the landowners, and the financiers were able to extract large profits from this industrial expansion, and the growth of accountancy and banking, which in turn led to further expansion. The people with financial power also wielded political power, and economic sanctions could be employed very effectively for political ends. The period was characterized by a sense of optimism, a rationalist attitude, and a firm belief in progress.
>
> At a certain point the dynamism of the Middle Ages began to fail and symptoms of decline became evident. The population ceased to grow, differences between the classes hardened, and there was less social mobility. Restrictive practices were introduced in many industries, and there was a growth of violent unrest in the big industrial centers. There were increasing

indications that the level of efficiency was dropping and at the same time there was a resistance to change. Energy production and mechanization had reached a peak and the standard of living began to decline. Inflation began to get out of hand; currencies were devalued and banks crashed.

There was a decline in the old moral values. People became less public-spirited, and with this went a growth of permissiveness. There was a growing awareness of aesthetic values. Many people turned away from traditional religion to embrace new esoteric cults. Rationalism gave way to mysticism.

If the picture of the medieval world does not sound like the Dark Ages, or like the age of romance and chivalry, it is because the history of technology has been so universally neglected, thanks largely to the age-old attitude of academics and intellectuals toward manual work and engineering. Plato, in the Gorgias, gives evidence of the contempt in which engineers were held by philosophers in his time: "You despise him and his art, sneeringly call him an enginemaker, and you will not allow your daughter to marry his son or marry your son to his daughter."

The scorn of men of letters for engineers throughout history has kept them, all to often, oblivious to the technology created by those engineers who were of lower social status and worked to earn their living. They had no idea that in this other world there was an uninterrupted tradition of technological writing. Leonardo da Vinci is a case in point. As an engineer he was despised by the literati of his time, and they, like the majority of Western intellectuals today, were ignorant of the fact that Leonardo had borrowed a great many of his inventions from technological treatises by engineers of previous generations.

Our Western civilization has seen the development of two parallel systems of education — that of the mechanical arts for engineers and that of the liberal arts for men of letters. These are the two cultures of C.P. Snow. Historians steeped in the prejudices of the liberal arts have rarely thought it worthwhile to cross the gap in order to study or to write the history of the mechanical arts, the history of technology. Since the Renaissance, whenever Western man has tried to make historical comparisons, he has usually turned to the Roman Empire, not the Middle Ages, in spite of the fact that the medieval industrial revolution is remarkably comparable to the English Industrial Revolution and its subsequent development in America. The creative time span of each of these great technological eras lasted for some two-and-a-half centuries before symptoms of decline became apparent. Our own last two decades demonstrate that today Western technological society is revealing much the same pattern of history as its medieval predecessor.

We are witnessing a sharp arrest in technological impetus. No more fundamental innovations are likely to be introduced to change the structure of our society. Only improvements in the field of preexisting innovations are to be expected. Like every previous civilization, we have reached a technological plateau.

A problem with both the Middle Ages and Western civilization is that both eventually elevated pride over humility, conflict over harmony, chance over certainty, cycles over linear time, and man's animal nature over his spiritual nature. When man's spiritual nature is primary and regenerated, and along with the natural order is recaptured by God's law (the Law of

Moses) of liberty and harmony, then both man and the earth prosper. Both man and nature must be disciplined by laws that arise from outside them to effect a harmony of interests and prevent relative arbitrary power (conflict) from reigning supreme and establishing its laws, leading inevitably to poverty and destruction.

August 2, 1984

Chapter Twenty-Three
OVERCOMING THE SLAVERY OF NATURE

Three primary aspects of nature are conflict, chance and cycles. The two parts of the economic equation are land and labor. By understanding the relationship between these three aspects of nature and the two ingredients in the economic equation, we can understand the important relationship between nature and economics. With this understanding we gain a tremendous advantage over those who are slaves to nature.

Economics has always been called the dismal science. This is because its underlying assumptions about the nature of land and labor are indeed dismal. If we assume, regarding the land, that resources are limited and scarce, economics is indeed dismal. If we assume, regarding labor, that man has unlimited wants, economics is truly dismal.

Both of these economic assumptions about land and labor imply that nature is god, and that man is a slave to nature. It quickly follows then, because the *modus operandi* of nature is conflict, that survival of the fittest is ultimate in economics. The problem is, conflict and prosperity are adversaries. Prosperity does not long exist where conflict rules supreme. Cooperation, by contrast, produces prosperity.

The conflict over land, over limited resources, is indeed a dismal prospect. The conflict between men (labor), who have unlimited wants, is indeed dismal. Men with unlimited wants, without discipline cannot and will not save. Thus, there is no long-term basis for the production of capital by the natural man. Capital is produced by savings. Without capital, without deferred gratification, there is no capitalism and thus no prosperity. Only capitalism has produced prosperity.

Furthermore, a man with unlimited wants and no deferred gratification is not self-governing. Men who do not govern themselves are governed by others. Where civil government rules comprehensively there is no freedom. The absence of freedom is slavery and results in poverty. Because freedom and prosperity are allies, and because slavery and poverty are allies, comprehensive civil government is indeed dismal, particularly since civil government is an economic parasite outside of its proper role of ensuring justice and providing for the defense. The bigger the centralized civil government, the less the freedom and prosperity. Big bureaucratic civil government is confirmation of the slavery of a social order to nature.

If all of us had to live directly off the land, the earth would only support about ten million people. It took ten square miles to support one American Indian. So, if we are to better man's condition in an economic way, we have to rise above, subdue, and overcome the conflict of nature. We see this overcoming in the labor side of the economic equation where there is savings and the specialization and division of labor leading to cooperation, harmony and trade. Indeed, economic prosperity is a result of trade, as Adam Smith pointed out in his *Wealth of Nations*.

Today, the earth is *not* overpopulated. On ten square miles, U.S. agriculture now feeds 250 people. In the United States alone 600 people live on ten square miles, compared to that one lonely American Indian 200 years ago.

Of the 4.6 billion people on the face of the earth, if we divided them up into families of four members each, and gave them a single family dwelling with a front and back yard, they would all fit in the state of Texas. Indeed, using just present technology and agricultural lands, the earth can feed thirty-one billion people, about seven times the world's population.

Food shortages are not the real problem now anyway. While over 100 million people have starved in Africa, food is rotting and overflowing in the warehouses rented by the European Economic Community and the U.S.D.A. The problem is government and distribution, not production.

Every day the sun shines, solar energy is transformed into commodities, which provide us with real new wealth as energy is transformed into matter. And because commodities can be monetized, we have potentially an endless source of honest money as well. With unlimited wealth, people can develop their talents. Work that is in line with the development of one's talents becomes fun and joyous. And with the specialization and division of labor that follows, we end up truly needing each other. Harmony results. Harmony is basic to economic prosperity, but foreign in a primary sense to conflict-oriented nature.

The deserts of the world could blossom. Desalinization plants could be built on the oceans, the water then pumped inland, which along with an organic soil build-up program would cause the deserts to bloom. What if desalinization plants were built along the coasts of this country and then the water pumped inland alongside existing railroad right-of-ways?

Land can be recaptured from the sea, too. That's what has occurred in Holland. New discoveries, innovations, and technologies are continually finding higher and better uses for natural resources. We are on the verge of an avalanche of technological innovations, the likes of which will bring to man a lifestyle he cannot even imagine, if we can transform ourselves and our archaic and conflict-ridden institutions before they destroy us all.

We are approaching important breakthroughs in the technology necessary to harness and control the weather and climate.

The cost of photovoltaic cells, which provide us with solar energy and enable us to unhook from the local utility once and for all, is rapidly falling. Harnessing solar satellite-power and beaming it to earth is on the horizon. The free energy work of Joseph Newman is revolutionary. Minerals, supposedly in limited supply on this earth, can be mined from deserts and seabeds, as well as from presently off-limit government land.

Gems and crystals can be best grown with unmatched purity in the vacuum of space.

Regeneration of human limbs is only a decade away. Understanding the computer blueprint of the human body has created breakthroughs in non-drug homeopathic medicine. Integration of the treatment of the skeletal, electromagnetic and chemical systems of the body, as well as individual cell analysis, allows diagnosis and forecasts, and therefore the prevention of diseases, months and even years before individual body cells are vulnerable.

The Collins engine, with only five moving parts, has won worldwide awards. It runs on nearly any fuel, including hydrogen. It is part of the wave of the future. The chain of discovery goes on and on.

Man only needs to overcome himself, the natural man, and then overcome nature, with its so-called natural laws of conflict and the deterioration that follows in the second law of thermodynamics. When we are able to do this, and civil government is no longer the custodian of the land or labor, such things as restricted lands in California will open up, from which we can ecologically mine all the rare minerals and metals that we need for our industrial processes, including the strategic minerals and metals. This will make the United States self-sufficient from southern Africa and the Soviet Union in this key area.

Man does not have to be a slave to his own nature. He can rise above conflict. In economic terms, he does not have to have unlimited wants. He can save. He can practice deferred gratification. He can be self-governing. He can exercise a long-term view. He is able to earn all he can, save all he can, and give all he can, thus bringing harmony between the individual and the masses. He can cooperate in the division of labor leading to trade, prosperity, freedom and minimal government. He can, that is, if he has an incentive, both spiritually and materially.

Since man is the ultimate resource or the ultimate parasite or predator, as goes man, so goes nature. Again, conflict runs in the same harness with poverty, whether it's in the bush or modern society, in the Third World, the U.S.A. or the U.S.S.R. Man must rise above the conflict of his nature so he can help nature rise above the conflict and deterioration intrinsic in nature itself for peace and prosperity to abound.

Research has shown that a primary factor contributing to health is economic status. When an economy is stable, and people's economic status is stable, the health of people is generally good. People need to feel that they can manipulate their environment, that they can control nature (exercise dominion) and rise above it. A sense of individual and collective destiny is thus important to the health and well-being of people. Therefore, the fact that the U.S. has more functional socialism than France, even though France has more structural socialism, means people feel they have less control over their destiny and thus are less healthy. This is insidious slavery.

Additionally, debt capitalism, which gives rise to the boom/bust economic cycle, is detrimental to the health of the population. It enslaves the masses long-term. This situation would be partially cured by equity capitalism, which brings harmony by balancing off the rights of the individual with the rights of the masses. The instability of the business cycle is checkmated with equity capitalism, and so economic and physical health is improved.

The chance characteristic of nature — nature in the wild — is stressful, too. Even in our national forests and wilderness areas, we have game and land management, where man helps nature. This management helps arrest the natural deterioration of nature. Dominion overcomes chance.

A cycle is by its very nature unstable. It oscillates. In economics we see cycles in terms of the entire inflation versus deflation phenomenon, resulting from the boom/bust economic cycle. How many hours of investors sleep have been lost by worrying about inflation or deflation?

A boom/bust economic cycle, an inflationary/deflationary economic system, is unnatural and unnecessary. It is a creation of fractional reserve credit money and compound interest. If we eliminate such credit and interest, and replace it with honest commodity money or the representatives thereof, there will be no business cycle. There will instead be steady, linear economic growth. People will be more wealthy and healthy.

Cycles found in nature are predictable, many almost infallibly so. But there is something very different about cycles when it comes to man. In terms of human action, cycles only work probabilistically. Discontinuous events upset human action cycles. Human action cycles often contract, expand, or disappear. Nevertheless, cycles are important because they tell us where we are in the natural human action sequence in the economic cycle.

Cycles aren't taught in our business schools and colleges. No small wonder. Economic cycles are artificially created. Who benefits? Those who understand the nature of cycles as well as the fractional reserve banking system. It's the fractional reserve credit system that creates the economic cycles. One can profit immensely if one knows what's going on in the economic/monetary cycle while the many are ignorant. Who would be left to greatly profit if economic cycles were widely understood by the general public? No one. Huge profits come when there is little information available.

Cycles and human action are more important, the more that fractional reserve credit money is utilized in an economic system. Cycles also become more important and accurate as a predictive tool as men in a society increasingly become slaves to nature and thus more uncivilized. Just as cycles accurately forecast behavior patterns in the animal kingdom, such as the seasonal migration of geese, so too have cycles enhanced forecasting accuracy for mankind as men fall victim to nature.

Today, emotion rules over logic. Selfishness and conflict have priority over harmony, debt over savings, and the short-term view over the long-term view. This means that human action cycles are more helpful now than ever before. This means that on a full moon, when the natural man tends to become more aggressive and violent, hospitals and police departments increase their staffs.

In medieval Germany, the werewolves that appeared at the time of the full moon were simply men who were on the ragged edge of insanity, who went berserk and ran with wolf packs at the full moon. In the Soviet Union, the mentally unstable are placed in lead-shielded rooms in order to protect them and keep them from going crazy when the earth's magnetic environment changes during the sunspot cycle peak. And, in markets, the natural emotion attached to money makes men vulnerable to cyclical natural influences, too.

In short, cycles are most useful and have more predictive value when men are less rational, have no knowledge of cycles, have little or no self-discipline, are conflict oriented, and are effective slaves to nature. When masses of people react, rather than think coolly and then respond rationally, cycles are invaluable.

As Edward R. Dewey, founder of the Foundation for the Study of Cycles, wrote, "Anyone who starts out in business without knowing what time it is on the economic clock will obviously owe much to luck if he succeeds. And many men who have engaged successfully in business for a long time owe much to their sheer good fortune in having started out when the economic sun was rising." In other words, many businessmen are lucky. They succeed in today's cyclical economic environment because they happen to be in the right place at the right time, not because they are wise.

The very nature of cycles makes survival of the fittest true in business because only the fittest are able to pick up and profit from the ebb and flow of the business cycle, or are smart enough to figure out the cycles. Few men have the psychological make-up to profitably adjust to new cyclical economic reality. So, we have the survival of the fittest in evolutionary terms, both in business and in the very nature of economic cycles today, in the long-term widening the gap between the haves and the have-nots, between the few and the many. Revolution eventually fills this gap, followed by tyrannical bureaucratic slavery.

November 15, 1984

"There is no such thing as a 'Law of Nature.' No such thing ever existed. What exists is a general rule of behavior of physical systems under very general conditions. But it is just a rule. There is nothing sacred about it. If you change those conditions you blow that rule right out the window. But when you elevate it to the phrase, 'Law of Nature,' you are substituting for the phrase, 'Law of God,' and you are now practicing religion, not science. And that is what Western science is doing today."

Tom Bearden.

Chapter Twenty-Four
VERTICAL OR HORIZONTAL LIFESTYLE

We all come into this world subjected to the vertical lifestyle. We are dependent. People, usually our parents, rule over us and provide for our spiritual, mental, emotional and physical needs. Thus, our earliest experiences, which form our most ingrained habits, are those of a vertical lifestyle, of dependency. And we all know that habits are difficult to break. Even the most determined of adults requires three weeks of disciplined, habit-breaking behavior to crack an ingrained habit.

Given that our earliest experiences are those of a vertical lifestyle, it comes as no surprise that *our natural tendency as we age is to remain in, or revert back to, the vertical lifestyle of dependency*. It follows that wherever we find a society that maximizes the vertical lifestyle, with bureaucracies of people ruling over other people, that we will also find the people of the culture behaving in a childlike manner. They will be dependent and will manifest the immaturity of dependency. Envy rather than admiration will rule the view of one's fellow man. Conflict rather than cooperation will reign. Pride rather than humility, illusion rather than reality, leisure rather than productivity, and appearance rather than performance will be the guiding principles of the lifestyle of a vertically-integrated culture. In such a society, the people simply have not grown up; they have not matured. There has been an escape from maturity. The short-term view predominates. Slavery is manifest.

A typical childlike attitude is the unwillingness to save. Saving money is seen as a short-term pain not worth experiencing for the long-term gain of capital formation and deferred gratification. Thus, *a sure sign of an economically immature, childlike, vertically-integrated slave state lifestyle is the unwillingness to save and undergo economically short-term pain for long-term gain. Instead, an immature society is marked by its willingness to incur debt. It is, in fact, addicted to debt.* A short-term oriented, childlike, vertically-integrated society embraces debt as surely as a moth flies into the flame of its own destruction. Debt means death long-term, with slavery along the way.

The individual and collective key to being free, prosperous and happy has always been found long-term in the horizontal lifestyle. But the horizontal lifestyle requires self-discipline, a willingness to grow up, to grow out of dependency, and undergo short-term pain for long-term gain. The hallmark of the free, prosperous and happy horizontal lifestyle is the willingness to responsibly contract for our needs on a horizontal level, rather than to be at the mercy of those who rule over us on a vertical level.

The horizontally-integrated lifestyle requires economic responsibility. It imposes the moral responsibility to contract honorably for goods and services, and to meet the terms and conditions of those contracts in order that our own needs will be met. We must be free to contract, and by contracting we maintain our freedom, for by so doing we do not establish a vertical bureaucracy (or bureaucrats) to rule over us.

The signs, symbols and architecture of a culture speak of its horizontally or vertically-integrated lifestyle. The natural growth pattern of the Third World and small town rural America is horizontal, that is, outward. By contrast, cities tend to grow vertically, upward. Historically, this is why there has been more freedom in the Third World and in the country, with less freedom in the cities. Cities have historically been identified as slave centers. Slaves are passive toward life, interested primarily in self-indulgence, entertainment and spectator sports. Cities today are hotbeds of such activities.

Freedom is, in part, an absence of externally imposed regulations. There are more regulations in the cities than in the country. And in cities, civil government regulations and controls get more bang for their buck. It's easier to control people who are concentrated into a city. Contrast America in the 1980s, where approximately 80% of the people live in the one hundred largest U.S. cities, with the late 1700s, when 90% of the people were involved in agriculture and/or lived in small town rural America. The contrast is one of a vertical versus a horizontal lifestyle.

Other common ground that small town rural America shares with the Third World (as opposed to the world's cities) includes:

1. The economies of small town rural America and the Third World are built upon agriculture, natural resources and small businesses. By contrast, cities are built upon large industry, finished goods, services, information and paper. The way the city is able to dominate the country and control its resources and labor is by controlling laws and money. The cities control the government in a democracy. The cities control the issue of fiat currency and credit, which is in stark contrast to the honest monetized commodities created in the country.

2. The horizontally-integrated lifestyles of small town rural America and the Third World cradle abstract truths and eternal principles, creating long-term stability for a society. Roots are put down in the country. For this reason, the country, small town rural America, and the Third World are slow to change. This is why a certain London city-dweller, the father of communism, Karl Marx, referred to "the idiocy of rural life." The city is the locus of ever-changing facts, of rootlessness and restlessness. It is the breeding ground for vertical, bureaucratically imposed communism.

3. There is a slower pace of life in the country and in the Third World. The pace is quite fast in the city, giving rise to the phrase: "the rat race." It's a paradox that the city, supposedly the most civilized aspect of a culture, is called "the jungle."

4. The emphasis in the Third World and in small town rural America is on friendliness. The emphasis in the city is on cold, distant individuality.

5. The emphasis in small town rural America and in the Third World is on community, where the individual finds self-expression in terms of his service to his fellow man. This is in contrast to the city, where the emphasis is on radical individualism and conflict rather than cooperation in human affairs.

6. Both the Third World and small town rural America lose their youth to the cities, who go seeking after better jobs and higher pay. As Oswald Spengler wrote in *The Decline of the West*, cities consume people, particularly youth. Slaves enslave free men.

7. The Third World and small town rural America are controlled and politically discriminated against by cities. In Third World countries, government grants go to city projects while peasants in the country starve. The U.S. government bails out the likes of Lockheed, Chrysler, and Continental Illinois Bank. Meanwhile, what happens to the small farmers in the country? Their status is much like that of Third World peasants. The city has the credit dollar and democratic voting clout.

Now ideally, we have seen that to maximize the freedom, prosperity and happiness of the individual and society-at-large, we must grow from a vertically-integrated lifestyle into a horizontally-integrated way of life. So, *a wise nation, run by sagacious governmental leaders, will look to provide incentives to decentralize its population base if it truly cares for the long-term welfare of its people.* (U.S. cities occupy only 1% of our land mass.) A good government will enact laws that provide for the harmony and balance between the horizontally-integrated country versus the vertically-integrated city. One should not dominate the other. Both should work together.

A natural harmony should exist betweeen raw materials and agriculture produced in the Third World and in the country, with the finished goods, large industries, services and information produced in the city. There should be a balance, the logical integration between the abstract truths and eternal principles, held dear in the country, and melted together with the ever-changing facts spawned in the city. The balance between community and individualism in country and city respectively, is also desirable.

What is necessary to maintain this perpetual balance between city and country, and to prevent the dominance of the vertically-integrated immature cities over the maturity that naturally grows in the country, is enactment of certain laws. Laws are needed which: 1) strictly limit the absentee ownership of land; 2) prohibit fiat currency, inflation, and the creation of fractional reserve debt-money and credit; 3) promote a free market and the monetization of commodities; and 4) encourage individuals to cooperate and act responsibly in their own self-interest long-term by first serving their fellow man. Such laws are much preferred to laws promoting conflict by government involvement in economics, redistribution of wealth, and the building of bureaucratic vertically-integrated empires. People always respond to incentives. The law structure of a society provides economic incentives.

At this point, it should become very obvious that *the United States today is an immature, childlike, vertically-integrated society.* Like a stubborn unyielding child who cannot and will not act in his own self-interest long-term, so too is our political system. It is no accident then that we are losing our freedom, that we are becoming increasingly poorer (96% of Americans are flat broke at age sixty-five), and that we are progressively more unhappy.

It is indeed tragic (according to the Department of Labor) that only 2% of Americans are financially self-sufficient at age sixty-five. We are no longer the home of the free, economically speaking. And how brave are slaves? The number one obsession of Americans now is money instead of sex, according to *Money* Magazine. Furthermore, we are doing exactly the wrong thing at the wrong time, at a time when we face our greatest competitive challenges ever economically from abroad (not to mention the military challenge). Now, some 25% of the world's work force, the Chinese, are moving into the twentieth century. The average Chinese works for $2.00 per day compared to the average American who earns $30-$40 a day. When the Chinese become our technological equivalents, Americans' labor and goods will be priced out of world markets and unemployment will soar. Either that, or protectionist barriers will be progressively established, which are historically a forerunner of war.

If the Chinese don't get us, Dorothy's tin men without hearts, the robots, surely will. There is no escape over the rainbow into the New Age. Dr. Iben Browning, writing about robotics in *The Browning Newsletter*, noted that education and high skills will cease to have high value because robots will be built with these skills and will be able to do anything humans can do, only better. "Robots as intelligent as humans will probably be in use by the turn of the century, or soon thereafter," he wrote.

Robots, by manufacture, will be able to reproduce themselves and will be relatively inexpensive, so they will be able to take over jobs that humans are ill-suited to do. Furthermore, the explosive growth in memory technology indicates that robots may be able to think and approach problems as intelligently as human beings by the end of this century. For example, the Associated Press in a Hunt Valley, Maryland release reported on a hamburger chain that will be run by a six-armed robot "that prepares meals to order, takes money and makes change, even sweeps the floor and clears tables."

Considering the fact that 80% of the jobs created in this economic recovery have been in the service sector, such as in the likes of the fast food industry, we are now seeing confirmed that the one growth area left where human labor was valued — services — is also being threatened. What then is to become of our economy, particularly when we don't need people, only a few technocrats and bureaucrats who run the show from the top of the immature vertically-integrated social order? There will be no need for human slaves.

We know from "Wealth For All" economics that the normal, logical state of affairs in a well-ordered, peaceful, horizontally-integrated society is for each generation to be wealthier than the preceding one. This cumulative wealth stems from the abundant and unlimited free energy coming from the sun and found in the atmosphere, along with the specialization and division of labor leading to trade, technology and inheritance, where succeeding generations accumulate the wealth of its forefathers. But this natural prosperity stemming from a "Wealth For All" integrated horizontal economy is suppressed and attacked by those who rule in a vertically-integrated social order. Again, *slaves always attempt to enslave the free men. Men who need to control others are slaves to their lusts and themselves. Free men are self-governing.*

We see the insidious suppression of the glorious lifestyle available to the horizontally-integrated free man in the works of too many historians. Historians love empires, the age of kings and queens, lords and serfs, presidents, prime ministers, and bureaucrats. For example, modern historians consider presidents who balanced the Federal budget to be losers. Warren G. Harding and Ulysses S. Grant have received hostile treatment at the hands of most historians, and yet they balanced the budget. Five presidents who balanced the budget during three years out of four are also considered losers by historians — Buchanan, Pierce, Coolidge, Fillmore, Tyler, and Taylor. By contrast, historians have raved about the presidents who have never balanced the budget, including George Washington, John Adams, Thomas Jefferson, Andrew Jackson, Abraham Lincoln, Theodore Roosevelt, Woodrow Wilson, Franklin Roosevelt, Harry Truman, and every president since Dwight D. Eisenhower.

Not only is this bias in favor of the vertically-integrated lifestyle and against the horizontally-integrated one a contemporary reality, it is also true regarding more ancient history. Historians, for example, love to call the "Middle Ages" — one of the most prosperous times in history for the common man — the "Dark Ages." Egypt and Babylon, by contrast, are glorified by historians.

When I was in England in November 1983, I had the opportunity to visit some of the magnificent cathedrals built in the thirteenth and fourteenth centuries. They are truly majestic works of art. The question immediately came to mind: How did the man of the Middle Ages find the time to create such works of art? We, in twentieth century America, have to spend every waking moment scrambling to make a living. And we are supposedly so much better off technologically than the Middle Ages man. Where did he find the time and the skills to be so creative and artistic? He had the same basic economic needs as we do today. And yet, those beautiful fourteenth century cathedrals are testimony to the reality that men of that day and era had more time to create true works of art than do those of us who scramble about in our so-called Modern Age. (The reason they had so much time to build ornate cathedrals is that the church did its job in meeting the needs of the people.)

A little research revealed that the fourteenth century man in England only had to work fourteen weeks to meet his yearly economic needs. The rest of the time he was free to be creative, to be artistic, to develop his talents, or to go fishing. How many of us can meet our annual economic needs in fourteen weeks? Most of us have to work longer than fourteen weeks just to pay the federal government our taxes. Then again, our government today extracts more in taxes from us than the Middle Ages lord did from his serf (which was one-third). So, when our politicians talk about a flat tax, where the top bracket is only 35% or so, they are doing us the small favor of restoring us to the dignity of serf status, which was common in the "Dark Ages."

In the U.S. and Canada around 1900, the average working man could buy a home for a little over one year's wages. Now he works all of his life to pay off his home.

In the 1340s, the Black Plague wiped out half of the population of Europe. The plague did its most devastating damage in the cities, the vertically-integrated societies, not in the country. Is the Black Plague of the Middle Ages any worse than the slaughtering of human beings today in the vertically-integrated communist empires, where the executed numbers approach 100 million? Is it worse than the abortion of 1.5 million babies annually in this country?

The first Industrial Revolution took place in the Middle Ages. Steel produced in the Middle Ages was called Damascus steel. It has long been the envy of the modern steel industry. Damascus steel is strong and flexible. It's a high carbon steel, which was then used for fighting weapons in the tenth century. Stanford University is just now able to duplicate Damascus steel.

In thirteenth century Europe, there was the general use of pulleys, screws, wrenches, and overshot water-wheels. Researcher Terry S. Reynolds, in the July 1984 issue of *Scientific American* authored an article entitled, "Medieval Roots of the Industrial Revolution." Mr. Reynolds said, "The origins of modern industry are often dated only to the late eighteenth and nineteenth centuries, when manual labor was displaced by steam-powered machines, first in the cotton-textile industry and later in other industries. This period is commonly called the Industrial Revolution, a term strongly suggesting that there had been a sharp break from developments in the preceding centuries."

> The history of water power in medieval and early modern Europe presents a different picture. Powered machinery had begun to displace manual labor long before the eighteenth century, and in some areas of Europe it had done so on a substantial scale and in many industries. In other words, the rise of European industry should more properly be regarded as an evolutionary process going back at least to the eighth or ninth centuries, when European engineers began to aggressively apply water power to industrial processes...
> ...Medieval technicians between the tenth and fifteenth centuries devised two solutions to the problem of transforming rotary motion into the linear motion needed to actuate hammers: the cam and the crank. (*The Medieval Machine*; Jean Gimpel).

So much for the economic myths of the Middle Ages. But most Americans don't know about this prosperous history of the Middle Ages with its great freedom and creativity. Why? Because there were no bureaucratic, vertically-integrated, freedom-killing empires that ruled comprehensively during that age in Europe. (The Byzantine empire existed in S.E. Europe and S.W. Asia from 395-1453 A.D.) The horizontal lifestyle was predominant in the Middle Ages. It automatically followed from the conversion to Christianity among the northern European tribes from the fifth to the tenth centuries. But because empires today rule the present, they can control what is written in history books. So, by controlling the present and the past, they can also attempt to control the future. This is why a truly free press, such as the newsletter industry, is an anathema in the age of vertically-integrated, slave-like, poverty-instilling, freedom-squashing, misery-producing, bureaucratic empires, such as rule today in the East, West, and communist civilizations.

And why is the free market, the prosperity-producing free market of Austrian and Christian economics, so ignored, ridiculed, and despised? Because it is based upon the moral contract, the self-governing acts of individuals who, collectively in society, choose the freedom, prosperity and happiness of a horizontal lifestyle.

The *American Economic Review*, after surveying nearly 1,000 economists from the United States, West Germany, Switzerland, Australia, and France, found that the overwhelming preference of all economic systems was the price mechanism as it operates in the free market. Specifically, of those economists surveyed, 80% felt the economy would be more efficient if we had less government regulation; 95% thought wage and price controls should not be used to control inflation; 97% applauded the removal of importation restrictions; 67% thought that the minimum wage increases unemployment among those it was designed to help; and most generally saw rent controls as reducing the quantity and quality of housing available.

In other words, government involvement in economics, the interference of a vertically-integrated empire into horizontally-integrated activity, leads to less freedom, less prosperity and greater human misery. *Civil government involvement in economics is a curse long-term.*

Men choose the lifestyle they will live. We reap what we sow. Wise men choose to grow up from the vertical lifestyle into the horizontal lifestyle. In so doing, wise men choose freedom, prosperity and happiness. The horizontally-integrated lifestyle is a lifestyle of life, the vertically-integrated lifestyle is a lifestyle of death. Free, prosperous and happy men have no time for slaves.

April 25, 1985

Chapter Twenty-Five
THE KEYS TO HUMAN FREEDOM

Man has five interconnected needs which, when correctly joined together, provide him with life's equivalent of a five-leaf clover. Man's needs are: spiritual, mental, emotional, biological, and personal security. While, for purposes of discussion, we can separate these needs, they are actually inseparable and intertwined.

Two familiar axioms: "We are what we eat," and "We are what we think," are interrelated with man's basic needs. What we think, of course, is based ultimately upon our religious assumptions about the nature of reality as they tie into the factual world. How we emotionally process what we think and believe also determines whether the food we eat becomes beneficial or toxic to our systems. It has been demonstrated medically that 75% of our health problems are related to lifestyle and diet. Furthermore, emotion has now been shown to be stored in our body tissues and organs, like data in a computer bank. We are truly integrated spiritual, mental, emotional and biological computers. Furthermore, in our relationships, we either positively (in harmony) or negatively (in conflict) affect each other. This in turn affects how we meet our security needs.

Man's basic *spiritual* need in an earthly sense is for freedom. His fundamental *mental* need is to work, to creatively develop his talents and dreams. His primary *emotional* need is for love (self-esteem and love from others). His rudimentary *biological* need is economic — food, clothing, shelter. And his *security* need is balanced against his need for freedom through the working out of his mental, emotional and biological needs.

Once we have identified these needs and defined the problem in a scientific sense, we next need to decide how to structure our affairs in order to see that these needs are maximized for as many individuals as possible.

It's important to note that in the drive for maximum fulfillment of any of these needs — freedom, work, love, security and economic — none comes naturally. In fact, we have to first overcome our natural instinct to "take," which creates a conflict of interests. We need to grow to the point where we can first "give," if the fulfillment of our own needs are to be maximized. We need to work toward a harmony of interests and overcome the natural conflict of interests enslaving us. Stated differently, we have to rise above nature and our natural selves. This requires humility, self-discipline, personal responsibility, a service orientation and a long-term view.

We are born into this world as potential tyrants. As takers, not givers, we maximize a conflict of interests. Babies are dependent slaves. They make incredible demands upon others, and require caretakers (parents) to meet their biological, mental, emotional, spiritual and security needs. Babies demand to be fed and changed (economic needs); they demand to be loved (emotional and security); babies demand stimulation (mental needs); babies demand to do what they want to do when they want to do it (spiritual; absolute freedom). And yet, without a mature, loving parent willing to give unconditionally to a baby in order to meet his biological, mental, emotional and security needs, and protect him from himself with regard to his spiritual/freedom needs, that baby will shortly die. A baby cannot feed or change himself. A baby will die or become retarded if he is not nurtured, stimulated and loved.

We see that the nature of maturity in the spiritual, mental, security, biological and emotional realms is rooted in several important character traits: humility, self-discipline, personal responsibility, enlightened self-reliance, sound knowledge applied (wisdom), knowing limits, and giving, not taking. All require a long-term view. It is only such unconditional giving by the parent that transforms the conflict of interests between the caretaker (parent) and the baby into a harmony of interests. It is giving versus taking which thus ultimately determines the difference between maturity and immaturity in the affairs of men. Giving first requires humility, self-discipline, responsibility and patience. Giving is rooted in love. And giving is based in the long-term view.

Psychologists have proven with innumerable studies that the first six years of a child's life, and particularly the first two, are critical in his spiritual, emotional, biological and mental development. This is also the time when a child requires total security. These critical formative years are foundational. What a child receives during this time will strongly influence whether he will be a giver or taker in later life, and whether he will be willing to assume the risks of freedom and handle freedom properly. Since we build from the bottom up, and society is composed of individuals, it follows that the most basic institution responsible for ensuring a mature harmony of interests in society is the nuclear family. It is the family, the natural mother and father of the child, that has the primary responsibility of meeting the child's biological, mental, emotional and security needs, as well as defining the limits of his initial spiritual need for freedom.

The willingness of the mother and father to give unreservedly to an all-consuming and taking child is based on the reality that the child is an extension of themselves. So, when parents give to their child, they are in effect giving to themselves. When a man and a woman, a husband and wife, join together and produce a baby, they naturally unite the conflict of interests between the two of them, first resolved in the marriage contract, into a total harmony of interests in their offspring.

The basic nuclear family unit is the natural way by which a conflict of interests between individuals is transformed into a harmony of interests or cooperation in society. Therefore, the nuclear family unit is the building block of society. It is the first earthly source toward meeting the spiritual, mental, biological, emotional and security needs of mankind, individually and collectively. No wonder that in the Old Testament Law of Moses, treason is against the family, not the civil government. The importance of the extended family follows as a safety net-type health, education and welfare agency. Here, genetic links and family concerns work in the common self-interests of both individuals and society.

Today in America, we are engulfed with all sorts of problems. And, not surprisingly, only 7%-12% of Americans now live in what was typically the American nuclear family unit. Cause and effect? Of course. Actions have consequences, just as ideas have consequences.

In order to give, one must first have something to give. A child who grows up in an environment where his emotional needs of love are met is better able to give love. He is more secure. Where a youngster's biological needs are met and there is excess, he is able to be more charitable in the economic realm and help other people meet their biological needs, too. He is more secure. Mental growth stems from shared knowledge. As a child grows up, he will hopefully earn more responsible freedom, also. He will feel secure in assuming the risks of freedom. He will believe in himself.

Freedom isn't free; it is earned. Freedom is based upon an individual learning and heeding the natural and spiritual laws rightfully limiting his freedom, and then operating within those boundaries.

Freedom has both natural and moral limits, which complement the physical and spiritual nature of man. Man is "made in the image of God," and "formed from the dust of the earth." Absolute natural laws establish limits on our physical freedom. Moral laws, too, have long been established because human nature has been constant down through time. In both moral and scientific law, there is nothing new under the sun. Children have to learn, for example, that if they attempt to defy the natural law of gravity and jump off a cliff, they are going to suffer the consequences of limiting their freedom in time either permanently (by death) or by injury. Likewise, those who abuse and breach the freedoms of their fellow man by such action as theft and murder, in a just legal restitutional system, quickly suffer the consequences by losing their own freedom and/or property.

Men can learn the natural and moral limits of freedom either the easy way or the hard way. The easy way should come through careful training first in the home, then in the local church, school, workplace and community. When an individual is taught to be humble and responsible, to first give when it comes to meeting one's own biological, emotional, mental, security and then spiritual needs, and receive as a by-product of that giving, a harmony of interests is manifested. Then the need for a costly, bureaucratic, tyrannical civil government is effectively nonexistent. Human needs are met on the local, decentralized level, primarily through church (collective) or contractual (individual) arrangements.

Exploitative and tyrannical centralized "guns and butter" civil governments exist and grow only in an environment of pride, conflict, immaturity and irresponsibility. Thus, government "gun" power is maximized externally where conflict is maximized during times of war, and internally by way of the police and court systems. Government "butter" power is maximized where people are first dependent and takers, and are irresponsible when it comes to their fellow man. Thus, a runaway federal government "guns and butter" budget is a sign of the bankruptcy of a culture and the individuals in it.

Government fills the spiritual, economic, emotional, mental and security vacuum. As a result of the individual sins of ignorance, omission and commission, civil government makes men poor through heavy taxation, frustrates and redirects men's work, makes them insecure, sharply limits or eliminates freedom, and replaces love with fear.

A truly mature individual will be mature in these five key need areas of life — biological, emotional, mental, personal security and spiritual. He will struggle for a balance between them with his limited resource — time. He will develop the humble, responsible self-discipline to first give, and as a by-product receive, in order to effect a harmony of interests. A mature individual will learn that if he is to have his emotional needs for love truly met, he must first give love. Receiving real love is a by-product of having first given love, whether it's to his wife, his children, his business associates, his friends, or a stranger. Ideally, a stranger is a friend we have not yet had the opportunity to get to know.

To meet his biological/economic needs, in order to produce a harmony of interests, a man will first serve. He will meet the goods or service needs of his fellow man. As a by-product of this service, he will be rewarded financially, economically, biologically, and probably emotionally, too. His self-esteem will increase as will his sense of security.

Man's mental need to work creatively finds its expression in the natural resources of the real world, as he develops his talents. Then work becomes joy and is emotionally satisfying. Whether he is working with his fellow man, with the resources of the environment, or with a combination of the two, the full expression of the harmony of his effort will flow back to him when he receives the approbation of his fellow man and/or sees the higher and better use of a more productive natural environment. He also profits economically and feels more secure.

These five need areas are interrelated. The buck stops at freedom which is best risked if men are secure. For example, a man who is mature and secure economically (free), will feel more emotionally secure and can give comfort and aid to others. In return he receives love. His self-esteem increases. He will also have the wherewithal to spend his time doing what he chooses, with whom he chooses and where he chooses. This is real freedom. Freedom further allows this man the time to work creatively, to put his mental abilities to good use for all mankind. In exchange, he further prospers economically, emotionally, mentally, spiritually and feels more secure.

There is no escaping the reality that mankind is either on a synergistic spiral up or a conflict-ridden spiral down. The social difference between these two is the willingness to first give (spiral up) or take (spiral down). The hallmark of taking, of conflict, indeed of approaching death in a social order, is a desperate, warlike, bankrupt federal government attempting to accomplish the impossible in these five areas. Ultimately, the result of taking is the curse of bureaucratic Mother Government. Government is no more of a kind mother than nature is.

Since we have been discussing man's mental need to work creatively, we should focus for a moment on competition. Competition is often thought of as conflict. And yet competition, correctly seen, is competition to serve, competition to cooperate — harmony! Economists know in perfect competition that competition/conflict ceases to exist because perfect competition results in perfect cooperation. Cooperation results in prosperity through the specialization and division of labor leading to trade. Here, in cooperation we see the unity of man's emotional, biological, spiritual, mental and security needs.

If we could just reach the growth point in human action where all men were secure and mature spiritually, biologically, emotionally, and mentally, (in the sense expressed in this chapter), then all men would work to develop their God-given talents. They would willingly assume such a risk.

The development of these individual God-given talents would yield maximum economic prosperity because each individual would perfectly meet the needs of his fellow man as well as serve his own self-interest, while serving his God. This is a win-win-win contract. As a by-product, love, joy, peace, prosperity, and freedom would fill the earth, too, because when men no longer have economic concerns and are working to fulfill their dreams and develop their talents, work becomes a joy rather than drudgery.

Furthermore, in an important twist, man's inequality in talents and work produces equality in the marketplace as men contract and trade with each other. So, the biological need for economic prosperity, the need for security, the mental need to work, and the emotional need for love can be maximized. The spiritual need is partially fulfilled, too, for man must be free to work creatively. When everyone works to develop his talents and serve his fellow man and is commensurately rewarded for it, appreciation of excellence replaces envy. True equality arises. The need for a strong central government decreases. By contrast, wealth redistribution and war are sure signs of the preceding mental conflict of envy and inequality.

More elaboration is required regarding man's ultimate need, his spiritual need for freedom. There is no freedom for man unless freedom is freely given. History has shown us with clear certainty that even tyrants are not free. Men like Hitler and Castro had their freedom limited by fear of others and by bodyguards. Such tyrants have their personal freedom limited as a result of having limited the freedom of others, unjustly so.

Only where men are free to work and develop (via service), their God-given talents, and thus simultaneously pursue their own self-interest, is there widespread economic prosperity. Basic economic necessity takes immediate precedence over man's emotional, mental, spiritual and security needs. Without the economic basics, man dies. So, freedom is fundamental in meeting man's security, emotional, biological, and mental needs because freedom maximizes man's economic production, which is also basic. It's a round robin affair. Freedom demands economic resources and economic resources are vital to freedom. The other needs dovetail in.

Freedom incurs two basic requirements: self-discipline and duty to others. Self-discipline has to do with bringing to fruition the full security, emotional, moral, biological (economic), and mental development of each man so that he is not dependent, so he can contract successfully, and can thus be spiritually free. In other words, man overcomes himself and grows up from being a dependent, slavelike child into a free, mature, self-reliant, giving adult.

Second, freedom requires that man perform his duty toward other men. He must allow other men their freedom to maximize their own economic, security, emotional, mental development and need fulfillment. Duty is expressed in giving, by service, which is a form of love. So man's spiritual need for freedom is rooted in his emotional ability to love, to give, which in turn maximizes his own mental, emotional, biological and security fulfillment. Unless each of us has it all together personally, in a harmony of interests, how can we collectively have a harmony of interests? We cannot.

Here is finally where civil government properly comes in. What rules and laws will be enacted, based on self-discipline and duty, in order to maximize freedom? What rules of conduct do we establish that will transform the natural conflict of interests between the individual and the masses into a harmony of interests? Who makes the rules? Not men. Not if we want true equality under law. Men who make laws play god and consider themselves "better" than the rest of us. How about God's laws? Furthermore, how de we decide who leads? How about those who serve the best? They earn the right to lead. Serving and giving are based on humility;

taking is rooted in pride.

Laws, rules of human conduct governing human action, are religious ideas about right or wrong, ethics, morality, and good and evil. Governments enact and administer these laws, these religious ideas about morality in human affairs. Thus, the purpose of civil government is the concrete application of religious ideas to the real world. A civil government is the overt expression of the god of a society. Government is religion applied to economics. Therefore, if we are to maximize human freedom, which in turn maximizes the fulfillment of man's security, emotional, mental and biological (or economic) needs, we must look at the religious ideas which in turn define the laws enacted by the civil government.

Empirically speaking, what country, without historical equal, has maximized man's economic prosperity (fulfilled his biological needs), provided security for its people, shown more love and charity to the world-at-large (at least in its early years), and allowed men to work to develop their God-given talents — all in an environment of freedom? The answer is obvious — the United States of America. What religious system, albeit imperfectly applied, gave rise to the civil government and laws which maximized human freedom and fulfilled these five basic needs of man in a way never before fulfilled in history? The answer is again obvious, decentralized Bible Christianity.

It is the linking up and correct understanding of the abstract truths of Christianity, administered in society by government at all levels, tied to factual technology and circumstances, applied in the realm of human action (economics), that offer us the hope of a glorious future, indeed, of life itself.

Human action is never static. It is ever moving toward either life or death. Men choose to live with either a conflict or a harmony of interests. We reap what we sow on this earth. The natural man, as an animal, moves naturally toward death, in a conflict of interests. In the natural order, man is either the ultimate predator or parasite. He is accordingly poor, unloved, frightened, insecure, frustrated and/or enslaved long-term. Man only becomes the ultimate resource long-term when he has the religious basis and motivation to work to overcome his natural instincts and move toward a harmony of interests. Then, and only then, can he personally maximize his human development, find his five-need clover and find love, freedom, prosperity, and work to pursue his dreams.

The Deity Link

Every man's thinking is inescapably circular and based upon some religious presuppositions about the nature of reality. Because the natural realm is, in essence, imperfect and impersonal, and one of conflict, the ultimate resolution necessary to bring about a harmony of interests in time and eternity is found in the Creator, who is above the natural realm, who has absolute authority over it, and who decrees laws to govern it. He harmoniously unifies all things unto Himself. Being consistent with His own principle of "whoever has served most shall be the greatest," God deserves to be God. He has solved man's eternal life problem through the work of His Son, Jesus Christ, and has also served up potentially perfect love, security, economic provision, work, and freedom for man.We are then free to love Him "because He first loved us." All proposed deities thus can be tested according to this criteria.

Since God has solved man's eternal life problem, and through a covenant/contract provision potentially realigned His perfection with a now imperfect creation, then man-made religion attempting to do what God has already done, or prove itself worthy to be as God, is a waste of time. Or worse, it is, as the communists declare man-made religion to be, "the opiate of the people."

After we consider God, the question then comes down to, "How do we spend our time while on earth?" What can we give in return to a perfect God who has and is the Source of everything. Other than worship and praise, nothing. We can only give to and serve our fellow man. In fact, this is how God tells us to serve Him. How do we best do this? By developing to excellence our own God-given talents and then using them and their fruit to give to and serve others through tithes, offerings, charity and contracts (love and law), as He commands us. But even such serving and giving to others in freedom is in our own self-interest long-term. It keeps the civil government out of the economy and the health, education and welfare business. It brings about for us personal prosperity, love, dream fulfillment in our work, security and freedom when we operate within His laws of harmony. Peace and prosperity, individually and collectively, are manifested.

This then is the manner in which a total harmony of spiritual and physical unity is brought about in a win-win-win contract between man, nature and God. Thus, we see in the realm of ideas, the unified truth, "government is religion, applied to economics." However, in the concrete, real world, the institutions of government, religion and economics must be totally separated, decentralized to the maximum degree possible, and run by different men, in order to provide the checks and balances necessary to ensure freedom, to ensure true security, to ensure the protection and peaceful recapture of nature, and thus to enable free men to have the opportunity to fulfill the win-win-win contract and maximize individual and collective human potential while simultaneously serving God.

April 5, 1984

"Give and it will be given to you, good measure...running over, they will pour into your lap."

Luke 6:38

"Every good thing bestowed and every perfect gift is from above, coming down from the Father of lights, with whom there is no variation, or shifting shadow."

James 1:17

"For the wages of sin is death, but the free gift of God is eternal life in Christ Jesus our Lord."

Romans 6:23

"The one who does not love does not know God, for God is love."

I John 4:8

Chapter Twenty-Six
THE ONE GUIDING PRINCIPLE

Unquestionably, the institutional separation of church and state has historically been vital to the maintenance of freedom, security, prosperity, and the protection of the rights of individuals. Indeed, a republican form of government is dependent upon the dispersal of power which comes with the institutional separation and decentralization of church and state. Men cannot handle a concentration of power. Power corrupts and absolute power corrupts absolutely. Men cannot play god.

On the other hand, it is equally important that we realize in the abstract realm, the realm of ideas, that separation of church and state is impossible. In fact, in all societies, government is inescapably religion applied to economics.

From religion comes our ideas about right or wrong, ethics, morality, good and evil. Civil government enacts these religious ideas into law, which form the rules which in turn frame the arena of economics. (The lawgiver of any society is always the god of that society.) This means that in order to harmonize abstract principles with concrete reality, the clergy of a country must critique and petition the lawmakers of a society if the religious, legal and economic will of the people is to be fulfilled. Indeed, *Titus 1:7* admonishes the clergy to be economists. And Jesus taught that those who did not teach Scripture (law) correctly would be least in the kingdom.

Furthermore, the centralization or decentralization of responsibility, law and power determines the prosperity or poverty of a civilization. Close at hand, we can witness the difference between the prosperity of the United States and the poverty of Mexico, stemming primarily from the differences between the centralized religious, political and economic systems dominating Mexico, versus the decentralized institutions historically governing the United States.

We know historically that prosperity only comes when freedom and harmony exist in a society. Freedom comes when men are self-governing under God and responsible at the local level, for themselves, their families, and the health, education and welfare needs of the community, as implemented by the private sector, local charities, and churches. Bureaucracies, which fill this vacuum of irresponsibility (and ultimately unbelief), are always expensive and wasteful, regardless of their institutional brand. The older the bureaucracy, usually the greater its corruption, too. Therefore, the greater the irresponsibility of the people, the greater the growth of bureaucracies, and the less freedom, security, peace and prosperity there is. (This is also true regarding defense bureaucracies. A well-armed militia and a solid civil defense system would go a long way toward securing our freedom and prosperity. Switzerland and Israel are classic examples.)

Next, harmony only comes to a society that first asks and then resolves the ultimate political/religious question: "How do we resolve the conflict between individual rights and group rights?" Because we have no religious consensus today, it follows that we also lack a political consensus. Therefore, conflict reigns and we become progressively poorer.

It is economic cooperation, the specialization and division of labor leading to trade, that results in harmony and prosperity in an economic system. But such a system rests upon the integrity and morality of a contract honoring citizenry, which in turn is based on a political and religious consensus.

The laws governing a society's economic system must be geared toward insuring a balance between individual and group rights. Both individual and group rights must co-exist. Today we are violating most of the God-given harmonious, economic, political and religious principles. Small wonder then that we are becoming a poorer, debt-burdened people, marked by political strife and religious impotence.

The religious principle which captures the essence of this ultimate political and economic question is found in Christ's Second Great Commandment, "to love our neighbor as ourselves." This commandment balances the rights of the individual with the rights of the group by providing for a balance between self-interest and service. For it is only when we are empathetic, as we see our self-interest as best first served by service, that we do first serve our fellow man and as a by-product are rewarded. Then do we simultaneously meet both the needs of the group and those of the individual. This is a win-win-win transaction, producing peace and prosperity for both the individual and society, and simultaneously fulfilling the will of God. When men operate under such principles, the enslaving, expensive, wasteful, corrupt bureaucratic institutions which dominate us today wither away and die. They become unnecessary.

We get the government we deserve. We reap what we sow. As a founding father William Penn put it, "Men must be governed by God or they will ruled by tyrants." When law does not come from God, it inescapably comes from men who are corrupted by the likes of money, sex, and power, who build huge bureaucracies to implement their will.

Christ's Second Great Commandment, which He restated from the Old Testament law, effectively the Golden Rule, must be our one guiding principle, both individually and collectively, for human action. Christ's Second Great Commandment is religious in essence because it is a statement made by God Himself. It is governmental, because it is a command which specifies a rule or law of behavior. It is economic because it governs human action in a contractual way between individuals and society. It is the very clear and certain reflection of Jesus Christ Himself — Creator of the universe (economic), King of kings (government) and Lord of lords (religion).

Jesus Christ earned and deserved the right to be God. He totally and perfectly completed His work in service to God and mankind (economics). He perfectly kept the law (government). Jesus Christ is the perfect union between government, religion and economics. His personal centralization of governmental, religious and economic power above and outside of nature permits man to decentralize governmental, religious and economic power on earth. This in turn allows man to meet his five interrelated biological/economic, security, love/self-esteem, mental/work and spiritual/freedom needs. For this, man gives God the thanks, praise, glory and worship, for "we love Him because He first loved us." In so doing, we fulfill the First Great Commandment, "to love the Lord, our God, with all our hearts."

September 16, 1985

Chapter Twenty-Seven
CHOOSING TRUTH OR TRADITION

Today, when the traditions of men in our society are captured by so much error, we have a hard choice to make: We can either be accepted by our culture and go along with the crowd and be wrong, or we can grow, cling to truth, and stand pretty much alone in small groups.

Cyclical historians' perspective of civilization, when it is as frozen as ours is, is that civilization can no longer respond effectively to the challenges it faces. This is another way of saying that the traditions of men are so rigid that the civilization can no longer respond to the truth and reality which bombard it. So, apparent security today is really false security. There is no security in going over the cliff with everybody else. There is only temporal security in facing reality, dealing with it, and assuming risk. Such is contrary to bureaucratic, slave state thinking. Apparent security in a bureaucracy, long-term, is insecurity. When the bureaucracy consumes its host, free men, the bureaucracy dies.

"Tradition" is another way of saying that men collectively are creatures of habit. Even when men know intellectually that their habits are wrong and destructive over the long-term, they will seldom change them until they are forced to change, dramatically and painfully. Generally, people keep on doing what they are doing, even when they know it is wrong or bad for them, until it no longer works. Trying to reform a people from tradition to truth, trying to change folks' habits, is akin to trying to pull a meager dog biscuit from the mouth of a ferocious dog who has not eaten for three weeks, even if it is to replace it with a juicy steak. The dog can't see beyond the biscuit. So, too, men have so much pride in their traditions, fear the unknown, and resist change, not to mention the social stigma of going against the crowd and becoming socially unacceptable, that they don't change easily. Instead they cling to tradition, which leads to their civilization fragmenting into chaos, rather than making vital progressive transitions into the future.

Look at it another way: Very few investors ever learn or are able to apply the profitable lessons of contrary opinion investing. Very few investors are able to go against the crowd as a consistent *modus operandi* in making money. How many investors really buy low and sell high? How much less should we expect of the tradition-bound bureaucratic minds, most of whom have not even heard of contrary opinion, much less understand it. Bureaucrats dominate today. Slaves dominate today.

A frozen civilization is the triumph of the bureaucratic collective over the individual. Balance between the individual and society is lost in a mature civilization. There is nothing more stifling to an individual's pursuit of his destiny than the road blocks built by a ripe civilization. A civilization is built upon the traditions of men. A useful definition of the traditions of men today is "secular humanism." Such is implemented by the bureaucracy. It is antagonistic to Bible Christianity.

Today, Western civilization is tradition bound. As Americans we are homogenized by nationwide radio, news publications, television and public schools. Our restaurants and hotels, as well as the freeway signs in cities all across the country, are uniform. And, at the heart of our cultural tradition we have bought a lie. We have bought the bill of goods that the federal government can take care of us when, in reality, the federal government is mostly an economic parasite that can only destroy us long-term. Every short-term economic problem government tries to solve creates a worse situation long-term. Today, Americans who directly depend upon goverment, and secondarily through government contracts, make up 76% of our population. Government, the parasite, first enslaves and then destroys its host, free men. It's only other option is to become imperialistic.

The absurdity of all of this can also be seen by the naming of wealth redistribution "entitlements." Entitlements, indeed. Involuntary wealth redistribution is legalized criminal theft. But, if one challenges these traditions of men, this cultural blindness, this secular humanism, the establishment media and book-publishing pipeline quickly shuts one down. This is why thinking writers usually starve. What civilization wants to financially support an individual who points out its fatal flaws?

We really don't want people to be different and unique today. We value traditions more than truth. We nurture the status quo. A society that values truth will nurture and protect the independent man and safeguard his uniqueness and independence. Wherever freedom is valued, dissent is encouraged. Original and individual thinking is stimulated. A society that values truth values this freedom of thought and peaceful dissent and sees the individual as very important.

Individuals make up society. It is individual creativity that leads society forward. This is not the case today. We live in an age where the big bureaucratic dinosaurs of government, banking, business, medicine, labor, and education dominate the landscape. And, they try to step all over us in the name of the greatest good for the greatest number — socialism. Socialism is the triumph of the traditions of men, of secular humanism. Socialism brings about the unity between debt capitalism and communism.

By giving primary value to money and materialism, which leads to power, we have enthroned pride, ruthlessness and conflict, and we have established dominant, insecure personalities to rule over us. Leaders no longer serve. They lust for the likes of money, sex and power. The worst do get to the top. They overcome oppression at the bottom, work through competition in the middle, and are lonely at the top due to compromise and treachery. Our Founding Fathers were correct. We were not able to keep our balanced republic. We instead turned it into a democracy, which is the rule of men (humanism), which is nothing more than a short breath between Left or Right Wing tyrannies. We should have servers who lead instead.

Long-term prosperity is conditional upon cooperation and harmony in a society, stemming from individual humility and carried into the marketplace by initiative, incentive, creativity, and responsibility. Since, by contrast, our society is conflict-ridden, and overemphasizes the collective, our illusion of prosperity has to be based upon the drug of debt.

Let's face it. People, taken collectively, in all societies and civilizations throughout history, are flat-out proud, ignorant, and rigid for the most part. They seldom learn a thing from history. Civilizations make pretty much the same mistakes over and over again. This is why human action cycles have validity.

Put another way, most people run with the crowd. If you're one step ahead of the thundering herd and going in their direction, you are considered a leader. If you are two steps ahead of the masses, you're a radical. However, if you are three steps ahead, they make you a martyr. This is again why avant-garde thinkers and authors starve to death. Unless you have a way to earn your daily bread in a culturally-accepted manner, a society won't pay you beans if you make them uncomfortable in their traditions and illusions.

Avant-garde thinkers have always had to pull the general public kicking and screaming into a future where they did not want to go, short-term. The masses first scoff at a new idea. Next, the establishment persecutes it on "behalf of the people." Finally, the masses wonder why the new idea wasn't with them all along.

Let's look at just how blind people can be when it comes to challenging their traditions. In the early 1800s, Dr. Ignaz Semmelweis was a physician in a maternity hospital in Vienna. He noticed that his fellow doctors examined mothers in the maternity ward after they finished dissecting corpses, and without washing their hands. He suggested that the doctors all wash up after they finished dealing with the dead before they examined the living. The mothers in the maternity ward, you see, were dying of infection and disease. Scornfully, Semmelweis' fellow physicians reluctantly agreed to wash up after Ignaz pressed the point. To the physicians' shock and surprise, the mothers in the maternity ward stopped dying. Was Semmelweis made a hero? No way. Far from becoming a hero who was uplifted, appreciated and praised, Semmelweis was kicked out of the hospital, forced to leave Austria, and finished his career in Hungary.

Question: Does the AMA treat creativity in health care approaches any differently today? No. Or the FDA? No, again. What happens when someone from inside or outside the medical profession strays too far away from drug therapy and the "crisis medicine," "you break it, we'll fix it" mentality? Doesn't the AMA act first to protect its own union members? Shouldn't individuals be allowed the freedom to assume the risk and pursue the medical approach they think is best for their own individual health care?

The moral of this story is simple: civilizations and their bureaucratic institutions do not allow men to progress freely. They do not like to have their traditions challenged. Civilizations reserve the right to be proud, arrogant and rigid, maintain the status quo — and the right to self-destruct. Today we cling bureaucratically to the death of secular humanism.

The highly educated establishment-bound, professional class, are the worst in this regard. To be an accepted member of a professional class, one can only disagree within well-defined, culturally-acceptable parameters. This is why approximately 80% of all new inventions come from the radical fringe, or from totally outside of a field of study. This is why meaningful reforms seldom come from inside of the established religious community. They nearly always come from laymen.

Men today can be traditional, comfortable, acceptable and wrong, or they can be radical, uncomfortable, and unaccepted, and be aligned with truth or on the road to truth. In the wintertime of this civilization, when traditions have frozen our institutions into rigidity, we have a polarized situation.

When a civilization no longer responds accurately to the challenges presented to it, when the bureaucrats stomp on truth, then men truly do love darkness more than light. They die in the illusions of their traditions. But frankly, they are more comfortable there. The long-term risk of freedom for these slaves is not worth forfeiting the short-term security of slavery.

It's lonely and painful to be loyal to truth. Tradition-minded bureaucrats blissfully skip along the mine field of life hand in hand. They are blind to the reality that "truth kills those who hide from it." Ignorance is bliss — until you're blown up.

Dr. John Lukacs, author of *Outgrowing Democracy: The History of the United States in the Twentieth Century,* stated in an interview in *U.S. News* the reason for the decline of the United States: "The main source of this decay is the rise of bureaucracy and of the bureaucratic mind...Large numbers of people adapt their entire personalities to the bureaucratic system — or lack of system. This is true in almost every field of life." Stated another way, people generally prefer slavery to the responsibility of freedom today. This is why they wallow in tradition, in secular humanism.

As I pointed out in my first book, *Cycles of War*, studies in both Europe and in this country have consistently confirmed that the most highly educated are the most removed from the world of reality and common sense. These people, in and out of government, have moved straight from their homes into the public school indoctrination centers, picked up the B.S. from the local state-supported college or university (or some culturally elite one), and from there moved directly into a government, religious, educational or some such bureaucracy, which is pro-statist at worst, or escapist and passive at least. (Most businessmen can't survive long-term living with such nonsense and folly, unless they secure special favors from the government. Somewhere along the line they have to meet the needs of the marketplace and thus touch base with reality. Of course, big businessmen today get trapped by bank and government-sponsored debt capitalism, which is almost as bad if not worse than the other bureaucracies.)

Ludwig von Mises wrote, "Innovators and creative geniuses cannot be reared in schools. They are precisely the men who defy what the school has taught them." George Bernard Shaw once commented that the only time his education was interrupted was when he was in school.

This reminds us of the Soviet dissident Aleksandr Solzhenitsyn, who told us that the only reason the bankrupt theology and political system of the West had survived so long was because of its prosperous economic and financial base. When this economic base crumbles, the theological and political systems will quickly crumble. Government is religion applied to economics. Religion ultimately comes down to economics with politics positioned between the two. Solzhenitsyn noted that those in the Gulag quickly harmonized their theology and political views with economic reality. There, they had no way to live with their illusions and survive.

The educated bureaucratic minds of administrators who are culturally blind to their traditional humanistic biases are inescapably and probably unintentionally at war with the philosophical ideas upon which avant-garde think tank-type organizations are built.

On a larger scale, what's going to happen to us, the thinkers of this country, a true avant-garde, when the traditions of men come crashing down on the masses? Won't we be likely candidates for scapegoats, for whipping boys? Wasn't Semmelweis? We are "Atlas Shrugged." Envy is nurtured in this country today, along with resentment. This is social polarization. A nation divided against itself cannot stand. Conflict never builds. It destroys.

It's not easy to live being torn constantly between truth and oppressive tradition. If one is by nature gregarious and extroverted, as opposed to being a loner and introverted, the pull becomes even more challenging.

Self-preservation alone requires some withdrawal and limited contact with society-at-large as a necessary step to shelter oneself from a great part of civilization's craziness. The need for privacy today is often a result of being unable to cope with or meet all the ridiculous social requirements and demands. Small, like-minded local groups and constructive releases such as a regular exercise program, or pets, can help.

It is not easy living with this frustration day by day. It becomes very easy to become at first critical, then angry, then hateful, cynical, bitter, and finally self-destructive. This is why many in the newsletter industry have found a way to self-destruct over the years through health failure, drugs, alcohol, suicide and divorce.

The survival rate among newsletter editors is not very high. Longevity is not the norm. My temporal salvation, my way of handling this thing, is to try to think like God thinks. God has to have a sense of humor (followed by compassion and love) about the stupidity of the human race or else He would have destroyed the world by fire long ago. He did it once by water.

One of the hardest lessons I have had to learn is to allow people the freedom and grace to self-destruct, to make their own mistakes, to make themselves miserable, to ruin their own lives, to cause me misery and still forgive and love them. How many times have I forgiven people who have not kept faith and broken their covenants?

As a rule, people do not like to learn the easy way. They are too proud, stubborn, fearful, humanistic and tradition bound. They have to learn the hard way. They like to be slaves to tradition. They love their secular humanism. This is why the greatest bargain available to mankind has always been the low cost of good advice. Few men are wise enough to take advantage of it.

The most difficult thing of all is to forgive men individually and specifically, and then generally, for their folly, and love them for who they are. After all, except for the grace of God we could have been in the same folly.

Short-term, meaning before 2010, Western civilization is headed for a lot of pain. The next great civilization of the 510-year cycle belongs to China. Just wait until Chinese resources and manpower link up with Japanese management, marketing, and technology. This has been expected by the elitist think-tanks since 1943. This is why the elitists in this country began planning the future of the Pacific Basin back in the 1950s. Oh yes, the Vietnam War was part of it. How else could a strategic thirteenth century country have been transformed into a twentieth century power in a few short years? And, I have finally confirmed that in super secret U.S. war games, Australia is painted red and labeled the New China.

There is an interesting irony here, too. The Western theologian whose work is attracting the most attention in the Far East is Cornelius Van Til. Van Til did his work in the United States. And yet, with the exception of a few brilliant discerning scholars, Van Til is only given lip service by the religious intellectuals in the U.S., and is totally unknown by the masses.

Van Til is to theology what von Mises is to economics. Van Til linked to von Mises, established the religious base for sound economic prosperity, with limited government in a free market. In other words, the Christian theological base is presently being built in the Pacific Basin to bring to fruition the cyclical projection that the next great civilization will be the Far East and specifically China. China will eventually have its religion, government, and economics straight. Civilization always moves west.

I have been pondering why, when the United States was a far more Christian country, as in its early years, there was far less religious involvement with the federal government than today. The answer, I think, is because the true practice of the Christian faith focuses on self-government, the government of the family, the local church, the school, the job, and the local community and county. Furthermore, since in all societies, government is always religion applied to economics, and since people can never agree totally on religion, therefore the best religion, and thus the best government, is self-government. Self-government focuses upon the development of individual character and talents, and looks to a harmony of interests. In this way, the federal government becomes and remains insignificant.

When it comes to the natural man, man is basically an energy machine. It will take harsh financial/economic reality (along with political, civil and military disruptions) to shake the tradition-minded humanistic Western bureaucrat and slave loose from his illusions. Long-term, we have to feel sorry for these people, who effectively now comprise 76% of our society. They will suffer the most. The change for them will be the most radical, both psychologically and in actuality. They won't even know what hit them, where to turn, or what to do for help. They will mistakenly try to rebuild the past, something that has never before worked. They will fall victim to the futile attempt to build a One-World Order. And, most ludicrous of all, they will blame us (freemen) for their troubles. And we're the very people who could bail them out of this mess.

It's crazy. Historical precedent says that odds favor us moving into a tyrannical slave state in the late 1980s. Perhaps if we're fortunate, and if we're provided a window of opportunity, then with a lot of grace and even more character and hard work, we'll be able to pull the blind out of the ditch before such a disaster occurs.

In our society today, where everyone is a specialist, we are by default ignorant in most other areas. We lack generalistic wisdom. This is why newsletter writers and readers, who seek broader understanding, tend to be aloof. Free men have no time for slaves.

October 18, 1984

Chapter Twenty-Eight
THE JUDAS "SINDROME"

Inherent in each of us are the seeds of the Judas "Sindrome," the tendency to betray truth, to cause misery to others around us, to self-destruct.

Judas, as one of Jesus' disciples, walked daily with the Living Truth. As he increasingly learned the truth from Jesus, Judas felt the growing tension between what Jesus taught and the "traditions of men" as taught by the Jewish religious leaders. Finally, unable to stand the internal conflict and cognitive dissonance, Judas betrayed Jesus and thus betrayed The Truth. Recognizing what he had done, Judas was no longer able to live with himself. In the ultimate act of self-pity, self-rejection, and humanism, he committed suicide. By so doing, Judas fulfilled *Proverbs 8:36*, "But he that sinneth against me wrongeth his own soul: all they that hate me love death."

The sin nature in the natural man feels this tendency to reject the truth in favor of the approval of men and social respectability. In a society, this tendency is expressed in the collectivist, socialistic impulse.

The Judas *Sindrome* results in this collectivist, socialistic tendency because we as members of mankind are gregarious. We want to be liked. We need to be loved. Thus, we have a natural tendency to get along, agree, and compromise in order to secure group approval. But one characteristic of any group, of society generally, is to resist truth, persecute it, resist change and fear the unknown. Men tend to destroy what they do not understand. They feel secure in their traditions. They love darkness more than light. This is essentially why the Jews, in conspiracy with the Roman political leaders of their day, crucified Christ. He was not the kind of Messiah the Jews wanted. As in Jesus' time, men today are culturally blind, slaves to tradition. Human nature has not changed.

The Judas *Sindrome* creates an immediate problem for all of us who are followers (disciples) of Christ. Through the power of the Holy Spirit we are disciplined to obey God's Law-Word, and principles, and grow in the knowledge and application of The Truth. As we learn of the person of Christ and His principles, we work out our temporal salvation. When this "head" knowledge through the power of the Holy Spirit becomes "heart" knowledge and is applied, and we move from milk to meat, we become Christlike and grow toward fulfilling Christ's two Great Commandments, exhibiting also the fruit of the Spirit. We then live consistently in keeping with *James 2*, where our works are the evidence of our faith. We also exhibit the characteristics of the elder or bishop as outlined in *Titus 1*. We produce fruit.

A funny thing happens, however, on the way to becoming a good disciple, steward, and an ambassador for Christ. As we move from the conflict of the natural man and his realm to the harmony of Christ's kingdom, we find ourselves paradoxically in increasing conflict with our culture and society, with other men's ideas, actions, habits and traditions. Now, we are not in conflict with people themselves. We are to live peacefully with all men as much as possible. But as we grow as Christians, we come increasingly into conflict with natural concepts, pagan laws, and ungodly traditions, which govern men in our social order. This is the spiritual conflict spoken of in *Ephesians 6:12*, where "we wrestle not against flesh and blood (not against our fellow man), but against principalities, against powers, against the rulers of the darkness of this world, and against spiritual wickedness in high places."

As we speak the truth in love in our society, and take stands against pride, conflict, irresponsibility, selfishness the short-term view and all other forms of ungodliness in our culture, we face inevitable persecution, perhaps prosecution. We are challenging the basic, psychological, fallen sin nature of man, individually and collectively. Inevitably, we run head-on into the Judas *Sindrome*, the tendency to be group oriented and herd bound, to blindly follow the "traditions of men." The Judas *Sindrome* causes men to be proud, to resist change, to fear the unknown, and to persecute it. (This is why, incidentally, 80% of the inventions that lead to a better material life for mankind in God's creation come from those courageous and creative individuals on the radical fringe of a profession, or from completely outside of it. Creativity is not an attribute of tradition bound socialism/collectivism).

It is truly paradoxical that as we become more Christlike, and grow in truth, at the same time we are persecuted by the natural, humanistic, evolutionary man for being different and for challenging cultural traditions and institutions. If it were otherwise though, we would be lukewarm. In our Christlike character, the natural man sees his own sinfulness, which brings to the surface his own guilt, inadequacy, resentment, and envy. It is natural that he will then persecute the followers of Christ. So as we grow in God's truth, we will see a decrease in the fulfillment of our natural, culturally-acceptable, social/love needs. This is why we need the local church, so we can grow together, so we can stand firm, fighting the good fight in the real world, while not being either escapist or worldly. And God provides his blessing in time, as well as eternally.

There is incredible pressure put upon the Christian man or woman, which can only be resolved by walking in God's grace, in His law, with His people, in the real world, through the power of the Holy Spirit. The more we adhere to God's Truth personally in our lives, and stand on principle in love as an example to the secular community, as a light on a hill which cannot be hidden, the more we are ostracized, persecuted, and maligned.

Inescapably again, the deeper our adherence to God's truth, the less our natural social/love needs will be met. And despite this tremendous challenge to live in a Christlike manner on a day-to-day basis, we are additionally told to love those who persecute us, to do good to those who do us evil. What an incredible commandment. This is why we need the whole counsel of God, His love, His law, His Holy Spirit, Christ's intercession, His church, as well as evangelism, praise, prayer and fasting, and our personal discipleship and stewardship. All of this must be covered and energized by the supernatural power of the Holy Spirit as we fight the Judas *Sindrome* in the natural world.

There is no such thing as a mature, noncontroversial Christian. The Christian who allows the Holy Spirit to apply God's Word to every area of his life is in spiritual conflict with the natural humanistic, evolutionary, satanic, fallen order — the unseen world. The Christian who works as a free man in God's creation, redeeming it to harmony, is in a struggle with those who are deceived and who love death that is both physical and spiritual. So, a Christian who has no controversy with the natural world is both immature and lukewarm. The Old Testament, the New Testament, and church history consistently confirm this point.

Sadly, too many Christians and churches today are slaves to the "traditions of men." They are socially acceptable coffin churches of cultural conformity. They are plunging us toward death, all the while in cahoots with the rulers of this natural world.

Jesus told us we would face such challenges as we grew to be edified believers. In *Matthew 10:32-37* He declared:

> Whosoever therefore shall confess me before men, him will I confess also before my Father which is in heaven. But whosoever shall deny me before men, him will I also deny before my Father which is in heaven. Think not that I am come to send peace on earth: I came not to send peace, but a sword. For I am come to set a man at variance against his father, and the daughter against her mother, and the daughter-in-law against her mother-in-law. And a man's foes shall be they of his own household. He that loveth father or mother more than me is not worthy of me: and he that loveth son or daughter more than me is not worthy of me.

Jesus is telling us that being His disciple and steward, and living according to His truth is not easy from the perspective of the natural man. Being

Christlike is more important than even our ties to our natural family, He says. And we know how important the family is. In *I Timothy* 5:8, Paul told us, "But if any provide not for his own, and specially for those of his own house, he hath denied the faith, and is worse than an infidel." That's how highly God thinks of family ties! He exalts loyalty to the person and the work of Jesus Christ even above the natural family ties. Given the incredible demands of Christ upon our lives, the ever-growing tension between becoming Christlike and the "traditions of men," it becomes painfully obvious why we must guard against our natural tendency to self-destruct, thus fulfilling the Judas *Sindrome*.

Keeping the Second Commandment

The Judas *Sindrome* is the natural tendency in all of us to fall away from and betray the truth. This results in our self-destruction. We see, in terms of the individual and society, the one and the many, how the natural tendency we have to fall away from the truth is nurtured by a fallen world order, by society at large. But individuals, loners, fall away from the truth, too. The popular social norm of "do your own thing" is the ruthless assertion of the individual as autonomous from all of society. It is the maximization of the evolutionary "survival of the fittest." This is contrary to Bible teaching. In economics this is evidenced by seeking the fulfillment of one's self-interest at all costs, including those harmful to our fellow man.

The Word of God teaches that man is either a slave to nature or a slave to God. It is an either/or thing. There is no middle ground. There are no other choices. Furthermore, man falls under obedience to the Word of God or the word of man (humanistic laws). Man does, however, maximize his freedom, security, prosperity, creativity, love, and joy when he is in "bondage" to God, and obeys His Word, rather than when he is a slave to the fallen order of nature and man.

Man is born into a nuclear family. He also has an extended family. He is a member of a school, a workplace, a church, and a community. He lives in a county, state and country. Man's responsibilities are thus always tied to a group. There a few hermits, mountain men, or true loners. As a result, we are always having to balance our personal goals and desires against those of society. It is in trying to find this balance where an individual allows either God's law or man's law to rule.

If the group (society) is a godly one, then the mutual support, service, and love extended one to another checkmates the Judas *Sindrome*, the tendency to fall away from the truth, to create conflict, and to self-destruct. Christians are intended to be mutually supportive, not in competition. However, this is increasingly rare as well as difficult in our social order today, which maximizes the pagan norm of alienation between individuals and autonomous survival of the fittest. This conflict is reinforced by the public schools and the mass media pressure to conform to the evolutionary, humanistic "traditions of men" which are hostile and antagonistic to the Word of God. This, in turn, breeds the parasite of big, bureaucratic, centralized government, which is called upon to mitigate conflict and meet man's every need.

This is far removed from Christ's Second Great Commandment: "Thou shalt love thy neighbor as thyself."

In quoting *Leviticus 19:18* in this Second Great Commandment, Jesus was establishing the fact that His doctrine was built upon the Law of Moses. Furthermore, He was defining man's relationship with his fellow man, the balance between the one and the many. Elsewhere, Jesus told us that the way we are to love Him is to keep His commandments. So when we love our neighbor as ourselves, we keep Christ's commandment regarding our responsibility and duties to our neighbor, as captured by New Testament principles and Old Testament law. Jesus was also establishing empathy as the underlying virtue in dealing peacefully with our fellow man, preceded by personal humility.

Jesus wisely knew that our own sin nature, our natural man, would understand our own self-interest. This is why He commanded us to see our neighbor's self-interest as if it were our own, but with an empathetic heart and mind. The works of the law written on the hearts of men make the balance between grace and law, between justice and mercy, readily possible when man loves his neighbor as he loves himself.

When we reflect on this Second Great Commandment, especially from God's perspective, we begin to see that He gave it to us for our own good. We all have a need for love. But we never truly receive mature love until, in reciprocity, we first give love away.

By developing our talents, our calling, not only are material rewards received in exchange for our service to our fellow man, so is the recognition, approbation, security and payment for our work honored as we have first served or loved our neighbor as ourselves.

Our economic needs in the marketplace are met by providing a desired good or service. Thus, by serving our fellow man first, we then serve ourselves economically. We love our neighbor as ourself.

Even freedom imposes a duty to allow other men to be free. In turn, other men allow us our freedom. Duty is a form of service. Service is an aspect of love. We are best served when we love our neighbor as ourselves.

So, in terms of the basic purpose of God's law with regard to all individuals — protecting the sanctity of life, liberty, and property — we see that His rules are all interconnected and also linked to Christ's Second Great Commandment. Thus, when we love our neighbor as ourselves, our neighbor allows us our life as we allow him his. We allow our neighbor his property, which is necessary to sustain his life, as he reciprocates. We allow our neighbor his freedom to live his life and develop his calling and talents, the fruits of which are his property, in return for his willingness to allow us our life, liberty and property. As a result we are both more loved, more secure, and enjoy more freedom. Christ's Second Great Commandment thus provides for peace and prosperity, the balance between the one and the many, between the individual and society.

Harmony is always necessary for life, liberty, security, work, prosperity and love. For it is only in a peaceful, free environment that men can develop their talents and pursue their calling, leading to the specialization and division of labor, resulting in cooperation, or trade, and good stewardship. This in turn results in prosperity, the wealth of nations. Religion always comes down to economics.

This contract between men, the agreement to love thy neighbor as thyself, is why restitution was the principle of punishment established for both civil and criminal offenses in the Old Testament. Restitution was the penalty for the breach of contract concerning a neighbor's life, liberty, or property. It reflected God's ethical and covenantal (contractual) dealings with man in both the Old Testament (Old Contract) and the New Testament (New Contract).

When the harmony of Christ's Second Great Commandment breaks down, and we fall away from this truth, we move inescapably toward the self-destruction of the Judas *Sindrome*. We fall back into the conflict of the natural order, which comes under the externally-imposed discipline of God's law (if not humanistic law, tyranny or anarchy), where the governing principle becomes an "eye for an eye, tooth for tooth, hand for hand, foot for foot." Restitution! We reap what we sow. How much better it is to grow from being a natural man before Christ (or as a new believer), effectively operating under conflict governed by the externally-imposed discipline of God's law, to the edification of harmony taught by the Holy Spirit, as Christ intended in His Second Great Commandment, and finally to the full fruit of the Spirit.

God's Word is progressive. The New Testament is built upon the foundation of the Old Testament. Upon Christ's two Great Commandments hang all the law and the prophets. We are saved eternally, chosen before the foundation of the world, elected and predestined. Then, in time, we are born again, awakened to the reality of our salvation by the Holy Spirit, and called to service in time for God's glory as disciples and stewards, to the good of our fellow man, for our own reward, both eternally and temporally.

In a sense, we work our way up in time. The Holy Spirit has to change us from being conflict-ridden, selfish children who feed on milk, to harmony-oriented adults who feed on meat, who see self-interest as best served by service in tune with Christ's Second Great Commandment. Of course, the fruit of the Spirit will begin to be the manifestation of a daily living of Christ's Second Great Commandment. The fruit and the work are the manifestation of faith. Words by themselves are cheap, the mark of religious men, of whitewashed tombs.

Christ's Second Great Commandment, to love thy neighbor as thyself, a restatement of the Golden Rule, has a religious, political, and economic unity to it. To reiterate, government is always religion applied to economics. Government's laws are the concrete enactment of religious ideas which in turn frame the arena of human action (economics). When men do not live in harmony with God's law, and therefore do not keep Christ's Second Great Commandment (The Golden Rule), as they fall away from the truth, they maximize the self-destruction, conflict, envy, and strife evident in the Judas Sindrome, and bring on the religious, political and economic curse of *I Samuel 8:11-18* and *Revelation 13:15-17*. In these verses are found the curse of centralized, pagan, governmental religion applied to economics.

Christ's Second Great Commandment, to love thy neighbor as thyself, is religious because it is the commandment of God Himself. Commandments are by definitions laws. They must be obeyed. So commandments are governmental. The commandment is also economic because it defines human action. Interestingly, the great Austrian economist, Ludwig von Mises, titled his treatise on economics, *Human Action*.

Rejecting the Judas *Sindrome*

The corporate church struggles today with the destructive nature of conflict between the rights of the individual and the rights of the group, because the church has not fully understood the harmony or balance between these different rights as defined religiously, governmentally, and economically by Christ's Second Great Commandment. Self-interest today is seen as being in conflict with service. Selfishness is viewed as contrary to selflessness. Capitalism, with its incentives, is considered antagonistic to the collective sharing of socialism, which is growing in popularity with the church. However, socialism is a product of evolutionary humanism, which always leads to conflict as per the survival of the fittest. Yet, conflict is not God's *modus operandi* for His people. As the Sovereign of the Universe, He brings all things into harmony with Himself. Indeed, the New Testament teaches both self-interest and service (in a sense, truth-in-tension), not one or the other, but both.

The Protestant work ethic is to earn all one can (incentive), save all one can (capitalism), and give all one can (service). We are commanded to work hard, save, and invest so we can give more. To whom much is given, much is expected. We are commanded to give to the church, provide for the needy, and yet provide for our own needs, especially those of our family. Thus, self-interest and service are different ends of the same interconnected linear chain.

In the fallen, evolutionary, natural, economic world, self-interest is seen as pitting man against every other man. The end of such conflict is destruction, both collectively and individually. This is the individual and collective manifestation of the Judas *Sindrome*. Christian economics, by radical contrast, sees self-interest being best served as a by-product of service. This requires a long-term view rather than a natural or evolutionary short-term one.

Even freedom, which of some sort is desired by all men, first requires individual responsibility and self-discipline, but next demands duty (service) to our fellow man, allowing our fellow man his freedom, in exchange for him allowing us our freedom. (Christ's Second Great Commandment again). Duty is a form of service and service is an aspect of love. Thus the self-interest of freedom is linked inescapably with duty toward our fellow man and service with love.

Forced sharing, government economic planning, redistribution of wealth, communism and socialism do not work long-term. They stifle incentive to produce. They have ever led to tyranny, ruthlessness, bloodshed, misery, poverty, and a corrupt bureaucratic elite who live royally like pagan gods at the expense of everyone else. This is true in the Soviet Union today. Under atheistic Soviet socialism there is no self-discipline, only externally imposed discipline. In the farm sector, for example, where Russia was once an exporter of foodstuffs, it is now the world's largest importer of grain. Yet some incentives are allowed on private family plots in the Soviet Union. These plots comprise only one per cent of the Soviet Union's agricultural land. Yet this freedom and incentive to produce encourages self-discipline, and these private sections of land produce up to 40% of all the poultry, milk, fruits, and vegetables grown and raised in the Soviet Union. Only grants, loans, subsidized food sales, and transfers of technology have allowed the Soviet Union to survive, 95% of which have come from Western civilization.

If the collectivist, socialistic, communistic ideas were going to work, they would have worked for the self-sacrificing, hard-working, self-disciplined Pilgrims. The Pilgrims pledged themselves to such a system when they established the Plymouth Colony in 1620 under Governor William Bradford. And yet for three years the Pilgrims nearly starved to death despite their pious Christian character. It was only, as Governor William Bradford wrote in *Of Plymouth Plantation*, when incentives were introduced that the Plymouth Colony finally prospered. It took incentives, captured first by service, to make Plymouth work. At Plymouth, God's laws, as captured by Jesus' two Great Commandments, resting on the Ten Commandments and the other laws of Moses protected the life, liberty, and property of the individual, with emphasis on the family, the local church, and the community. Christian men saw their incentives for personal gain in terms of first providing the goods or services desired by their neighbors. They economically loved their neighbors as themselves. Self-interest was captured by service. Selfishness was captured first by selflessness.

There was the other side of the coin, too. If a man did not work, he did not eat. This was effectively an economic death penalty. If a man doesn't eat, he dies. So those who created jobs enabling other men to have the dignity of work, and thus allowed men to provide economically for themselves and their families, were seen as superior to the man who simply provided dead-end charity, which kept the needy in bondage to the dole.

People respond to incentives. Biblically, however, personal incentives must be captured first by service, balancing the rights of the individual with the rights of society (Christ's Second Great Commandment). The numbers on welfare will increase if the incentive to be irresponsible and lazy and to not work, exists. On the other hand, if the "traditions of men" promote the incentives of ruthless, conflict-ridden selfishness (like debt capitalism), then a society will reap what it sows — death. The spread between the rich and the poor will grow, resulting in more conflict and eventually revolution, anarchy and finally tyranny. The self-destruction of the Judas *Sin*drome will then cause havoc everywhere as men flee from the truth. By contrast, if men operate under the harmony of Christ's Second Great Commandment, the Golden Rule, and see that their self-interest is only served first in terms of meeting their neighbors' needs, God's balanced equation between the rights of the individual and the rights of the group — the harmony between the one and the many — then exists. The Judas *Sin*drome wilts under this truth of God applied to life.

The stages in the development of a civilization are from paganism, to Christianity, then to perverted religious Christianity. It's relatively easy to convert conflict-ridden, miserable pagans to Christianity once the Holy Spirit moves and they finally understand the Christian spiritual, governmental, and economic issues and benefits, and break through their bankrupt "traditions of men." They have nothing to lose and everything to gain, both spiritually, governmentally, and economically from Christianity. God gives it all.

The Christian stage of the civilization is the most glorious of all, marked by harmony, security, self-government, freedom, limited civil government, prosperity, charity, and growth. However, the post-Christian era, the era of perverted religious Christianity, is the most difficult one of all in which to communicate truth. It is in the post-Christian era of today that our civilization is still covered by "Christianity," but all too often in name only.

People today believe they are Christians. But with the reinfiltration of the pagan empire-building, humanistic, evolutionary "traditions of men," we have become religious pagans in practice. Too many Christians nod to God on Sunday and live like hell the other six days of the week. Religion has no relationship to reality. This was the problem Jesus faced in His day, and the problem the Christian church faces today. Today, institutional Christianity is for the most part a whitewashed tomb, the whitewash covering the ungodly "traditions of men."

It's ironic that in theory, both communism and capitalism, the two dominant political/economic systems of today — one atheistic, the other claiming to be Christian — both hold to self-government and the elimination of government bureaucracies. Capitalism holds that the free marketplace, governed by God's unseen hand, best meets man's economic needs, and that the only purpose of government is a limited one, to protect life, liberty, and property, ensure justice, and provide military protection against all enemies, foreign and domestic. Communism in its final stage, envisions the withering away of the state, where people live in perfect harmony. Thus, in theory both capitalism and communism see the evil of big, bureaucratic, socialistic government. But both capitalism in the West and communism in the Soviet Union (and China) today operate under a bureaucratic socialistic form of government. This speaks to the bankruptcy of both theories. There is no uniformity between theory and substance. This confirms that we are living in an age maximizing the ungodly "traditions of men." Men do not seek the truth because they do not want to find it. They do not want to alter their traditions by embracing Christian government, which is self-government first, and then the government of the family, local church, job, community, county, and so on.

No wonder more people have starved, more wars have been fought, and more men have died on battlefields in the twentieth century than in any previous historical era. Our religion, government, and economics are ungodly. And we are headed for an economic, political, and military disaster that will only be celebrated by the hounds of hell. Our "traditions of men" have maximized the Judas *Sindrome*. We await our approaching death, in fact, our suicide. We need repentance and reconstruction now, based on the power of God's Word and applied to His creation by the Holy Spirit, to overcome the natural downward spiral of the Judas *Sindrome*, and to bring His Kingdom on earth peace as it is in heaven.

March 17, 1986

Chapter Twenty-Nine
IN A NUTSHELL

It is ironic that both capitalism and communism idealistically share a common goal — the minimization or elimination of external government. Capitalism ideally sees government's functions as strictly limited to maintenance of the peace, ensuring justice, and enforcing contracts. Communism's final stage is when the state (government) has withered away. So, capitalism and communism, apparent enemies today, both have the same philosophical long-term objective of effectively eliminating civil government.

Let's take at face value the concept that the two major world political systems today see big centralized bureaucratic government in the long-term as evil. The obvious difference between these two systems then, is the means used to achieve this end of eliminating the evil of a federal government. Capitalism formulates its economic system by means of the private ownership of capital goods, wherein private decisions are made by individuals with regard to the production, distribution, and use of resources in a competitive free market. Communism, on the other hand, as practiced today, holds to civil government (group) control and decision making regarding the production, distribution, and use of resources.

Both political systems are unequivocally economic in nature as well as religious. Capitalism has "faith" in the "bottom-up" approach, stressing the individual. Communism's "faith" is in the "top-down" approach, stressing the group, the collective. Thus the capitalism-versus-communism argument is a statement of the recurring problem man faces: *How does man resolve the conflict between the individual and the group? Between the individual and society?*

Conflict has never produced prosperity or eliminated civil government for too long. If this observation were not true, then all of us would rush to invest in Lebanon and Nicaragua. However, the very nature of "flight capital" is to seek a haven of safety, a location of peace and tranquility, where conflict is not in evidence. Furthermore, conflict always leads to a larger government, which in a wasteful bureaucratic fashion consumes resources.

Both capitalism and communism today exhibit the reality that government is always religion applied to economics. As mentioned, capitalism has "faith" in the individual. Communism has "faith" in the group. This "religious" faith is expressed in "political" systems which attempt to effect "economic" theories in time on earth. Both are failing because neither is achieving its stated objective — to minimize and ultimately eliminate the power of the civil government. Instead, both are increasing the size of the central government through bureaucracies.

It doesn't matter if a bureaucracy is communistic or capitalistic, a bureaucracy is a bureaucracy. It breeds dependent, nonthinking, slavelike conscienceless behavior. It consumes prosperity, and is the oppressor of free men. Bureaucracies have ever been the greatest institutional manifestation of human evil. But a bureaucracy, a short-circuited solution to human problems, is what we should expect from both systems, because neither system has come up with the answer to providing the harmonious balance between the individual and the group. Thus, neither capitalism nor communism has eliminated conflict. Further, as each system builds its bureaucracy contrary to its stated philosophical objective, it consumes and economically bankrupts its respective society and turns its citizens into distrusting, alienated cynics, if not criminals.

Bureaucracies consume wealth. Bureaucrats add nothing by way of goods and services to the wealth of the social order. They only redistribute wealth. Furthermore, bureaucracies limit freedom and personal responsibility. (Prosperity, individual freedom, personal responsibility, and morality are all linked together.) Why should a civil government be trusted when it does not accomplish what it sets out to do?

Both communism and capitalism have opted for socialism as an escape valve by which their respective bureaucracies mask their failures. While both promise peace on earth, prosperity, and either limited government or none at all, neither delivers. This is because socialism is still the collective government ownership and administration of the means of production and distribution of goods. Ultimately, under socialism, there is no private property.

Today, communism never gets beyond socialism in practice. Capitalism, as practiced today, moves toward socialism and stops there. So, why shouldn't communism and capitalism unite, when both are socialistic?

Both communism and capitalism today acknowledge no force or source higher than nature itself. Since in the conflict of nature, power finally rules, it logically follows that the greatest power in nature is the collective synergy of man in a group, manifest by civil government. Socialism then is the ultimate statement of this power. So, communism and capitalism have moved logically toward socialism. A One-World order, as it continues to emerge, will be socialistic. It will be a global slave state.

Next, because both communism and capitalism utilize the natural, relativistic methodology of Hegel's dialectic, the thesis of capitalism and the antithesis of communism will logically unite in the synthesis of socialism. But socialism, as earlier discussed, is the hallmark of failure of both the capitalistic and communistic philosophical systems. This failure gives rise to the socialist governmental bureaucratic parasite which first creates and then mediates conflict, consumes the wealth of a society, brutalizes its people, and ultimately bankrupts them. This happens more rapidly when the "land" side of the "land and labor" economic equation becomes unstable.

As Winston Churchill commented, "Socialism is the philosophy of failure, the creed of ignorance, and the gospel of envy. Its inherent virtue is the equal sharing of misery." (It must be recalled, too, that communism is a creation of Western civilization. Karl Marx researched and wrote his communist doctrines in London. The Russian Revolution was financed by American debt capitalists.)

Western civilization correctly understood the true basis of civil government in the formulation of this country. It is historically self-evident that *government is religion applied to economics.* The United States produced the most economically prosperous nation on the face of the earth in the fastest time ever. The economic prosperity of the U.S. was a reflection of its preceding governmental and theological soundness, (even though many of the pioneers were in error in their abuse of the environment).

Let's break this down and examine it more closely. First, consider that the United States was established as a Christian nation. (This was discussed in considerable detail in Chapter 5 of my book, *Wealth For All: Religion, Politics and War.*) In short, this was important governmentally and economically, because it was the Christian foundation that established the balance or harmony between the individual and the group.

It cannot be stressed enough that all governmental laws are concrete enactments of religious ideas. When men agree religiously, they will concur politically and then act accordingly in economic terms. In America, individual rights were seen in terms of self-discipline, personal responsibility, duty to others, and service. The rights of the individual, from the American Christian perspective, were defined in terms of duty or service to the group, the collective.

Jesus' First Great Commandment directed man to a God who is above the conflict of man and nature, who created and rules over nature, a God whose primary characteristic is love, which balanced with His law, produces harmony for both man and nature — peace and prosperity.

Christ's Second Great Commandment defined man's individual self-interests in terms of those of his neighbor. In this country, the New Testament theme of love then became the *modus operandi* by which the laws of the Old Testament were enacted and made operational on earth by government. Justice was tempered with mercy. This created social harmony as the Law of Moses held in dialectic tension the natural conflict between the individual and the group.

Recognizing correctly that man is never autonomous, never totally free, but rather in subordination to the tyranny of nature and other men, or to God, the Founding Fathers of this country established a legal framework based on biblical law. (It was no accident that in some of the original colonies lawyers were outlawed. For example, in Virginia, in 1658, all lawyers were expelled. In Massachusetts in 1641, it was made illegal for a man to take money for representing another in court. This was because everyone knew — or was expected to know — the biblical legal standard. Ignorance of God's law was no excuse. Lawyers who argued for any law other than the law of God were considered heretics).

Thus, in the United States, a republic was established, not a democracy. In a republic, not everyone votes — voting is not a "right." There are qualifications and responsibilities that must be met in order to have the "privilege" of voting. (In the Greek "democracy," only about 30,000 of a population of over 100,000 voted.)

Also, in a republic, the importance of the central government, seen as an economic parasite and a potential tyrant, is rightfully minimized. Legislators only have the responsibility of applying the exact law and the abstract principles of biblical law to the concrete facts of the situation at hand. As such, legislators do not make laws. This was seen as God's responsibility. It truly kept all men equal under the law. It kept government decentralized.

By contrast, our democracy today, like all humanistic democracies before it, is nothing more than mob rule — the rule of the majority — where the federal government becomes a criminal, stealing from the productive and giving to the unproductive; where the government makes ungodly laws and politicians play god, relying ultimately upon the force of violence. Governments today legislate immorality rather than God's morality. All laws are the legislation of some type of morality.

When a man's wealth and property are stolen, his life and time is also stolen. Human rights cannot be separated from property rights. A man spends his time, his life, earning money to buy property. So, the criminal act by civil government of wealth redistribution via taxation, inflation or draft conscription for that matter, is a form of slavery, a sure sign of a welfare democracy enroute to the total slavery of socialism.

The nature of slavery is religious, political, and ultimately economic. Under communism, economic slavery is first covered by overt atheism and then by a brutal political and military hammer. In the West, slavery is more subtle. It is first achieved by subverting religion to the traditions of men, then by convincing men that the federal government can solve all the problems. Finally, slavery is accomplished economically by means of progressive taxation, inflation, alphabet agency legislation, the redistribution of wealth (with resulting poverty), the draft, and the use of fractional reserve debt and compound interest.

In God's reality, the individual is as important as the group, because any group is no better than the character, dedication, and professional efforts of the individuals who compose it and contribute to it. Religiously, each individual also has a calling from God to be fulfilled, which means freedom has to be maximized for individuals. And yet freedom is defined not only in terms of personal responsibility, but also in terms of duty to the group.

The group has to allow an individual his freedom for freedom to exist. Individual fulfillment is found only in self-disciplined responsibility, as a by-product of service to the group. This provides for harmony and balance between self-interest and service. Thus, the character development of the individual is primary. The individual has to rise above his natural self as a dependent child and move from pride to humility, from dependency to personal responsibility, from taking to empathy and service, in order to be free and prosperous in Christian American society. The natural man, the natural self, is seen as the enemy to be overcome. Only when such character is established in man individually by the Holy Spirit does he have the ability to carry through with his legal contracts and his covenants, which are the moral/religious basis of the prosperity-producing free market. It's a bottom-up, bootstrap approach accomplished supernaturally, mentally, and through hard work. (Ironically, case study after case study has shown that the minority groups that get ahead economically emphasize family, hard work, learning skills, and saving. By contrast, the government today tries to "help" minorities to get ahead by the opposite approach, by destroying families and by providing incentives not to work, learn skills or save. Government involvement in economics is always a curse.)

Government must be first and foremost *self*-government, then family government, next church government, school and work place government, city/county government, state government, and finally, federal government. When everyone maximizes self-government, then the "state" — that is, the federal government — truly withers away. There is no law against men who individually manifest the "fruit of the Spirit" — love, joy, peace, long-suffering, kindness, goodness, faithfulness, gentleness, and self-control. *Thus, the curse of the growth of external, bureaucratic, civil government is a direct result of a lack of character in a people. If we want to be above the law and truly free, we must allow the Holy Spirit to fulfill the character of the law in us!*

Freedom, decentralization, individual development, security, self-esteem, love, group satisfaction, prosperity, and happiness come through "horizontal" covenant/contract transactions, not through bureaucratic "vertical" ones. There is strength when a group of individual men come together voluntarily, each possessed of the individual characteristics of humility, responsibility, and service, enabling them to covenant and contract successfully. Then true synergy exists. The whole is indeed greater than the sum of its parts. By contrast, when weak men who are proud, irresponsible, and selfish come together in a group, the inevitable result is failure due to conflict. This is most evident in communism, which effectively translates into socialism, which is nothing more than tyranny at the top, resulting in bloodshed below (100 million killed as a result of communism).

Early Christian America put a priority on establishing character in the individual, enabling him to carry through on his contracts and covenants as he worked to develop his talents. It stressed self-interest as a by-product of service, with the economic arena of human action framed by biblical law. This balanced and eliminated the conflict between the individual and the group, and stopped the cycle from order to disorder, the cycle from tyranny to anarchy. It could not help but produce prosperity. Government involvement in the economy was shunned. Government economic interference in the economy was correctly seen as a long-term curse. Prosperity was further enhanced by three important factors: an emphasis on the family (inheritance), a strict limitation on the absentee ownership of land, and honest free market money in equity capitalism, which condemned the use of compound interest and unbridled debt.

It must be remembered, biblical treason in God's law is primarily against the family, not the established civil government. Why? Because when a man and woman naturally come together in a family and voluntarily through their covenant relationship, produce offspring, the natural conflict between these adult individuals is automatically harmonized into the unity of the group, biologically, spiritually, and economically through the children. In the nuclear biological family, the rights of the individual and the rights of the group become inescapably and naturally one, in intertwined mutual self-interest. For this reason, the family is the basic building block of any godly society.

Spiritually and governmentally, the local church, local community and county, local school, and local workplace, in line with freedom and decentralization, become the primary non-family social governing units. We can see that even the architecture of these local entities is "horizontal," rather than "vertical," as is the case in cities. (Cities have historically always been "vertical" in nature. The skyscraper (Tower of Babel) is historically the architectural hallmark of bureaucratic slave centers.)

Ninety percent of the early Americans worked the land. They were, in keeping with biblical ideals, rooted in the land. In many states, land ownership was actually a requirement for voting. Only in the cities and specifically designated recreational areas should absentee ownership of land be allowed. Ideally, no man should be allowed to own more land than he is able to transform into a garden. This gives people roots, encourages personal responsibility and duty toward others, promotes decentralization and the continual development of the earth. It provides for the continuity of the economic chain from agriculture and other resources to small business, to large industry, to a service economy, and finally to an information-based economy. This provides an economic base for government and real estate development long-term. It maintains the balance between the city and the country. (A civilization can survive even if its cities are destroyed, as long as the countryside is left alone. But if the countryside is ravaged, the culture does not come back. The city depends upon the country for survival.)

By establishing free enterprise equity (non-debt) capitalism rather than pagan debt capitalism, men can balance the rights of the individual with the rights of the group. The entrepreneurs, who inevitably lead society forward, have their antisocial and power-lusting weaknesses checked by equity capitalism. Entrepreneurs can then only obtain financing through stock offerings, partnerships, and joint ventures, which keep them accountable to the group as they seek the fulfillment of their individual self-interests. The group gets rich as entrepreneurs become wealthy by financing other entrepreneurs through equity capitalism. None of this OPM (other people's money) or OPE (other people's energy) evolutionary slavery is permitted.

Debt capitalism, accompanied by the infinite compounding effect of interest (which finite man cannot handle successfully), and money that is no longer tied to physical reality, are both anti-biblical positions. Debt capitalism severs this critically delicate balance between the productive entrepreneur and the group. Self-interest is no longer tied to service, and so the age old war between the "haves" and the "have-nots," the conflict of the survival of the fittest, again emerges.

The biblical criteria for promotion, leadership and financial reward is service. This is true in religious government and economic institutions, and in all other institutions as well. Whoever serves the most is uplifted and elevated the most. Likewise, the individual who serves the group best is rewarded the most. By contrast, the greater the degree of conflict of interests that exists, the greater will be the degree of poverty, government regulation, and religious apostasy that will appear in a society over the long-term. This is true because economic prosperity is based on cooperation, not conflict, as the specialization and division of labor, leading to cooperative, harmonious trade demonstrates. This is further based on the theological position that God has a perfect plan for each individual, that each individual is uniquely gifted with a God-given talent and calling, which if fully developed, leads to maximum service to his fellow man as well as benefits to himself. This is why Christian evangelism must be followed by discipleship and stewardship — character development and the development of the individual's talents into economic work and production. Governments then keep their laws few in number so that human freedom has little restriction.

Today we have lost most of this, and as a result we are dying — religiously, governmentally and economically. Our religious institutions are marked by status orientation, the traditions of men, materialistic lust, escapism, socialism, and "feel goodism." The runaway nature of the federal budget and the ever increasing Federal Register laws are a clear sign of our government's financial and legal bankruptcy. The actuarial bankruptcy of our multinational banking system with its nonperforming loans is awaiting its horrific fruition in reality. And, as we fall, that brutal, bureaucratic, military slave state, the Soviet Union, created by the loans and technology of Western civilization, will fall also if it does not enslave us first.

These out-of-date dinosaurs of atheistic, evolutionary debt capitalism and atheistic communism will not go down without a fight. They will either attempt to merge into a One-World, bureaucratic socialist state (quite logically so), or maximize their philosophical and operational death in a military nuclear holocaust. One is no better than the other, as far as we the people are concerned.

Human nature and the traditions of men strongly indicate that we all resist change, even if we have the truth and know it. The rigidity of our personal habits and institutions, our traditions, established by years of planned conditioning, strongly suggests that we will not successfully respond to our present environmental challenges. We naturally won't change our individual and collective habits until they simply no longer work, even if we know they are wrong. This means the rigidity of our habits and traditions will lead us inevitably into an attempted One-World socialist slave state, or a nuclear war, either alternative aggravated by the abrupt climatic changes that will occur in the late 1980's — unless we have a Christian revival and reformation now.

Communism, caving in on itself, also looks with militarily, imperialistic ambitions to conquer the West in order to survive. A socialistic, fully-developed parasite, as the Soviet Union is today, must have a bigger host in order to maintain itself and its bureaucracy.

The West, on the other hand, seeing its own atheistic, evolutionary, humanistic, debt capitalistic and socialistic bureaucratic government caving in, is now looking to the atheistic East for answers. There is certainly no help there. The natural religions and philosophies of the East have always yielded nothing better than vertical, bureaucratic, human-enslaving institutions, and brutal treatment of individuals. It could not be otherwise. The religions and philosophies of the East, as worked out in their governments and economies, have always been enslaved by and/or passive to nature. The East has never been able to rise above nature. And so, the East has always found itself in an irreconcilable philosophical conflict, leading to confusion, fatalism, apathy, and despair.

The East claims that its primary philosophical idea is that of harmony. And yet the systems of the East are based on submission to nature. But nature's primary means of achieving balance is conflict through the survival of the fittest. Effectively, the harmony of the East is only found in terms of submission to the conflict of nature, which elevates nature and conflict to the stature of a god and thus diminishes the dignity of man, ensuring poverty, dependency, and slavery for the masses. Vertical bureaucracies of one sort or another have ruled the East. If not a bureaucracy, then tyranny or anarchy.

Three primary characteristics of nature are conflict, chance and cycles. There is no long-term prosperity, freedom or true longlasting harmony under nature's *modus operandi* of conflict. There is no long-term hope or meaning to life in a world of randomness and chance. Why should a man sacrifice in the present and practice deferred gratification for the long-term when he knows his life is always at risk in a realm of conflict, and when life ultimately has no purpose or meaning? Why work when there is no true linear progress in the fatalistic endless cycle of Yin and Yang? Why not instead, eat, drink, and be merry? Reincarnation is the acknowledgment of failure. The same ground is covered over and over again in cyclical reincarnation.

This naturalistic basis of the philosophy of the East falls back onto power as the means of controlling society, with vertical bureaucracies ruling over other men, with all the resulting corruption, brutality, oppression, and poverty.

The West, in its original philosophical purity, is superior to the East. The primary idea of Western civilization is law. The primary idea of Eastern civilization is harmony. Harmony is only achieved, however, when man, who is the transitional bridge (via Christ's work) between God and nature, stands in the gap and recaptures the conflict of disorderly nature into the harmony and organization of a garden by means of God's laws. By the use of God's law — which stands in the gap between nature's Yin and Yang and holds them in perpetual dialectic tension — cycles, chance and conflict are brought to a halt. In their place come progressive linear time, useful planning, certainty, prosperity, freedom, love and true harmony.

Effectively, the East is rooted in conflict. The West has been rooted in natural conflict since it adopted evolutionary Darwinism. And the communist system is also rooted in natural conflict. All three are moving toward the ultimate conflict, a global holocaust. The world is in a downward spiral, moving toward death, after an attempted One-World Order. Only a Christian revival and reformation can turn things around. God with His Son and Holy Spirit have the love and law necessary to harness man's nature and the natural order.

To reiterate, as the rigid bankrupt institutions of the East, West, and communistic systems are shaken during the worldwide changes beginning in the latter part of the 1980's, desperation will give way to either the Third World War or an attempted One-World socialistic government. Either way, mankind loses. A socialistic One-World Order is a parasite which has no host left to consume. It can only cave in on itself. It will fail.

The key, the answer for our earth and the human race, comes by man individually overcoming his nature, his attitudes of pride, conflict, irresponsibility and selfishness through the work of Christ and the power of the Holy Spirit. Rising above his nature, he can establish in his individual character, humility, personal self-discipline, responsibility, duty to others, service, and cooperation as primary if he allows the Holy Spirit to work in his heart. With such a character, he can then successfully covenant and contract in all areas of life, and see that his self-interest is served only as a by-product of his primary service to the group. The resulting emphasis will be upon the basic nuclear family, the local institutions of church, school, workplace, and city/county government. With biblical law established as the basic moral order from which all laws are legislated, with honest money and non-debt oriented equity capitalism, limiting the absentee ownership of land, he can then fight the pagan traditions of men, particularly in his centralized bureaucratic institutions. Not only will he be able to recapture (evangelize) mankind so that humanity can rise above nature, but he will also, through his work and his calling, reclaim nature from conflict to harmony. In the process he will overcome the fatalism of cycles and chance. This is what discipleship and stewardship are all about.

All of these economic aspects of the Law of Moses, interestingly enough, are common to the Christian, Hebrew, and even Islamic cultures. (Mohammed took his economics from Moses.) They are summarized in Christ's Two Great Commandments. Again, Christ's First Great Commandment establishes God as outside of and above nature, a personal God Who both created man and nature and ultimately unifies all things unto Himself. Such a God gives man an ultimate spiritual, governmental and economic basis for harmony, which is expressed in the very character of the Christian Trinity — three in one, the individual and the group, separate yet united (Father, Son, Holy Spirit).

The Second Great Commandment harmonizes the natural conflict between man and his fellow man, between the individual and the group. "Love thy neighbor as thyself" ties man's self-interest to his service and responsibility to the group, inevitably promoting harmony. Whenever and wherever there is harmony among men, there is subsequent harmony in nature. When men overcome themselves and nature (through the power of the Holy Spirit), they have no drive to rule over other men in a predatory sense.

Finally, and most importantly, the work of Christ on the cross on behalf of mankind becomes the death knell to both man's concerns about his eternal welfare and human religions generally. God solved man's religious problem. This turns man's focus to his work and his calling on earth, to discipleship and stewardship.

Again, government is religion applied to economics. The basis of prosperity is the successful operation of human covenants and contracts. The ultimate prosperity — the gift of eternal life — was the result of a fulfilled "contract." Christ's free-will decision to die for the sins of man on the cross was the fulfillment of a covenant/contract. Restitution had to be made to God for the breach of contract between a perfect God and man, who violated the old covenant/contract and originally sinned. The atonement, the restitution, which effectively restored to its original position the contract between a perfect God and imperfect man, was what Christ's work on the cross was all about. God's love for man was simultaneously evident in His sacrifice of His Son. Christ restored eternal harmony between God and man and set up the potential for temporal harmony as well. Man can requisition this eternal life contract through faith in Christ, which faith is also given to him by God. With man's eternal life problem then solved, man is free to grow by allowing the Holy Spirit to perfect him (becoming like Christ), to his own and his fellow man's benefit and to God's glory. It's a win-win-win contract/covenant between God, man, and nature, harmonizing the supernatural with the natural.

It's all very logical, very consistent, very harmonious and not at all religious in the typical use of the word. In Christianity God seeks man. In human religion, however, man seeks God. Religion thus leads to escapism and subsequent hell on earth. The communists were correct when they dubbed religion as "the opiate of the people." Human religion allows man to escape from reality into a never, never fantasy land. It is imperfect man futilely seeking God, rather than God seeking man.

Economics is inescapably covenantal, contractual, and practical. It relates directly to reality. So it dovetails perfectly with biblical Christianity. Bible Christianity and godly economics both focus on service and covenants in the real world. It therefore follows that the Christian-rooted governmental system which yields the maximum in economic productivity on earth will simultaneously maximize harmony, human freedom, and dignity; it will reward responsibility and glorify God, while being contractual and practical. Religion comes down to economics, with government in the middle, a reflection of both religion and economics. When men are on target religiously, their economy prospers, and the state, the civil government, all but withers away.

August 15, 1985

— *Epilogue* —
AN END TO CONFLICT

Over the years, I have given a great deal of thought to the causes of conflict and to the nature of man. Man has basically three ways of resolving individual and collective conflict: 1) with brute force (e.g., fists; military); 2) with logic (negotiation and debate; the law and the court system); and 3) spiritually (resolution coming from above and from within man himself). All three are effective in varying degrees.

The last, the spiritual resolution of conflict within each individual man, is the most effective. Why? Because it is the only method of preventing man from warring within himself. In terms of human institutions, it is the only solution to conflict which is totally peaceful and is not imposed from the top down by a bureaucracy. Both the military and legal systems are bureaucratic in capitalistic and communistic social orders and involve physical and mental conflict respectively.

In order to transform conflict into harmony in society generally, to balance out the rights of the individual with those of the group, *each individual must first resolve the conflict within himself.* Each of us is torn between our various personal self-interests, our need for economic provisions, our need for security, our need for incentives to produce, our need to work creatively, and our need for self-esteem — all legitimate needs — versus our need for group approval, our need for group security, our need to be loved, to be touched — our belonging or group needs.

Now, we can resolve this conflict intellectually, and through the pain of subsequent self-discipline, pretty much put our convictions into actions. This is a struggle, however, a real battle. It puts us in a conflict with ourselves. In a limited sense, it makes the rational man "sovereign."

The spiritual way of resolving this dilemma is the best way. It requires first the intellectual recognition of the internal conflict (brought to our attention by the Holy Spirit), and then yielding to God. Next, in humble prayer, asking for a supernatural resolution of the problem by the Holy Spirit, there comes a change of the heart. In this way, over time, the personal change from conflict to harmony is realized peacefully, without the internal self-willed battle.

Personally, I am finally at peace in this matter. For years I struggled to resolve this internal conflict, because I understood the answers intellectually. But it was my iron-willed, self-disciplined attempts to apply the answers I intellectually knew were correct that kept falling short. It was only when I yielded to God in prayer that the change I had sought to bring about on my own for so long flowed easily and quickly, like the morning dew which rolls off a rose petal. Of course, I was subsequently tested again and again on the matter in the real world. (What reinforcement!)

The self-interests and personal incentives that I have in terms of my own legitimate needs are now natural by-products of having first served my fellow man, thereby bringing into harmony my individual rights with group rights.

My self-esteem is and was built upon a solid base, when it comes to my rights versus the rights of everyone else. I am free to work and creatively develop my talents, which is a joy, a blessing, not drudgery. Because I am good at my work, I feel good about what I do and who I am. This work achievement, the product of my toil, results in approbation and love returned to me by my fellow man, who appreciates the fruits of my labor, my service to him. Thus, through meaningful, productive work and service, my self-esteem and love needs are met. I feel very secure, too. And I prosper.

Furthermore, because I know every other man has a talent, which if properly developed, in turn serves both God and me, I can rejoice at his achievement. Therefore, I need my fellow man. Every one is important to me. There is something I can and should learn from everyone else. This helps keep me humble, empathetic, and free from envy.

Life in God is integrated, spiritually, intellectually and materially. Life in Christ flows readily to the physical world. After all, it too, is His creation, as we are. I take nothing that I have not contracted for or first given in order to receive. And, when it is appropriate, I give it all with no strings attached, without expectation of return, a stance which is, alas, often abused by my fellow man. But, there is no longer the strain of internal or external conflict, no need for government from without, from the top down. Because I am a self-governing, productive, harmony-bringing man, the need for an imposed military or legal government by other men over me vanishes. The spiritual rules supreme over the mental and the material. I am a free man.

True joy in this life, true peace, comes from living first at peace with God, then at peace with yourself, and finally at peace with your fellow man and God's creation. Peace with God originates with a yielded spirit and a broken heart. When this perspective covers the earth, implemented by prayer, study and work, blessed by a God whose love and peace passes all understanding, then this world will have true peace, prosperity, and joy unimaginable. There will be no time for slaves.

March 20, 1986

An Invitation from R.E. McMaster to Become a Serious & Wealthy Investor:

You are invited to begin receiving **THE REAPER**, a weekly newsletter personally written and published by R.E. McMaster for an exclusive group of investors who are serious about building wealth and staying on top of an economic world in turmoil.

R.E. McMaster's track record for making extremely accurate forecasts and specific investment recommendations in **THE REAPER** is truly unparalleled in the industry. Voted "best of the bunch" in a *Futures* magazine survey of the nation's financial newsletter readers, **THE REAPER** has surpassed every other financial newsletter in making relevant, accurate and above all profit-oriented recommendations.

Subscribe now to THE REAPER and receive FREE:

✔ Bonus Report: *McMaster on Markets*

✔ Special **REAPER** issue *The End of the Age of Oil*

✔ One month of *Cycle III*, an exclusive daily, call-in advisory hotline ($200 value)

"A top commodity expert."
U.S. News & World Report

"Timing is McMaster's forte."
Business Week

"You are still the best in the business."   **Howard Ruff**

☐ **YES,** I want to accept R.E. McMaster's invitation. Sign me up for a **one year** subscription to THE REAPER. That's a full 44 issues, for only **$195.** Please bill me quarterly for my subscription ($48.75). I understand that you'll send me FREE the bonus report, *McMaster on Markets*, the special Reaper issue *The End Of The Age Of Oil*, and that I'll receive a month of Cycle III absolutely FREE (a $200 value!).

☐ I'd like to try THE REAPER on a **3-month** trial basis — that's 11 issues for only **$60**. Also, send me *McMaster on Markets*.

☐ I've enclosed payment of $_____

CHARGE MY CREDIT CARD: ☐ MC   ☐ VISA

Card No. _____ Expires _____

Signature _____

NAME _____

ADDRESS _____

CITY _____ STATE _____ ZIP _____

100% MONEY BACK GUARANTEE!
Satisfaction Guaranteed or Your Money Back!
On your unused subscription.

Mail to:
THE REAPER
P.O. Box 39026
Phoenix, Arizona 85069

**OR CALL TOLL FREE
1-800-528-0559**

For More Information:

If you would like more information on the books, newsletters and services offered by R.E. McMaster, Jr., call Research Publications, 1-800-528-0559, or write:

R.E. McMaster, Jr.
Research Publications
P.O. Box 39026
Phoenix, AZ 85069

R.E. McMaster, Jr. writes and edits a weekly philosophical, economic and financial newsletter, *THE REAPER*. (A free sample of *THE REAPER* may be obtained from Research Publications.) He is also the editor of *CYCLE III*, a daily market trading financial hotline. His six other books are also available through Research Publications:

CYCLES OF WAR *(1977)*
THE TRADER'S NOTEBOOK #1 *(1978)*
THE TRADER'S NOTEBOOK #2 *(1979)*
THE TRADER'S NOTEBOOK #3 *(1980)*
WEALTH FOR ALL:
   VOL. I: RELIGION, POLITICS, AND WAR *(1982)*
   VOL. II: ECONOMICS *(1982)*

☐ **Yes,** please send me information on the publications and services offered by R.E. McMaster, Jr. I would like a free sample copy of *THE REAPER*.

Name _____

Address _____

City _____

State _____ Zip _____

Phone (_____) _____-_____

Mail to: **Research Publications**
       P.O. Box 39026, Phoenix AZ 85069